Shelby Foote

THE CIVIL WAR

A NARRATIVE

Shelby Foote

THE CIVIL WAR

A NARRATIVE

4

★ ★ ★

SECOND MANASSAS
TO POCOTALIGO

40th Anniversary Edition

BY SHELBY FOOTE
AND THE EDITORS OF TIME-LIFE BOOKS,
ALEXANDRIA, VIRGINIA

All these were honoured in their generations,
and were the glory of their times.

There be of them,
that have left a name behind them,
that their praises might be reported.

And some there be, which have no memorial;
who are perished, as though they had never been;
and are become as though they had never been born;
and their children after them.

But these were merciful men,
whose righteousness hath not been forgotten.

With their seed shall continually remain
a good inheritance,
and their children are within the covenant.

Their seed standeth fast,
and their children for their sakes.

Their seed shall remain for ever,
and their glory shall not be blotted out.

Their bodies are buried in peace;
but their name liveth for evermore.

ECCLESIASTICUS XLIV

Contents

★ ★ ★

PROLOGUE 6

1   **Return to Manassas**   8

2   **Invasion West: Richmond, Munfordville**   64

3   **Lee, McClellan: Sharpsburg**   80

4   **The Emancipation Proclamation**   134

5   **Corinth, Perryville; Bragg Retreats**   146

6   **Lincoln's Late-Fall Disappointments**   188

7   **Davis: Lookback and Outlook**   226

8   **Lincoln: December Message**   262

EPILOGUE 278

BIBLIOGRAPHICAL NOTE 280

PICTURE CREDITS 282

INDEX 283

★

Prologue

———— ⌇ ————

★ ★ ★   *I*n the early summer of 1862, Southerners were hopeful. Confederate force of arms and Union hesitation had stopped Yankee incursions into rebel-held territory.

In the East, Federal General McClellan had moved his army down Potomac into the Chesapeake Bay and landed it on the tip of the York/James peninsula in Virginia, preparing for a march toward the Confederate capital at Richmond. Fearing he was outnumbered and undersupplied, he moved cautiously. Elaborate ruses by Confederate "Prince John" Magruder slowed McClellan's advance at Yorktown, and small but stubborn rear-guard actions at Williamsburg and elsewhere, coupled with heavy rains and knee-deep mud, slowed him even more. Rebel forces under Joe Johnston slowly withdrew, drawing as much Yankee blood as they could as they retired up the Peninsula, and regrouped in intrenchments astride the Chickahominy River within earshot of Richmond.

Meanwhile, Stonewall Jackson, in the Shenandoah Valley, toyed with three separate Union commands under Banks, Frémont, and Shields, both avoiding them and whipping them when he chose. With these units tied up and Lincoln and Halleck, who thought Washington itself was in danger, frightened into withholding more men and supplies from the Peninsula, McClellan grew even more cautious.

McClellan and Johnston faced off along the Chickahominy and bloodied each other at Fair Oaks/Seven Pines. Johnston was severely wounded there, and the Confederate Army of Northern Virginia received a new commander: Davis pulled Robert E. Lee from behind his desk to lead the army in the field. For Seven Days, as McClellan attempted to swing to the Confederates' right in what he euphemistically called a "change of base" to the James River, Lee, joined by Jackson's force from the Valley, countered McClellan's every move. They met head on at places like Oak Grove, Mechanicsville, Gaines's Mill, and Savage Station, until on the Seventh Day, Federal artillerists atop Malvern Hill stopped the Confederate pursuit.

While McClellan reorganized on the James, Lee faced another threat from Pope's Federals moving toward Richmond from the north. Jackson was sent to counter the move, outfighting Pope at Cedar Mountain.

Out West, recent Union thrusts along the Mississippi and into western Tennessee and northern Mississippi had left the Federals with lengthy and unsecured supply lines. While the Yankees rested and re-grouped, Confederate Braxton Bragg managed to outmaneuver Buell and gain control of Chattanooga, from which he could threaten eastern Tennessee and perhaps even Kentucky. Taking further advantage of the hiatus in Union action, cavalry thrusts under Morgan and Forrest devastated the extended Yankee lines. To top it all off, one lone, not-quite-finished southern ironclad wheezed and blazed her way through the Union gunboats on the Mississippi. Although the C.S.S. *Arkansas* was finally destroyed, she had forced the Federal fleets to withdraw, leaving the central Mississippi River open to southern traffic and causing the Union to abandon Baton Rouge.

The momentum appeared to have changed. Following Cedar Mountain, Lee would move north to join Jackson and defeat Pope at a Second Manassas. With the Union army in disarray and McClellan's troops strung out between Washington and James River, and with Bragg in position to attack the soft underbelly of Tennessee, Lee and Davis decided to change their basic strategy. They would abandon the defensive posture maintained thus far and go on the attack. A two-front invasion would take pressure off the southern regions recently savaged by northern aggression, and any successes might sway France and England to support the Confederacy.

In the East, Lee opted to advance through Maryland, planning to strike north along the Blue Ridge, threatening perhaps Baltimore, Philadelphia, or even the Federal capital. He expected two things to aid him—that pro-southern Marylanders would rally to his support and that McClellan, again in charge of the forces facing Lee, would exhibit his usual slowness. Neither expectation would be realized. Lee sent Jackson to capture the Federal garrison at Harpers Ferry and sent the rest of his army northwest, using the mountains to screen their movements. McClellan, with rare celerity, moved in pursuit almost as soon as the threat was realized. Lee and McClellan would meet just west of Antietam Creek, near Sharpsburg, for the single bloodiest day's battle in American history. The battle was a draw, and late next day Lee withdrew across the Potomac into Virginia. McClellan did not pursue.

Bragg and Kirby Smith struck into Tennessee and Kentucky, the former heading for Louisville, the latter toward Cincinnati. Both were stopped in Kentucky—Bragg at Perryville and Kirby Smith at Franklin.

With both Confederate invasions thwarted, the North-South confrontation returned to where it had been before those strikes; except for one huge difference. Lincoln chose the days after Antietam to issue the Emancipation Proclamation—a document that would turn the conflict, for Northerners at least, into a moral crusade.

★ ★ ★

★

*F*leeing their masters, fugitive
slaves ford Virginia's Rappahannock River along with John Pope's
army during the Federal withdrawal in mid-August 1862.

ONE

Return to Manassas

1862 ★ ★ ★ ★ ★

Lee saw the Cedar Mountain confrontation otherwise. Pleased with Jackson's repulse of Banks, he congratulated him "most heartily on the victory which God has granted you over our enemies" and expressed the hope that it was "but the precursor of others over our foe in that quarter, which will entirely break up and scatter his army." However, the withdrawal to Gordonsville on August 12, despite Stonewall's subsequent double-barreled explanation that it was done "in order to avoid being attacked by the vastly superior force in front of me, and with the hope that by thus falling back General Pope would be induced to follow me until I should be reinforced," not only ended the prospect that his lieutenant would be able to "suppress" Pope and return to Richmond in time to help deal with McClellan; it also re-exposed the Virginia Central. This was as intolerable now as it had been a month ago, and Lee moved promptly to meet the threat the following day by ordering Longstreet to Gordonsville with ten brigades, which reduced by half the army remnant protecting the capital from assault on the east and south. Simultaneously he sent Hood, who now commanded a demi-division composed of his own and Law's brigades, to Hanover Junction in order to block an advance from Fredericksburg; or if Burnside moved westward to join Pope, Hood could parallel his march and join Jackson. Something of a

★

11

balance was thus maintained in every direction except McClellan's, potentially the most dangerous of them all.

Still, potential was a long way from kinetic: especially where McClellan was concerned. A week ago, when the bluecoats marched up Malvern Hill and then back down again, Lee had said of him: "I have no idea that he will advance on Richmond now." He took the risk, not thinking it great, and presently found it even smaller than he had supposed. On this same August 13, while Longstreet's men were boarding the cars for their journey out to the piedmont, an English deserter came into the southern lines with a story that part of McClellan's army was being loaded onto transports. Next day this was confirmed by D. H. Hill, whose scouts on the south side of the James reported Fitz-John Porter's corps already gone. That was enough for Lee. Convinced that Pope was about to be reinforced from the Peninsula — though he did not know to what extent — he decided to turn his back on Little Mac and give his undivided close-up personal attention to "the miscreant" on the Rapidan. The time was short. Before he went to bed that night he notified Davis: "Unless I hear from you to the contrary I shall leave for G[ordonsville] at 4 a.m. tomorrow. The troops are accumulating there and I must see that arrangements are made for the field." Tactfully — for he expected to be busy and he understood the man with whom he dealt — he added: "When you do not hear from me, you may feel sure that I do not think it necessary to trouble you. I shall feel obliged to you for any directions you may think proper to give."

In this sequence of events, Halleck's worst fears moved toward realization. The Federal dilemma, as he saw it, was that the rebels might concentrate northward and jump Pope before McClellan completed his roundabout transfer from the James to the Rappahannock. The southern commander had already proved himself an opponent not to be trusted with the initiative; yet that was precisely what he would have so long as the Army of the Potomac was in transit. The contest was in the nature of a race, with the Army of Virginia as the prize to be claimed by whichever of the two superior armies moved the faster.

Lee was not long in seeing it that way, too, and once he had seen it he acted. In fact — necessity, in this case, being not only the mother of invention, but also first cousin to prescience — he acted before he saw it: first, by detaching Jackson: then by reinforcing him with Hill: finally, by sending Longstreet up to reinforce them both: so that, in a sense, he was already running before he heard the starting gun. And now that he heard it he ran faster. As a result he not only got there first, he got there before McClellan had done much more than lift his knees off the cinders. Yet that was all: Fortune's smile changed abruptly to a frown. Having reached the finish line, Lee found himself unable to break the ribbon he was breasting.

The ribbon was the Rapidan, and Pope was disposed behind it.

★

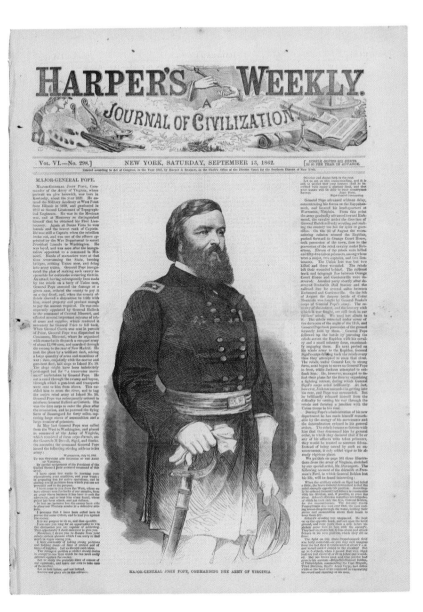

HARPER'S WEEKLY.

JOURNAL OF CIVILIZATION

Vol. VI.—No. 298.]　　NEW YORK, SATURDAY, SEPTEMBER 13, 1862.　　[SINGLE COPIES SIX CENTS.
[$2.50 PER YEAR IN ADVANCE.]

MAJOR-GENERAL JOHN POPE, COMMANDING THE ARMY OF VIRGINIA.

Harper's Weekly devoted the entire front page of its September 13 edition to John Pope. By the time this issue hit the stands, however, the newly minted commander had already been whipped by Lee two weeks earlier.

However, it was not the Union commander who forestalled the intended destruction, but rather a recurrence of the malady which had plagued the Confederates throughout the Seven Days: lack of coördination. Detraining at Gordonsville on August 15, Lee conferred at once with Longstreet and Jackson, who showed him on the map how rare an opportunity lay before him. Nine miles this side of Fredericksburg, the Rapidan and the Rappahannock converged to form the apex of a V laid on its side with the open end to the west. Pope's attitude within the V, and consequently the attitude of the fifty-odd thousand soldiers he had wedged in there between the constricting rivers, was not unlike that of a browsing ram with his attendant flock. Unaware that the butcher was closing in, he had backed himself into a fence corner, apparently in the belief that he and they were safer so.

In this he was considerably mistaken, as Lee was now preparing to demonstrate. Across the open end of the V, at an average distance of twenty miles from the apex, ran the Orange & Alexandria Railroad, leading back to Manassas Junction, the Army of Virginia's main supply base. While the infantry of the Army of Northern Virginia was being concentrated behind Clark's Mountain, masked from observation from across the Rapidan, the cavalry would swing upstream, cross in the darkness, and strike for Rappahannock Station. Destruction of the railroad bridge at that point, severing Pope's supply line and removing his only chance for a dry-shod crossing of the river in his rear, would be the signal for the infantry to emerge from hiding and surge across the fords to its front. Pope's army, caught off balance, would be tamped into the cul-de-sac and mangled.

Both wing commanders approved of the plan. Jackson, in fact, was so enthusiastic that he proposed to launch the assault tomorrow. But Longstreet, as on the eve of the Seven Days, and no doubt recalling the Valley general's faulty logistics on that occasion, suggested a one-day wait. Moreover, though he approved of the basic strategy proposed, he thought better results would be obtained by moving around the enemy right, where the army could take up a strong defensive position in the foothills of the Blue Ridge, forcing Pope to attack until, bled white, too fagged to flee, he could be counterattacked and smothered. Lee agreed to the delay — which was necessary anyhow, the cavalry not having arrived — but preferred to assault the enemy left, so as to come between Pope and whatever reinforcements might try to join him, by way of Fredericksburg, either from Washington or the Peninsula. Next day it was so ordered. The army would take up masked positions near the Rapidan on Sunday, August 17, and be prepared to cross at dawn of the following day, on receiving word that the bridge was out at Rappahannock Station.

That was when things started going wrong: particularly in the cavalry. Stuart had two brigades, one under Wade Hampton, left in front of Richmond, the other under Fitzhugh Lee, the army commander's nephew, stationed at Hanover Junction. The latter was to be used in the strike at Rappahannock Station; he was expected Sunday night, and Stuart rode out to meet him east of Clark's Mountain, in rear of Raccoon Ford. Midnight came; there was no sign of him; Jeb and his staff decided to get some sleep on the porch of a roadside house. Just before dawn, hearing hoofbeats in the distance, two officers rode forward to meet what they thought was Lee, but met instead a spatter of carbine fire and came back shouting, "Yankees!" Stuart and the others barely had time to jump for their horses and get away in a hail of bullets, leaving the general's

Confederate cavalry commander Jeb Stuart was rarely seen without one of his distinctive plumed hats.

plumed hat, silk-lined cape, and haversack for the blue troopers, who presently withdrew across the river, whooping with delight as they passed the captured finery around. Subsequently it developed that the ford had been left unguarded by Robert Toombs, who, feeling mellow on his return from a small-hours celebration with some friends, had excused the pickets. Placed in arrest for his neglect, he defied regulations by buckling on his sword and making an impassioned speech to his brigade: whereupon he was relieved of command and ordered back to Gordonsville, much to the discomfort of his troops. This did little to ease Stuart's injured pride and nothing at all to recover his lost plumage. Skilled as he was at surprising others, the laughing cavalier was not accustomed to being surprised himself. Nor were matters improved by the infantrymen who greeted him for several days thereafter with the question, "Where's your hat?"

Fitz Lee's nonarrival, which required a one-day postponement of the attack — it was as well; not all the infantry brigades were in position anyhow — was explained by the fact that, his orders having stressed no need for haste, he had marched by way of Louisa to draw rations and ammunition. When this was discovered it caused another one-day postponement, the attack now being set for August 20. Even this second delay seemed just as well: Pope appeared oblivious and docile, and in the interim Lee would have time to bring another division up from Richmond. Before nightfall on the 18th, however, word came to headquarters that the Federals were breaking camp and retiring toward Culpeper. Next morning Lee climbed to a signal station on Clark's Mountain and saw for himself that the report was all too true. The sea of tents had disappeared. Long lines of dark-clothed men and white-topped wagons, toylike in the distance, were winding away from the bivouac areas, trailing serpentine clouds of dust in the direction of the Rappahannock. After watching for a time this final evidence of Pope's escape from the destruction planned for him there between the rivers, Lee put away his binoculars, took a deep breath, and said regretfully to Longstreet, who stood beside him on the mountain top: "General, we little thought that the enemy would turn his back upon us thus early in the campaign."

If there could be no envelopment, at least there could be a pursuit. Lee crossed the Rapidan the following day: only to find himself breasting another ribbon he could not break. This time, too, the ribbon was a river — the Rappahannock — but the failure to cross this second stream was not so much due to a lack of efficiency in his own army as it was to the high efficiency of his opponent's. Pope knew well enough now what dangers had been hanging over his head, for he had captured along with Stuart's plume certain dispatches showing Lee's plan for his destruction, and in spite of his early disparagement of defensive tactics he was displaying a real talent for such work. After pulling out of the suicidal V, he skillfully took position behind its northern arm, and for two full days, four times around the clock, wherever Lee probed for a crossing there were solid ranks of Federals, well supported by artillery, drawn up to receive him on the high left bank of the Rappahannock.

Notified of the situation, Halleck wired: "Stand firm on that line until I can help you. Fight hard, and aid will soon come." Pope replied: "You may rely upon our making a very hard fight in case the enemy advances." Halleck, preferring firmer language, repeated his instructions: "Dispute every inch of ground, and fight like the devil till we can reinforce you. Forty-eight hours more and we can make you strong enough." Encouraged by this pep talk, as well as by his so-far success in preventing a crossing of the river to his front, Pope reassured the wrought-up Washington commander: "There need be no apprehension, as I think no impression can be made on me for some days."

★   ★   ★   Once more Lee was in disagreement. He not only intended to make what his opponent called an "impression," he knew he had to make one soon or else give up the game. Information from Richmond, added to what he gleaned from northern papers, had convinced him by now that the whole of the Army of the Potomac was on its way to the Rappahannock. Burnside's troops, under Major General Jesse L. Reno, had already joined Pope, bringing his total strength to 70,000 according to Lee's computations, and this figure would in turn be more than doubled when McClellan's men arrived. To oppose this imminent combination, Lee himself had 55,000 of all arms, plus 17,000 still at Richmond. Manifestly, with the odds getting longer every day, whatever was to be done must be done quickly. At any rate, the present stalemate was intolerable. Perhaps one way to break it, Lee reasoned, would be to startle Pope and make him jump by sending Stuart to probe at his rear, particularly the Orange & Alexandria Railroad, which stretched like an exposed nerve back to his base at Manassas. Stuart thought so,

★

too. Ever since the loss of his plume, five days ago near Raccoon Ford, he had been chafing under the jibes and begging Lee to turn him loose. "I intend to make the Yankees pay for that hat," he had written his wife.

He took off on the morning of August 22, crossing the Rappahannock at Waterloo Bridge with 1500 troopers and two guns. His goal was Catlett's Station on the O & A, specifically the bridge over Cedar Run just south of there, and he intended to reach it by passing around the rear of Pope's army, which was drawn up along the east bank of the river north of Rappahannock Station to contest a crossing by Lee's infantry. During a midday halt at Warrenton a young woman informed him that she had wagered a bottle of wine against a Union quartermaster's boast that he would be in Richmond within thirty days. "Take his name and look out for him," Stuart told one of his staff. The column pushed on toward Auburn Mills, rounding the headwaters of Cedar Run, and then proceeded southeastward down the opposite watershed. At sunset a violent storm broke over the troopers' heads. Night came early; "the darkest night I ever knew," Stuart called it; but he pressed on, undetected in the rain and blackness, and within striking distance of Catlett's was rewarded with a piece of luck in the form of a captured orderly, a contraband who, professing his joy at being once more among his "own people," offered to guide them to the private quarters of General Pope himself. Stuart took him up on that. Surrounding the brightly lighted camp, he had the bugler sound the charge, and a thousand yelling horsemen emerged from the outer darkness, swinging sabers and firing revolvers. The startled bluecoats scattered, and the troopers pursued them, spotting targets by the sudden glare of lightning. It was strange. A lightning flash would show the road filled with running men; then the next would show it empty, the runners vanished.

Despite the effectiveness of evasive tactics which appeared to enlist the aid of the supernatural, more than 200 prisoners and about as many horses were rounded up, including a number of staff officers and blooded animals, along with a good deal of miscellaneous loot. From Pope's tent — though the general himself, fortunately or unfortunately, was away on a tour of inspection — the raiders appropriated his personal baggage, a payroll chest stuffed with $350,000 in greenbacks, and a dispatch book containing headquarters copies of all messages sent or received during the past week. The railroad bridge over Cedar Run, however — the prime objective of the raid — resisted all attempts at demolition. Too wet to burn, too tough to chop, it had to be left intact when Stuart pulled out before dawn, returning the way he had come.

By daylight, one bedraggled trooper remarked, "guns, horses, and men look[ed] as if the whole business had passed through a shower of yellow mud last night." But Stuart's spirits were undampened. At Warrenton he called a halt in front of the young woman's house and had the captured quartermaster

★

*B*roken barrels still litter the ground around
Catlett's Station in this Alfred Waud sketch
made shortly after Stuart's raid in August 1862.

brought forward to collect the wagered bottle of wine for drinking in Libby Prison. Fitz Lee was in equally high spirits. Safely back across Waterloo Bridge that afternoon, he hailed an infantry brigadier and said he had something to show him. Stepping behind a large oak, he presently emerged wearing the cockaded hat and blue dress coat of a Federal major general. The infantryman roared with laughter, for the coat was so much too long for the bandy-legged Lee that the hem of it nearly covered his spurs. Stuart laughed hardest of all, and when he saw the name John Pope on the label inside the collar, he extended the joke by composing a dispatch addressed to the former owner: "You have my hat and plume. I have your best coat. I have the honor to propose a cartel for a fair exchange of the prisoners." Although nothing came of this — the coat was sent instead to Richmond, where it was put on display in the State Library — Stuart was quite satisfied. "I have had my revenge out of Pope," he told his wife.

Pope's coat was a prize R. E. Lee could appreciate as well as the next man, not excepting his charade-staging nephew; but more important to him, by far, was the captured dispatch book which reached his headquarters the following

★

morning, August 24. In it he found laid before him, as if he were reading over his adversary's shoulder, a sequent and detailed account of the Federal build-up beyond the Rappahannock. In addition to Reno, whose two divisions had already joined, Pope had other forces close at hand, including one on its way from western Virginia by rail and canal boat. Most urgent, though, was the news that Porter, whose corps was the advance unit of McClellan's army, had debarked at Aquia Creek three days ago and marched next day to Falmouth, which placed him within twenty miles of Pope's left at Kelly's Ford, five miles downstream from Rappahannock Station. He might have joined today — or yesterday, for that matter — along with Heintzelman, whose corps was reported steaming northward close behind him. "Forty-eight hours more and we can make you strong enough," Halleck had wired Pope, and Pope had replied: "There need be no apprehension." That, too, was three days ago, while Porter's men were filing off their transports. The race was considerably nearer its finish than Lee had supposed.

In point of fact, it was over. Pope was already too strong and too securely based for Lee to engage him in a pitched battle with anything like certainty of the outcome. Unless he could maneuver him out of his present position, and by so doing gain the chance to fall on some exposed detachment, Pope would go unscathed. And unless Lee could do this quickly, he could not do it at all; for once McClellan's whole army was on the scene, or even the greater part of it, the odds would be hopeless. Lee, then, had two choices, neither of which included standing still. He could retreat, or he could advance. To retreat would be to give up the piedmont and probably the Shenandoah Valley; the siege of Richmond, lately raised, would be renewed under conditions worse than those which had followed Joe Johnston's retreat. That would not do at all. And yet to advance might also worsen matters, since Pope might retire on Fredericksburg and thereby hasten the concentration Lee was seeking to delay.

The gray-bearded general studied his map, and there he found what he thought might be the answer. Pope's supply line, the Orange & Alexandria

Railroad, extended northeastward in his rear, so that to maneuver him in that direction would be to make him increase the distance between his present force and the troops coming ashore at Aquia Creek. Twice already Lee had tried to cut that artery: once with a blow aimed at Rappahannock Station, which had failed because Pope pulled back before it landed, and once more with another aimed at Catlett's, which had failed because the rain soaked the bridge too wet for burning. Now he would try again, still farther up the line. If successful, this would not only provoke a longer retreat by threatening Pope's main base of supplies, miles in his rear, but would also repeat the months-old Valley ruse of seeming to threaten Washington, which had yielded such rich dividends before. In reasoning thus, Lee was not discouraged by his two previous failures; rather, he resolved to profit by them. This time he would swing a heavier blow. Instead of using cavalry, he would use infantry. And he would use it in strength.

Infantry in this case meant Stonewall: not only because his three divisions were on the flank from which the march around Pope's right would most conveniently begin, but also because he knew the country he would be traversing and his men had won their "foot cavalry" fame for long, fast marches such as the one now proposed. Conversely, Longstreet too would be assigned the kind of work he preferred and did best: holding, with his four divisions, the line of the Rappahannock against possible assault by Pope's ten divisions across the way. This was risky in the extreme, both for Jackson and Old Pete. Pope was not only stronger now than both of them combined; he was apt to be heavily reinforced at any time, if indeed he had not been already. Furthermore, in dividing his army Lee was inviting disaster by reversing the basic military principle of concentration in the presence of a superior enemy. Yet he did not plan this out of contempt for Pope (Pope the blusterer, Pope the "miscreant" had handled his army with considerable skill throughout the five days since his escape from the constricting V); he planned it out of necessity. Unable on the one hand to stand still, or on the other to retire — either of which would do no more than postpone ruin and make it all the more ruinous when it inevitably came — Lee perceived that the only way to deal with an opponent he did not feel strong enough to fight was to maneuver him into retreat, and to do that he would have to divide his army. Thus the argument, pro and con, came full circle to one end: He would do it because there was nothing else to do. The very thing which made such a division seem overrash — Pope's numerical superiority — was also its strongest recommendation, according to Lee, who later remarked: "The disparity . . . between the contending forces rendered the risks unavoidable."

Today was Sunday. Shortly after noon, having made his decision, he rode to left-wing headquarters at Jeffersonton to give Stonewall his assignment. Jeffersonton was two miles back from the river, where a noisy artillery duel was in progress from opposite banks; Lee spoke above the rumble of the guns. The

*Just as he had in
the Shenandoah Valley
three months before,
Stonewall Jackson made
up for his fewer numbers
at Manassas with au-
dacity, guile, and a lot
of hard marching.*

march would begin tomorrow, he said. Moving upstream for a crossing well above Pope's right, Jackson would then swing northward behind the screen of the Bull Run Mountains, beyond which he would turn southeast through Thoroughfare Gap — the route he had followed thirteen months ago, coming down from the Valley to reach the field where he had won his nickname — for a strike at Pope's supply line, far in his rear. No precise objective was assigned. Anywhere back there along the railroad would do, Lee said, just so Pope was properly alarmed for the safety of his communications, the welfare of his supply base, and perhaps for the security of Washington itself. Lee explained that he did not want a general engagement; he wanted Pope drawn away from the reinforcements being assembled on the lower Rappahannock. Once that was done, the two wings would reunite in the vicinity of Manassas and take advantage of any opening Pope afforded, either through negligence or panic.

Jackson began his preparations at once. After sending a topographical engineer ahead to select the best route around the Bull Run Mountains, he set his camps astir. The march would begin at earliest dawn, "with the utmost promptitude, without knapsacks" — without everything, in fact, except weapons, the ordnance train, and ambulances. Beef on the hoof would serve for food, supplemented by green corn pulled from fields along the way. Ewell would lead, followed by A. P. Hill; Winder's division, now under Brigadier General W. B. Taliaferro, would bring up the rear, with orders to tread on the heels of Hill's men if they lagged. During the night, Longstreet's guns replaced Jack-

★

son's along the Rappahannock south of Waterloo Bridge, and Lee, who would
be left with 32,000 troops — including Stuart's cavalry, which would join the
flanking column the second day — prepared to stage whatever demonstrations
would be needed to conceal from Pope the departure of Jackson's 23,000.

What with the moving guns, the messengers coming and going, the
night-long activity in the camps, Stonewall himself got little sleep before the
dawn of August 25. He rose early, ate a light breakfast, and took a moment,
now that the Sabbath was over, to write a brief note to his wife. In it he said
nothing of the march that lay ahead; merely that "I have only time to tell you
how much I love my little pet dove." Presently he was in the saddle, doubling
the column. The men looked up and sideways at him as he passed, the bill of
his mangy cadet cap pulled down over his pale eyes. As usual, they did not
know where they were going, only that there would most likely be fighting
when they got there. Meanwhile, they did the marching and left the thinking
to Old Jack. "Close up, men. Close up," he said.

★ ★ ★ **T**en days ago, still down on the Peninsula, preparing
for the withdrawal he had unsuccessfully protested, McClellan had warned Halleck: "I don't like Jackson's movements.
He will suddenly appear where least expected."

This was not exactly news to Halleck, coming as it did on the heels
of Banks' repulse at Cedar Mountain. Besides, Old Brains had other problems
on his mind: not the least of which was the situation in the West, where his carefully worked-out tactical dispositions seemed about to come unglued. Kirby
Smith left Knoxville that same week, bound for Kentucky, and Bragg had his
whole army at Chattanooga, apparently poised for a leap in the same direction.
Lincoln was distressed, and so was Halleck. So, presently, was McClellan. Earlier, to encourage haste in the evacuation, Halleck had assured him: "It is my intention that you shall command all the troops in Virginia as soon as we can get
them together." McClellan's spirits rose at the prospect. To Burnside, who arrived with further assurances of Halleck's good will, he said as they stood beside
the road down which his army was withdrawing to Fort Monroe: "Look at
them, Burn. Did you ever see finer men? Oh, I want to see those men beside of
Pope's." But there were subsequent delays, chiefly the result of a shortage of
transports, and Halleck's cries for haste once more grew strident: so much so, in
fact, that McClellan felt obliged to take official exception to what he called his
"tone." Privately he protested to his wife that Halleck "did not even behave
with common politeness; he is a *bien mauvais sujet* — he is not a gentleman.
. . . I fear that I am very mad."

All the same, he made what haste he could. Porter left for Aquia
Creek on August 20, and Heintzelman left next day for Alexandria. Both were to

★

join Pope at once, the former by moving up the left bank of the Rappahannock, the latter by moving down the Orange & Alexandria Railroad. But Lee was across the Rapidan by now. "The forces of Burnside and Pope are hard-pressed," Halleck wired, "and require aid as quickly as you can send it. Come yourself as soon as you can." The bitter satisfaction McClellan found in this appeal was expressed in a letter to his wife: "Now they are in trouble they seem to want the 'Quaker,' the 'procrastinator,' the 'coward,' and the 'traitor.' *Bien*." Two days later, Franklin followed Heintzelman to Alexandria, and Sumner embarked the following day to follow Porter to Aquia Creek. Four of the five corps were gone, leaving Keyes to man the Yorktown defenses: McClellan had answered Halleck's cries for haste. But he no longer put any stock in any promises made him, either by the general in chief or by any other representative of the Administration. In fact, he told his wife as he left Old Point Comfort, August 23, "I take it for granted that my orders will be as disagreeable as it is possible to make them — unless Pope is beaten," he added, "in which case they will want me to save Washington again. Nothing but their fears will induce them to give me any command of importance or to treat me otherwise than with discourtesy."

Sure enough, when he got to Aquia next morning — Sunday — he found that Porter and Heintzelman had already been released to Pope, and when he wired for instructions Halleck replied: "You can either remain at Aquia or come to Alexandria, as you may deem best, so as to direct the landing of your troops." In other words, it didn't matter; the Young Napoleon was merely to serve as an expediter, dispatching the rest of his men to Pope as fast as they came ashore at those two points. He chose Alexandria, presumably to be close at hand for the call he believed would follow the calamity he expected. Monday and Tuesday were doubtful days; Pope's scouts had spotted a column of "well-closed infantry" moving northward, up the far bank of the Rappahannock, and Pope reported Lee's whole army bound for the Shenandoah Valley "by way of Luray and Front Royal." Then Tuesday night the line went dead. All was silent beyond Manassas Junction, where there had been some sort of explosion. . . .

The next five days were smoke and flame; McClellan ran the gamut of emotions. With Porter and Heintzelman committed, he sent Franklin to join them, saying: "Go, and whatever may happen, don't allow it to be said that the Army of the Potomac failed to do its utmost for the country." Sumner followed. "You now have every man . . . within my reach," McClellan told Halleck, requesting that "I may be permitted to go to the scene of battle with my staff, merely to be with my own men, if nothing more. They will fight none the worse for my being with them." Halleck replied, "I cannot answer without seeing the President, as General Pope is in command, by his orders, of the department." When McClellan asked where this left him, the answer came from the War Department: "General McClellan commands that portion of the Army of the

Potomac that has not been sent forward to General Pope's command." In all, this amounted to nothing more than his staff and the handful of convalescents at Alexandria. Instead of being removed from command, as he had feared at the outset, he now perceived that his command had been removed from him.

He was left, he told his wife, "flat on my back without any command whatever. . . . I feel too blue and disgusted to write any more now, so I will smoke a cigar and try to get into a better humor." It did no good. Far off, beyond Fairfax, he could hear the rumble of guns from a field where his soldiers were fighting under a man he despised and considered professionally incompetent. Unable to go, yet unable to sit still, doing nothing, he took up his pen. "They have taken all my troops from me! I have even sent off my personal escort and camp guard, and am here with a few orderlies and the aides. I have been listening to the sound of a great battle in the distance. My men engaged in it and I away! I never felt worse in my life."

---

*L*et us look before us," Pope had said, "and not
★ ★ ★ behind." In taking advantage of this policy, obligingly announced for all to hear, Jackson not only fulfilled McClellan's prediction that he would "suddenly appear where least expected," but he did so — in accordance with Lee's instructions — by landing squarely and emphatically astride those lines of retreat which Pope had said could be left "to take care of themselves."

In point of fact, however sudden his appearance was to Pope, to his own men it was something else again, coming as it did at the end of two of the longest and hardest days of marching any 23,000 soldiers ever did. At the outset the two views coincided. Like Pope, whose lookouts promptly reported the upstream movement, when they first marched into Monday's dawn they thought they were headed for another bloody game of hide-and-seek out in the Valley. That was fine with them. Rations had been scarce of late, and they recalled the largess of Commissary Banks. They swung on through the dust and heat, a long column of striding men whose uniforms, as one of their number later said, were "of that nondescript hue which time and all weathers give to ruins": Jeffersonton to Amissville, then northward across the river to Orlean, halfway through the first day's march, which would end just short of Salem, a station on the Manassas Gap Railroad. Where they would go from there they did not know. Nor did they seem to care. Approaching that place, with twenty-five leg-aching miles behind them, they forgot their weariness when they saw Jackson standing upon a large stone by the roadside, cap off, watching the sun turn red as it went down beyond the Blue Ridge. But when they cheered him, as was their custom, he made a startled gesture of protest and sent an officer to explain that the noise might give away their presence to the Yankees. So they raised their hats in mute salute as they swung past him, smiling, proud-eyed, silent except for the shuffle of feet in the dust. Flushed with pleasure, for their silence was more eloquent than cheers, Stonewall turned to his staff. "Who could not conquer with such troops as these?" he asked.

Wherever it was they were going, they knew next morning it was not to be the Valley; for at Salem they turned east toward White Plains, then southeast, following the railroad into the sunrise, blood red at first, then fiery in the broad notch of Thoroughfare Gap. That was the critical point. If it was held, there would be fighting and the loss of a large portion of the element of surprise. They quickened the step. Then word came down the column, Ewell to Hill to Taliaferro: the gap was empty, not a Federal in sight. They pressed on, eastward to Hay Market, then south-southeast to Gainesville, where they struck the Warrenton Turnpike, which led east-northeast from Pope's position on the Rappahannock, traversing the scene of last year's triumph on the plains of Manassas, across Bull Run at Stone Bridge, then on to Centreville and Alexandria. Tactically — so far, at least, as it had been kept from the marchers themselves — the secret was more or less out. "Disaster and shame lurk in the rear," Pope had said. Now Jackson lurked there, too.

It became obvious at once, though, that he intended to do a good deal more than simply lurk there. Stuart having arrived with all the cavalry — Lee had released him late the night before; he had ridden hard to catch up by midafternoon, when the head of the infantry column got to Gainesville — Jackson fanned the troopers out to the right, protecting the flank in the direction of the Rappahannock, and pushed on southward across the turnpike. Six miles ahead was Bristoe Station, where the Orange & Alexandria crossed Broad Run; destruction of the bridge there would sever Pope's supply line for days. "Push on, men. Push on," he told the marchers. But this was easier said than done. They were showing the effects of strain, and there was much less talk and horseplay up and down the column. Nearing Bristoe they had covered more than fifty miles, most of it in blazing heat and on secondary roads, with little to eat but green corn and apples along the way. Still, now that the goal was nearly in sight, according to one admiring cavalryman, "the feeling seemed to be a dread with each one that he would give out and not be there to see the fun." Many did give out, especially during this last half-dozen miles. As usual, however, though the column dribbled blown and blistered stragglers in its wake, Stonewall showed no pity for either the fainting or the stalwart, whatever their rank. Just short of Bristoe he dismounted and went onto the porch of a roadside cabin to wait for the column to close. He sat in a split-bottom chair, tilted back against

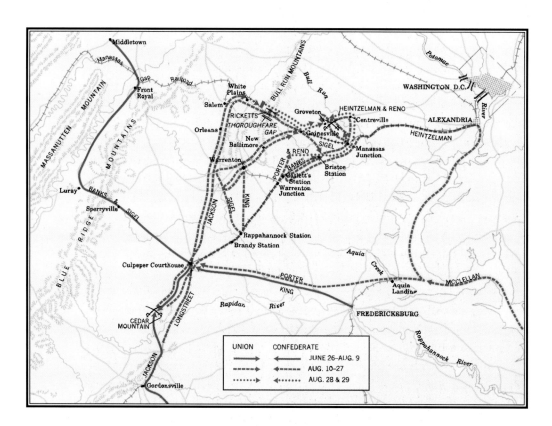

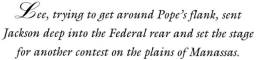

*Lee, trying to get around Pope's flank, sent
Jackson deep into the Federal rear and set the stage
for another contest on the plains of Manassas.*

the wall, and fell asleep. Presently a staff officer arrived and shouted him awake:
"General Blank failed to put a picket at the crossroads! and the following
brigade took the wrong road!" The eyelids lifted; two pale blue chinks appeared
in the thin-lipped mask. "Put him under arrest and prefer charges," Jackson
snapped. The eyelids dropped and he was back asleep at once.

The lead brigade hit Bristoe just at sunset. Coming forward on the
run, the whooping graybacks overpowered the startled guards and were taking
charge when they heard the approaching rumble of a northbound train. Hur-
riedly they threw crossties on the track and began a frantic attempt to unbolt a
rail. Too late: the engine was upon them, scattering ties and men, then clattering
out of sight in the gathering dusk — doubtless to give warning up the line.
Their disappointment was relieved, however, by news that this was the hour
when empty supply trains made their run, one after another from Pope's advance depots around Warrenton, back to Manassas and Alexandria. When the

next prize came along the raiders were ready. Riflemen lining one flank of the right-of-way gave the locomotive a volley as it thundered past, struck an open switch, and plunged with half its cars down the embankment, where it struck with a gaudy eruption of red coals and hissing steam. Delighted with this effect, the Confederates gathered round and were pointing with elation at a bullet-pocked portrait of Lincoln on the steam dome — the engine was called *The President* — when the whistle of a third train was heard. It rammed into the cars left on the track, creating another rackety tableau of splintered wood and twisted iron: whereupon still a fourth whistle sounded. But while the watchers were getting set to enjoy another eruption of sparks and steam, they heard instead a screech of brakes as the locomotive stopped, then backed rapidly away and out of sight. The raiders cursed the engineer for his vigilance. Now the alarm would be sounded below as well as above the captured station; the fireworks fun was at an end.

Though he had enjoyed all this as much as anyone, now that it was over Jackson wasted no time on regret that it could not have lasted longer. Instead, he put his troops to work at once on the job for which he had brought them here in the first place: destruction of the Broad Run railroad bridge. While this was being done he stood beside a fire, hastily kindled for light, and began to interrogate one of the captured engineers. Across the way, a Federal civilian was laid out on the ground; a middle-aged man — probably a politician, for he had come down from Washington on a visit to Pope's army — he had suffered a broken leg in one of the train wrecks. Hearing who his captors were, and that their commander was just on the opposite side of the campfire, he asked to be lifted, despite the pain, for a look at the famed rebel. When the soldiers obliged, he saw beyond the dancing flames a stoop-shouldered figure in outsized boots and road-colored clothes slouched with a crumpled cadet cap pulled far down over his nose. For half a minute the civilian stared at the plain-looking man his captors assured him was the gallant Stonewall, scourge of the Yankee nation. Then, anticipation having given way to incredulity, which in turn gave way to disillusionment, he said with a groan of profound disgust: "O my God! Lay me down."

Jackson himself knew nothing of this: which was why he never understood the basic implication of the expression used by his soldiers in almost every conceivable situation from now on, whether confronted with an issue of meager rations or a charging Union line: "O my God! Lay me down!" In any case, even if he had heard it, he had no time for laughter. Interrogation of the engineer, along with other captives, had divulged that Pope's main base of supplies, four miles up the line at Manassas, was lightly guarded and wide open to attack. How long it would remain so, now that the alarm had been sounded in both directions, was another matter. Jackson decided to take no chance on being shut off from this richest of all prizes. Leg-weary though the men were, some of them would have to push on through the darkness to Manassas, block the arrival of reinforcements sent by rail from Alexandria, and hold the place until their comrades joined them in the morning. Two of Ewell's regiments drew the duty; or, more strictly speaking, were volunteered for it by their commander, Brigadier General Isaac Trimble. It was Trimble, a sixty-year-old Virginia-born Kentucky-raised Marylander, who had wanted to make a twilight charge up the blasted slope of Malvern Hill the month before; Stonewall had restrained him then, but he remained undaunted; "Before this war is over," he declared as the army started northward, "I intend to be a major general or a corpse." He set off into the night, riding out of Bristoe at the head of his two foot-sore regiments, a burly white-haired West Pointer with a drooping black mustache. On second thought, Jackson sent Stuart and his troopers along to support him. Then the rest of the command bedded down, too weary to worry overmuch about the fact that they were sleeping between an army of 75,000 bluecoats and the capital whose safety was supposedly that army's first concern.

Early next morning, August 27, leaving the rest of Ewell's division to guard the Broad Run crossing in his rear, Jackson moved on Manassas with the troops of Hill and Taliaferro. The sight that awaited them there was past the imagining of Stonewall's famished tatterdemalions. Acres — a square mile, in fact — of supplies of every description were stacked in overwhelming abundance, collected here against the day when the armies of Pope and McClellan combined for another advance on Richmond. Newly constructed warehouses overflowed with rations, quartermaster goods, and ordnance stores. Two spur tracks, half a mile long each, were jammed with more than a hundred brand-new boxcars, similarly freighted. Best of all, from the point of view of the luxury-starved raiders, sutler wagons parked hub-to-hub were packed with every delicacy their vanished owners had thought might tempt a payday soldier's jaded palate. There it all was, spread out before the butternut horde as if the mythical horn of plenty had been upended here, its contents theirs for the taking. So they supposed; but when they broke ranks, surging forward, they found that Jackson, frugal as always, had foreseen their reaction and had moved to forestall it by placing Trimble's men on guard to hold them back. For once, though, he had underrated their aggressive instincts. Veterans of harder fights, with infinitely smaller rewards at the end, they broke through the cordon and fell on the feast of good things. Canteens were filled with molasses, haversacks with coffee; pockets bulged with cigars, jackknives, writing paper, handkerchiefs, and such. However, the chief object of search, amid the embarrassment of riches, was whiskey. This too their commander had foreseen, and by his orders the guards staved in the barrels and shattered the demijohns; whereupon the looters dropped to their hands and knees, scooping and sipping at the pools and rivulets before the liquor soaked into the earth or drained away. Some, more abstemious, were satisfied with loaves of unfamiliar light-bread, which they ate like cake. Others, preferring a still richer diet, found pickled oysters and canned lobster more to their taste, spooning it up with grimy fingers and washing it down with bottles of Rhine wine.

Off to the east, a troublesome Federal battery had been banging away in protest all this while. Jackson sent one of his own to attend to it, but presently word came back that enemy infantry was crossing the Bull Run railroad bridge and forming for attack. Most of Hill's division was moved out quickly to meet the threat, which turned out to be a brigade of four New Jersey regiments sent down by rail from Alexandria under a zealous and badly informed commander, Brigadier General George W. Taylor. His orders were to save the bridge, but he decided to press on to the junction itself and drive away the raiders, whom he mistook for cavalry. The Jerseymen came on in style, green and eager, not knowing that they were up against the largest and proba-

---

Canteens were filled with molasses, haversacks with coffee; pockets bulged with cigars, jackknives, writing paper, handkerchiefs, and such.

---

bly the hardest-fighting division in Lee's whole army. Jackson opened on them with his guns — prematurely it seemed to Little Powell's men, waiting with cocked rifles for the interrupters of their feast to come within butchering distance. But the bluecoats took their long-range losses and kept coming, bayonets fixed and fire in their eyes.

Then Stonewall did an unfamiliar thing. Admiring their valor, which he knew was based on ignorance — the charge, he said later, "was made with great spirit and determination and under a leader worthy of a better cause" — he called a cease-fire and rode out in front of the guns, waving a handkerchief and shouting for the Federals to surrender and be spared extermination. By way of reply, one attacker took deliberate aim and sent a bullet whistling past him. Cured of his lapse into leniency, Jackson rode back and ordered the fire resumed. By now the Jerseymen were nearer, and this time it was as if they struck a trip-wire. Suddenly demoralized, they turned and scampered, devil-take-the-hindmost. Their losses were surprisingly light, considering the danger to which their rashness had exposed them: 200 captured and 135 killed or wounded, including their commander, who, as he was being carried dying to the rear, appealed to his men to rally "and for God's sake . . . prevent another Bull Run."

★

They paid him no mind; nor did Jackson. Already burdened with more spoils than he could handle — victim, as it were, of the law of diminishing utility — for once he was unconcerned about pursuit. The whole comic-opera affair was over before noon. After burning the railroad bridge to insure against further interruption from that direction, he brought Hill's men back to the junction, where some measure of order had been restored in their absence. It was maintained, at least temporarily. While the plunderers were held at bay, the ambulances and ordnance wagons — all the rolling stock he had — were filled with such Federal stores as were most needed, principally medical supplies. Once this was done, the rest were thrown open to the troops, who fell upon them whooping, their appetites whetted by the previous unauthorized foray. Painful as it was to Stonewall, watching the improvident manner in which his scarecrow raiders snatched up one luxurious armload only to cast it aside for another, he was reconciled to the waste by the knowledge that what was rejected would have to be given to the flames. Word had come from Ewell that he was under attack at Bristoe from the opposite direction; Jackson knew the time had come to abandon his exposed position for one in which he could await, with some degree of security, the arrival of Longstreet and reconsolidation of the army under Lee.

★ ★ ★ **By now, of course, Pope had learned the nature of the explosion in his rear.** Instead of heading for the Shenandoah Valley, as had been supposed when the signal station reported a well-closed gray column moving north two days ago, Lee had divided his army and sent half of it swinging around the Bull Run Mountains for a strike at Manassas; that half of it was there now, under Jackson. But Pope was not dismayed. Far from it; he was exultant, and with cause. He had forty brigades of infantry on hand, including a dozen of McClellan's, with others on the way. It seemed to him that Lee, who had less than thirty brigades — fourteen in one direction, fifteen in another, more than twenty air-line miles apart, with 75,000 Federals on the alert between the two segments — had committed tactical suicide. Hurrying to Bristoe, where Hooker's division of Heintzelman's corps was skirmishing with the enemy, Pope arrived as night was falling, and found that the rebels, soundly thrashed according to Hooker, had retreated across Broad Run. Encouraged by today's success, he decided to bring up six more divisions and with them crush Jackson's three before the sun went down tomorrow. A depot of supplies, however vast, seemed a small price to pay for bait when it brought such a catch within his reach.

To Phil Kearny, commanding Heintzelman's other division at Warrenton Junction, went a wire: "At the very earliest blush of dawn push forward . . . with all speed to this place. . . . Jackson, A. P. Hill, and Ewell are in front of us. . . . I want you here at day-dawn, if possible, and we shall bag the whole crowd. Be prompt and expeditious, and never mind wagon trains or roads till this affair is over." To Reno, at Greenwich with Burnside's two divisions, went another: "March at the earliest dawn of day . . . on Manassas Junction. Jackson, Ewell, and A. P. Hill are between Gainesville and that place, and if you are prompt and expeditious we shall bag the whole crowd. . . . As you value success be off at the earliest blush of dawn." A third wire went to McDowell, whose three divisions were helping to hold the line of the Rappahannock: "Jackson, Ewell, and A. P. Hill are between Gainesville and Manassas Junction. We had a severe fight with them today, driving them back several miles along the railroad. If you will march promptly and rapidly at the earliest dawn of day upon Manassas Junction we shall bag the whole crowd. . . . Be expeditious, and the day is our own."

Northeastward, exploding ammunition dumps imitated the din of a great battle and the night sky was lurid with the reflection of a square mile of flames: Jackson's graybacks were evidently staging a high revel, oblivious to the destruction being plotted by their adversary, five short miles away. But next morning, after fording Broad Run unopposed and marching past the wreckage at Bristoe Station, when Pope reached Manassas all he found was the charred evidence of what one of his staff colonels called "the recent rebel carnival." The scene was one of waste and desolation. "On the railroad tracks and sidings stood the hot and smoking remains of what had recently been trains of cars laden with ordnance and commissary stores intended for our army. As far as the eye could reach, the plain was covered with boxes, barrels, cans, cooking utensils, saddles, sabers, muskets, and military equipments generally; hard bread and corn pones, meat, salt, and fresh beans, blankets, clothes, shoes, and hats, from brand-new articles, just from the original packages, to the scarcely recognizable exuviae of the rebels, who had made use of the opportunity to renew their toilets." Of the revelers themselves there was no sign. Nor was there agreement among the returning guards and sutlers as to the direction in which they had disappeared. Some said one way, some another. As far as Pope could tell, the earth had swallowed them up.

As things now stood, last night's orders would result in nothing more than a convergence on a vacuum. Presently, however, reports began to come in, pinpointing the gray column first in one place, then another, most of them quite irreconcilable. Pope sifted the conflicting evidence, rejecting this, accepting that, and arrived at the conviction that Stonewall was concentrating his three divisions at Centreville. Revised orders went out accordingly, canceling the convergence on Manassas; Centreville was now the place. If they would still be expeditious, the day would still be Pope's.

His exuberance and zest were undiminished; he kept his mind, if not his eye, on the prize within his reach. But for others under him — particularly the dust-eating soldiers in the ranks, left hungry by the destruction of their commissary stores — the chase, if it could be called such, had already begun to pall.

★

Marched and countermarched since the "earliest blush of dawn" in pursuit of phantoms, they were being mishandled and they knew it. The very terrain was of evil memory. It seemed to them that they were heading for a repetition of last year's debacle on these same rolling plains, under some of these same commanders. McDowell, for example; "I'd rather shoot McDowell than Jackson," men were saying. Now as then, they turned on him, muttering imprecations. Nothing about him escaped suspicion, even his hat, a bamboo-and-canvas affair he had invented to keep his scalp cool in the Virginia heat. They suspected that it was a signaling device, to be used for communicating with the rebels or as an identification to keep him from being shot by mistake. "That basket," they called it, contemptuous not only of the helmet, but also of the general it shaded. "Pope has his headquarters in the saddle, and McDowell his head in a basket."

All through the long hot afternoon of August 28 Pope kept groping,

★

Federal soldiers stand watch over a burned-out train of boxcars torched by Jackson's "foot cavalry" during their raid on Manassas Junction.

like the "it" in a game of blindman's buff, arms outstretched, fingers spread, combing the landscape for the ubiquitous, elusive rebel force: to no avail. Riding into Centreville at sunset, in advance of most of the twelve divisions he had slogging the dusty roads — all, that is, but the two with Banks, which, being still unrecovered from the shock of Cedar Mountain, had been left behind to guard the army trains — he found that he had ordered another convergence on another vacuum. The graybacks had been there, all right, but they were there no longer. They had vanished. Once more it was as if the earth had swallowed them, except that this time he would have to look for them in darkness, with troops worn

★

down by fourteen hours of fruitless marching. Pope felt the first twinges of dismay. Not because of fear; he was afraid of nothing, not even Stonewall; but because the time allotted for the destruction of Lee's army, wing by isolated wing, was running out. Such fear as he felt was that Jackson would make his escape and rejoin Longstreet, who by now would be moving to meet him.

Pope's dismay was short-lived, however. After nightfall, two dispatches reached him that changed everything and sent his spirits soaring higher than ever. The first informed him that Longstreet's column, after penetrating Thoroughfare Gap, had been driven back to the west side of Bull Run Mountain. This afforded considerable relief, allowing as it did additional time in which to catch the rebel host divided. But the best news of all came just before 10 o'clock. Late that afternoon, marching as ordered toward Centreville, one of McDowell's divisions had found Jackson lurking in the woods beside the Warrenton Turnpike, two miles short of Stone Bridge, and had flushed him. There on the field of last year's battle, Pope wired Halleck, "a severe fight took place, which was terminated by darkness. The enemy was driven back at all points, and thus the affair rests."

Determined not to let it rest there long, he sent peremptory orders to the commanders of his five converging corps for the execution of a plan he improvised, then and there, for the absolute destruction of his just-found adversary. McDowell and Sigel, with 30,000 men, would attack at dawn from the south and west, blocking any possible withdrawal by way of Thoroughfare Gap, while Heintzelman, Porter, and Reno, with another 30,000, would attack from the east: twin hammers whose concerted blows would pound to a pulp the 23,000 butternut marauders, pinned to the anvil by their own commander.

FEDERAL GENERALS ON THE LOOKOUT FOR "STONEWALL" JACKSON.

A northern newspaper cartoon parodies inept
Federal generals who never seemed able to figure
out Stonewall Jackson's whereabouts.

★

Pope's instructions were explicit: "Assault him vigorously at daylight in the morning." Exultant — and with cause; Jackson's 14 gray brigades were about to be mauled simultaneously by 34 in blue, 17 from one direction, 17 from another — he added: "I see no possibility of his escape."

★ ★ ★ *S*toutly conceived though the plan was, and stoutly though he strove to put it into execution, Pope was again the victim of several misconceptions. For one thing, Jackson was not trapped; nor was he trying to "escape." He very much wanted to be where he was, and he very much hoped that Pope could be persuaded to attack him, whatever the odds. In fact, if he could have been at Federal headquarters, with control over the messages coming and going, he scarcely would have changed a line in a single one of them. His luck was in and he knew it — the old Valley luck, by which even his worst errors worked to his advantage. The night march out of Manassas, for example:

When Ewell came up from Bristoe about sunset, having disengaged from the skirmish with Hooker's division across Broad Run, Stonewall gave these late arrivers a chance at the fag end of the feast — "What we got was . . . not of a kind to invigorate," one cannoneer grumbled, "consisting as it did of hard-tack, pickled oysters, and canned stuff generally" — then put all three divisions in motion while the rear guard set fire to the picked-over wreckage left behind. What followed, as the troops slogged more or less northward in three columns, looking back over their shoulders at the spreading glow of flames, was one of the worst executed marches in the history of his command. Heavy-stomached, with bulging haversacks and pockets, the men fell by the wayside or crawled under bushes to sleep off their excesses of food and drink. The result was confusion and a great deal of lost time as the file-closers probed the countryside, rounding them up and persuading them to fall back into column. Taliaferro did best, moving almost due north up the Sudley Springs road to Groveton, the designated point of concentration, where that road intersected the Warrenton Turnpike. Hill did worst; he went all the way to Centreville, then swung west. Ewell, following Hill for a time, crossed Bull Run at Blackburn's Ford, then recrossed it at Stone Bridge, Hill coming along somewhere behind. Morning found the three divisions badly scattered and dangerously exposed; it was midday before they were reunited at Groveton. For this there were various causes — Jackson's sketchy instructions, inefficient guides, the droves of stragglers — but even this blundering performance worked to Stonewall's advantage, providing as it did the basis for the conflicting Federal reports of his whereabouts, which led Pope off on a tangential pursuit.

Whatever blame he deserved for the confusion in all three columns along the way, Jackson had chosen their destination with care and daring. A rapid withdrawal to rejoin Lee beyond the mountains was in order, but it was not Stonewall's way to turn his back on a situation, no matter how risky, so long as possible benefits remained within his reach. Tomorrow or the next day, Longstreet would be coming down through Thoroughfare Gap or up the Warrenton Turnpike. At Groveton, Jackson knew from last year's extended stay in the area, there was an excellent covered position in which to await Old Pete's arrival by either route, and if the pressure grew too great his line of retreat would be reasonably secure. Meanwhile, the Federals — or, as he preferred to express it, "a kind Providence" — might afford him a chance at the infliction of another "terrible wound." About midday, when he finally got his scattered divisions back together, he put the men in position just north of the turnpike, behind a low ridge and under cover of some woods. One soldier later remembered that they were "packed [in there] like herring in a barrel." They stacked arms and lounged about, all 23,000 of them (minus stragglers) snoozing, playing cards, and munching at more of the good things they had in their haversacks by courtesy of Commissary Pope. The bands were silent; the troops were instructed not to shout; but as that same soldier remembered it, there were "no restrictions as to laughing and talking . . . and the woods sounded like the hum of a beehive in the warm sunshine."

Jackson himself remained on the ridge, which afforded a clear view of the pike in both directions. When a report arrived that a strong Union column was advancing from Gainesville, he moved Taliaferro and Ewell two miles west and posted them in the woods adjacent to the pike for a surprise attack on the flank of the passing bluecoats. Nothing came of this; the column turned off south toward Manassas before it came abreast. Stonewall was cross and restless, reminding one observer of "an explosive missile, an unlucky spark applied to which would blow you sky high." Lee had told him to avoid a general engagement, but he did not like to see the Federals escape the ambush he had laid. Besides, he knew now that reinforcements from the Peninsula were at Alexandria — better than 30,000 of them, in addition to the two corps already joined. If Pope withdrew in that direction, the combined might of his and McClellan's forces would be too great for a strike at them, even after Lee arrived with Longstreet. So Jackson continued to patrol the ridge, trotting back and forth on his horse, peering up and down the pike. His staff and several brigade and regimental commanders sat their mounts at a respectful distance, not wanting to come near him in his present frame of mind or take a chance on interrupting his prayers that Providence would send another blue column into the trap the first had avoided.

Along toward sunset, his prayers were answered after the flesh. A well-closed Federal column was approaching, trudging hard up the turnpike in the direction of Stone Bridge, flankers out. Jackson rode down off the ridge for a closer look and trotted back and forth, within easy musket range of the bluecoats, who gave him no more attention than a casual rebel cavalryman deserved. Back on the ridge, the officers watched in horror and fascination. "We could almost tell his thoughts by his movements," one declared. "Sometimes he would halt, then trot on briskly, halt again, wheel his horse, and pass again along the [flank] of the marching column." They thought they knew what he would do, and presently he did it. When the head of the blue column drew abreast, he whirled and galloped back toward the group on the ridge. "Here he comes, by God!" one shouted. Jackson pulled up, touched his cap, and said calmly: "Bring your men up, gentlemen." At this, they turned and rode fast toward the woods where the infantry was waiting. "The men had been watching their officers with much interest," the same observer remarked, "and when they wheeled and dashed toward them they knew what it meant, and from the woods arose a hoarse roar like that from cages of wild animals at the scent of blood."

The artillery led off. Three batteries emerged from the woods, went into position in the open, and began to slam away at the compact column on the pike. As the cannonade got under way, Taliaferro's men swarmed down the

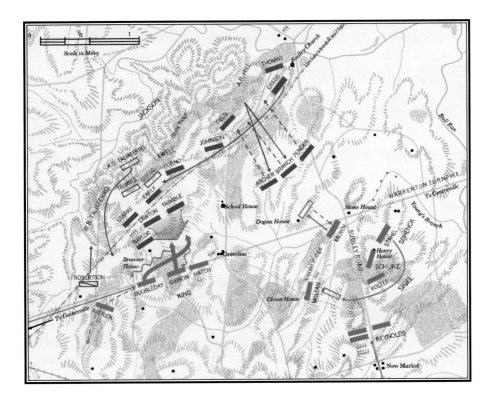

*P*ositioned behind an unfinished railroad cut,
Jackson opened the three-day battle when he jumped
the first Federal column to march past.

slope, yelling as they came, the battle flags of the Stonewall Brigade gleaming blood-red in the fading light. The result should have been panic, for the blue-coats taken thus unawares were from Rufus King's division — specifically, John Gibbon's brigade of four regiments, three from Wisconsin and one from Indiana — one of the largest but also one of the greenest in Pope's conglomerate command. However, instead of panicking at this abrupt baptism of fire, the Western-ers wheeled to meet the attackers and stopped them in their tracks with massed volleys. Gibbon was regular army, loyal to the Union despite the fact that three of his North Carolina brothers went with the Stars and Bars. Supported by two regiments sent forward from Abner Doubleday's brigade, he handled his troops skillfully, holding off Taliaferro, who presently was reinforced by two brigades from Ewell. What ensued, first by the red glare of sunset, then on through dusk and twilight into darkness, with 2800 Federals facing nearly twice as many Con-federates, was one of the hardest close-quarter fights of the whole war.

Jackson did not attempt to maneuver. Contrary to his usual practice once the advance had stalled, he was content to let the weight of numbers settle the issue. In point of fact, however, neither the pressure nor the savagery of his veterans settled anything at all. If the Wisconsin and Indiana farm boys were in a hopeless predicament, outnumbered nearly two to one by fighters whose fame was the highest in either army, they did not seem to recognize the odds. Experi-ence had afforded them nothing by way of comparison; for all they knew, com-bat was supposed to be like this. The opposing lines stood face to face, parade-style, and slugged it out for two solid hours. Gibbon, who at thirty-five had a long career ahead of him, said afterwards that this was the heaviest in-fantry fire he ever heard, and Taliaferro referred to the engagement as "one of the most terrific conflicts that can be conceived of."

Finally the firing slacked; by 9 o'clock it died away, by mutual con-sent. The Federals withdrew across the turnpike, unpursued. More than a thou-sand of them had fallen, well over a third of the number engaged; the 2d Wis-consin, which had gone into the fight 500 strong, came out with 202, having begun tonight to establish the record it would set, before the war was over, by having more of its members killed in combat than any other regiment in the U.S. Army. Gibbon and Doubleday wondered what to do. Their latest orders called for a march on Centreville, but if the two-hour fight proved nothing else, it certainly had proved that the way was blocked in that direction. King was sick in an ambulance; no one knew where McDowell was. (He was in fact lost in the woods, having strayed from the pike in the darkness, and would not himself know where he was till morning.) So Gibbon and Doubleday, conferring with the ailing King, decided that the best thing to do would be to swing on down to Manassas, the original objective, taking such of their wounded along as could be recovered from the field. Grass-green three hours ago, the western soldiers fell

One of the Black Hat Brigade's regiments, the 2d Wisconsin, carried this national flag during the bloody fight on the evening of August 28.

back in and set off down the road as veterans. They were known as the Black Hat Brigade, Gibbon having seen to it that they were equipped with nonregulation black felt hats. In time, the rebels too would know them by that name; "Here come them damn black hat fellers!" the gray pickets would yell. But presently they changed it. Within a month they were calling themselves the Iron Brigade.

Few men anywhere were inclined to question their right to call themselves by any name they fancied — least of all Taliaferro's and Ewell's, who had suffered about as heavily as the troops they sought to ambush. The Stonewall Brigade took 635 soldiers into the twilight conflict and came out with 425, a ghost of the proud 3000-man command that won its *nom de guerre* on nearby Henry Hill the year before and then passed through the glory of the Valley Campaign and the carnage of the Seven Days. Some of its most famous regiments were reduced to the size of a small company; the 27th Virginia, for example, was down to a scant two dozen men by the time the firing stopped. Murderous as these figures were, they told but part of the story, for they included a high percentage of officers of all ranks. The 2d Virginia had only one captain and one lieutenant left with the colors, and others were stripped almost as bare of leaders. Nor were the losses restricted to those of field and company grade. This fight brought down generals too, including two of the three ranking just under Jackson himself. Taliaferro, who had succeeded Winder less than three weeks ago, was thrice wounded. He kept on his feet till the melee ended, but then, bled white, was carried off the field. His successor, Brigadier General William E. Starke — a former New Orleans cotton man, professionally untrained in arms — had been promoted on the eve of Cedar Mountain and had led a brigade in action for the first time tonight. Now suddenly he found himself in command of the most famous of all Confederate divisions.

The other high-ranking casualty was Ewell. Unable to resist the lure of close-up combat, he had gone forward to direct a charge by the 21st Georgia.

As he knelt, squinting under the smoke for a glimpse of the enemy line, several of the Georgians called out proudly: "Here's General Ewell, boys!": whereupon the Federals, hearing the cheering, cut loose with heavy volleys in that direction. The regiment scattered, taking such losses here and elsewhere that it emerged from the battle with only 69 of its 242 men unhurt. Old Bald Head himself was found on the field when the fight was over, unconscious from loss of blood, one knee badly shattered by a minie. The surgeons assessed the damage and pronounced the verdict: amputation. Apparently he was out of the war for good. His successor was Alexander R. Lawton, who had held the rank of brigadier for sixteen months — longer than any other general in the army — apparently because Jackson, who had by-passed him in favor of Winder, did not consider him competent for divisional command. Now, as a result of attrition, his seniority could no longer be denied.

Any fight that cost the Confederacy the services of the profane and eccentric Ewell, along with those of the fast-developing Taliaferro and nearly a thousand other veterans of all ranks, could scarcely be called an unclouded victory, no matter who held the field when the smoke cleared. Moreover, Jackson himself had displayed symptoms of a relapse into tactical lethargy once the thing was under way. Yet if he felt either dismay or dissatisfaction at being thus deprived of two of his three chief lieutenants — all, in fact, but the one he trusted least, the thin-skinned and erratic A. P. Hill — he showed no signs of it, any more than he showed signs of apprehension for what Pope would surely try to do to him tomorrow. He seemed in fact, according to one of his soldiers, "calm as a May morning." What was left of the night he devoted to sleep. Purposely, as if with a shout of Boo! in the game of blindman's buff he was playing, he had attracted Pope's attention, hoping to hold him there by absorbing his attacks until Lee arrived with Longstreet and made possible a shift to the offensive he preferred.

* * * *Longstreet was nearer than Jackson knew:* near enough, even, to have heard the tearing rattle of musketry in the twilight west of Groveton, six miles off, and to wonder at the silence that ensued. For Lee, who was with the approaching column, this was one more enigma to be added to the many that had fretted him since Stonewall marched away, four days ago. The first day had been spent continuing the artillery demonstration along the Rappahannock. That night, after wiring Davis to ask if more troops could be spared from the Richmond defenses, he sent Stuart off with all the cavalry. Next morning, August 26, he continued the cannonade, hoping to keep Pope's attention fixed on his front while Jackson

moved around his flank to strike his rear. By midday, however, there were signs that the Federals were beginning to pull back: which might or might not mean that the ruse had been detected. Lee sent for Longstreet. The time had come to reunite the two wings of the army, he said, and he left to him the choice of routes, either up the Warrenton Pike or roundabout through Salem. Old Pete chose the latter. Leaving Major General R. H. Anderson's division, formerly Huger's, to hold the fords and mask the movement, he set out that afternoon with his other three divisions — Hood's, reinforced by Shanks Evans, whose brigade had come up from South Carolina; Brigadier General D. R. Jones', formerly half of Magruder's; and Longstreet's own, now split in two, under Brigadier Generals Cadmus Wilcox and James Kemper. This gave him, in effect, five divisions, each with three brigades; 32,000 men in all.

He made eleven miles before bivouacking near Orlean after nightfall, and by noon of the following day the head of the column had passed through Salem, matching the performance of Stonewall's fabled marchers over these same roads, thirty-six hours ago. That was gratifying indeed. Even more so, however, were two dispatches Lee received before going into bivouac on the outskirts of White Plains. The first was from Jackson, informing him that he had taken Bristoe and Manassas the night before. He was concentrating now at the latter place, he added, squarely in Pope's rear, and saw no evidence, so far, that the Federals were massing against him. The second welcome dispatch, brought by a courier from the opposite direction, was from Davis, replying to Lee's request for reinforcements. They were on the way, the President told him: Wade Hampton's cavalry brigade and two divisions of infantry under Harvey Hill and Major General Lafayette McLaws, the latter having been assigned the other half of Magruder's old command. Howls of protest might ordinarily be expected when his critics learned that the seat of government was being stripped of defenders, Davis said, but "confidence in you overcomes the view which would otherwise be taken of the exposed condition of Richmond, and the troops retained for the defense of the capital are surrendered to you on a new request."

Lee's anxiety, both for the present and the future, was considerably relieved. In addition to the badly needed brigade of cavalry — he had none at all for the screening of Longstreet's column; riding point that morning near Salem, he and his staff had barely avoided capture by a roving Federal squadron — the arrival of the promised ten brigades of infantry would add 17,000 veteran bayonets to his army. That would by no means even the odds Pope and Burnside and McClellan could bring to bear, combined, but it would at any rate reduce them to the vicinity of two to one: 150,000 vs 72,000. If the present odds were less heartening — McClellan, after all, might be with Pope already — in other respects the situation appeared quite promising. Reinforcements on the way, Jackson astride the railroad in Pope's rear, the main Union supply base

*Georgia troops under General Longstreet fire
down on Federals blocking the Confederate
passage through Thoroughfare Gap.*

up in flames: all this was much, besides which it held out interesting possibilities for maneuver. Manassas being just twenty-two miles from White Plains, Longstreet's present bivouac, Lee could reasonably expect to have the two wings of his army reunited by tomorrow night, prepared to undertake the completion of the "suppression" already begun. Before dawn, more good news arrived. Jackson informed him by courier that he was withdrawing from his exposed position at Manassas and would concentrate at Groveton, thus reducing by three full miles the interval between himself and Longstreet.

Refreshed by sleep, Old Pete's veterans swung off into a rising sun that seemed destined to shine today on a reunited Army of Northern Virginia. Only one natural obstacle lay in their path: Thoroughfare Gap. If the Yankees held it in strength there would be the delay of an uphill fight or a roundabout march, either of which would throw the schedule out of kilter. This seemed unlikely, though, since Jackson's couriers had been coming through unhindered, and presently another arrived, bringing further assurance that the pass was open and that his chief had reached Groveton, unmolested and unobserved, and was concentrating his troops in the woods overlooking the turnpike at that place. At 3 o'clock, topping the final rise that brought the gap into view, Longstreet's lead division pushed rapidly forward. Back with the main body, Lee presently heard from up ahead the reverberant clatter of musketry in the gorge. "Its echoes were wonderful," one staff officer later recalled. "A gun fired in its depths gave forth roars fit to bring down the skies."

Lee's reaction was less esthetic, for this of all sounds was the one he least wanted to hear. Then came the message that confirmed his fears: The Federals not only held the pass itself, they also had a reserve line posted on a dominant ridge beyond. John Pope had turned the tables, it seemed. Instead of panicking when he found Stonewall interposed between himself and Washington, the Union commander apparently had seized the initiative and posted his superior force between the two Confederate wings, preparing to crush them in sequence.

This was the darkest possible view. But Longstreet — "that undismayed warrior," his chief of staff afterwards called him, adding that he was "like a rock in steadiness when sometimes in battle the world seemed flying to pieces" — put his troops at once in motion to test the validity of such gloom. While Jones, supported by Kemper, kept up the pressure dead ahead, Hood probed for an opening near at hand and Wilcox set out for Hopewell Gap, three miles north. These dispositions took time. Near sunset, during lulls in the firing here at the pass, Lee heard from the direction of Groveton the mutter of distant musketry, mixed in with the grumble of guns. This was presently blotted out, however, by the stepped-up firing close at hand: Hood's men had found a cleft in the ridge and were on the Federal flank. Promptly the bluecoats retreated, unplugging the gap and withdrawing from the ridge beyond. (They were only a single division, after all, sent by McDowell on his own initiative, shortly before he wandered off and got himself lost in the woods.) Jones and Kemper marched through unopposed, joining Hood on the eastern slope, and the three divisions settled down to await the arrival of Wilcox, who had likewise penetrated Hopewell Gap.

Now that their own guns were silent, they heard again the growl and rumble of those near Groveton, half a dozen miles away. The uproar swelled to climax. Then it sank. At 9 o'clock it stopped. This might mean almost anything; all that was certain was that Jackson had been engaged. Whether he had won or lost — whether, indeed, that wing of the army still existed — they would know tomorrow. Whichever it was, it was over now. After sending a courier to inform Stonewall that the main body was safely through the pass, Lee told Longstreet to bed his men down for a good night's sleep in preparation for a fast march at sunup.

Friday, August 29, Hood's troops took the lead, marching so fast that their commander later reported proudly, "General Longstreet sent me orders, two or three times, to halt, since the army was unable to keep within supporting distance of my forces." There was need for haste. Ahead, the guns were booming again and a great white bank of smoke was piling up against the hot, bright blue, windless sky. Comforting though this was as proof that Jackson's men were still alive and kicking, it also demonstrated Pope's determination to destroy them before reinforcements got there. The Texans pushed on through Hay Market, raising a red cloud of dust with their feet, then down to Gainesville, where they struck the Warrenton Turnpike and swung left, advancing another three miles toward the ground-jarring thunder of guns, until they came upon Stonewall's right flank, above Groveton. It was now about 10 o'clock: Lee's army was reunited. Hood went into position north of the pike, establishing contact, and the other divisions filed into position on his right, extending the line generally southward, across the pike and down toward the Manassas Gap Railroad. From left to right, Longstreet's order of battle was Hood, Kemper, Jones, Wilcox. Anderson, who had masked the withdrawal from the Rappahannock line, was due to arrive by nightfall.

★ ★ ★ *M*oving from the scene of last night's bloody encounter, Jackson had placed his three divisions along the grade of an unfinished railroad. Part cut, part fill, it furnished an excellent defensive position, practically a ready-made system of intrenchments, roughly parallel to the turnpike across which Longstreet's line was drawn. When the Valley soldiers heard that their comrades had completed the march from Thoroughfare Gap and were filing into position on the right — "covered with dust so thick," one cavalryman observed, "that all looked as if they had been painted one color" — they rose and cheered them, despite the cannonade, which had scarcely slacked since sunup. Presently, though, they had more to worry about than bursting shells. The blue infantry was swarming to the attack.

The Federal chieftain's plans for a simultaneous double blow at both of Stonewall's flanks had gone astray, Porter having been delayed by darkness and two of the missing McDowell's three divisions having fallen back on Manassas after their twilight fights at Groveton and the Gap. "God damn McDowell, he's never where I want him," Pope was saying, angry but undaunted. He sent staff officers to locate them and hurry them along. Meanwhile, Sigel, Reno, and Heintzelman were at hand, and he flung them forward, still convinced that Jackson was trying to escape. One after another, they surged across the open fields, breaking in waves against the embankment where Stonewall's bayonets glittered. The closest they came to success was on the rebel left, where some woods afforded a covered approach. This was on Little Powell's front, the extreme flank of which was held by Brigadier General Maxcy Gregg's South Carolinians. Kearny's division struck hard here, effecting a lodgment astride the ramp and pressing down on the end of the line as if to roll it up. On a rocky knoll, here on the far-east margin of the conflict, Rebs and Yanks fought hand to hand. Bayonets crossed; rifle butts cracked skulls. A bachelor lawyer, somewhat deaf, Gregg strode up and down, brandishing an old Revolutionary scimitar and calling for a rally. "Let us die here, my men. Let us die here," he said. Many did die, something over 600 in all, but the knoll was held. The Federals withdrew.

Hill did not think it would be for long. He sent word to Jackson that he would do his best, but that he doubted whether his men could withstand another such assault. Jackson sent the courier back with a sharp message: "Tell him if they attack him again he must beat them!" Riding toward the left to see for himself, he met the red-haired Hill coming to speak to him in person. "General, your men have done nobly," Jackson told him. "If you are attacked again, you will beat the enemy back." At this, the clatter broke out again in the woods on the left. "Here it comes," Hill said. As he turned his horse and rode back into the uproar, Jackson called after him: "I'll expect you to beat them!" The clatter rose to climax, then subsided. A messenger came galloping out of the smoke and pulled up alongside Jackson: "General Hill presents his respects and says the attack of the enemy was repulsed." Jackson smiled. "Tell him I knew he would do it," he said.

That was how it went, touch and go, all along his line all afternoon. Pope paid no mind to Longstreet, being unaware that he was even on the field: which, indeed, might practically as well have

"Let us die here, my men. Let us die here."

— Maxcy Gregg

been the case, so far as relief of the pressure on Jackson was concerned, except for some batteries in brisk action on a ridge to Hood's left where the lines were hinged, like widespread jaws gaping east-southeast. Lee was quick to suggest that Old Pete swing the lower jaw forward and upward in order to engage the bluecoats and absorb some of the single-minded pressure they were applying to the weary men along the unfinished railroad. But Longstreet demurred. He never liked to go piecemeal into battle unprepared; Anderson was not yet up, and he had not had time enough for a thorough study of the ground. Besides, Stuart reported a force of undetermined strength gathering on the right; this, too, would have to be investigated. Regretfully Lee agreed to a delay. Longstreet left on a personal reconnaissance, then presently returned. He did not like the look of things. More Federals were coming up from the south, he said, in position to stab at his flank if he moved east. If they would venture squarely into the jaws, he would gladly clamp and chew them with gusto; but for the present he saw little profit, and much risk, in advancing.

★

Jackson rode up, dusty and worn. The two generals greeted him, and in reply to his statement that his line was hard pressed Lee turned to Longstreet. "Hadn't we better move our line forward?" he suggested.

"I think not," Longstreet said. "We had better wait until we hear more from Stuart about the force he has reported moving against us from Manassas."

A step-up in the firing toward the east caused Jackson to ride off in that direction. Federal dead and wounded were heaped along the forward slope where the Confederates, drawing their beads under cover of the cuts and fills, had dropped them. Charge after charge was repulsed all down the line, but this was accomplished at a high cost to the badly outnumbered defenders: especially when the fighting was conducted at close quarters, as it often was today. In Starke's division, on the right, not a single brigade was under a general officer, and one was led by a major. In Lawton's, when bull-voiced old Ike Trimble was hit and carried from the field, command of his brigade passed for a time to a captain. For the survivors, fighting their battle unrelieved and unsupported, this was the longest of all days. One remembered, years afterward, how he spent the infrequent lulls "praying that the great red sun, blazing and motionless over-head, would go down." He added, looking back: "For the first time in my life I understood what was meant by 'Joshua's sun standing still on Gibeon,' for it would not go down."

At last, however, as it approached the landline, Lee suggested for the third time that Longstreet attack. But Longstreet still demurred. Stuart had identified the hovering bluecoats as Porter's corps, two veteran divisions. Besides, Old Pete had a new objection: There was too little daylight left. The best thing to do, he said, would be to make a forced reconnaissance at dusk; then, if an opening was discovered, the whole army could exploit it at dawn tomorrow. Once more Lee deferred to Longstreet, who assigned the task to Hood.

The Texans moved out at sunset, advancing up the Warrenton Turn-pike, "the light of battle in our eyes — I reckon," one recalled — "and fear of it in our hearts — I know." They collided in the dusk with King's division, return-ing from Manassas, in a fight so confused that one Union major was captured when he tried to rally a regiment that turned out to be the 2d Mississippi. Hood held his ground, driving the weary Federals back, but when he reported to Lee and Longstreet after dark, he recommended that his troops be withdrawn to their original position. Nor did he think that an attack next morning would suc-ceed in that direction; the enemy position was too strong, he said. Thus Longstreet's daylong judgment was apparently confirmed. Lee gave Hood per-mission to withdraw, which he did, encountering in the darkness the men of An-derson's division, just arrived from Thoroughfare Gap, and thus prevented them from stumbling blindly into the Union lines.

★

The long day's fight was over. Out across the night-shrouded fields and in the woods behind the corpse-strewn embankment, the groans of the wounded were incessant. "Water! For God's sake, water!" men were crying. Jackson's medical director, reporting the heavy casualties to his chief, said proudly: "General, this day has been won by nothing but stark and stern fighting." Stonewall shook his head. "No," he said. "It has been won by nothing but the blessing and protection of Providence."

★ ★ ★ *D*awn found Pope in excellent spirits. His headquarters were on a little knoll in the northeast quadrant formed by the intersection of the Manassas-Sudley road with the Warrenton Turnpike, and as he stood there in the growing light, burly and expansive, smoking a cigar and chatting informally with his staff and those commanders who found time to ride over for a visit, the gruffness which was habitual — one of his aides referred to it as "infusing some of his western energy into the caravan" — seemed merely a form of bantering this morning, pleased as he was with the overall success of his efforts to keep Stonewall from escaping. He had cast his net and the foe was entangled; now all that remained, apparently, was the agreeable task of hauling him in, hand over hand.

By no means had all gone to suit him yesterday. The attacks, though pressed with vigor, had been delivered somewhat piecemeal. Most irksome of all, Fitz-John Porter had declined to advance against Jackson's right flank, claiming that Longstreet barred the way with something like three times as many men as he himself had. Pope did not believe this for an instant. At 4.30 he repeated his orders for Porter to "press forward into action at once on the enemy's flank, and, if possible, on his rear." Porter balked, still insisting that he had more than half of the rebel army to his front, and darkness fell before Pope could budge him. Disappointed, the Federal commander moved the sluggish Porter around to the main line, paralleling the turnpike, and prepared for an all-out assault at dawn, when he wired Halleck a summary of his achievements: "We fought a terrific battle here yesterday . . . which lasted with continuous fury from daybreak until dark, by which time the enemy was driven from the field, which we now occupy. Our troops are too much exhausted yet to push matters, but I shall do so in the course of the morning. . . . The enemy is still in our front, but badly used up. We have lost not less than 8000 men killed and wounded, but from the appearance of the field the enemy lost at least two to one. He stood strictly on the defensive, and every assault was made by ourselves. Our troops behaved splendidly. The battle was fought on the identical battlefield of Bull Run, which greatly increased the enthusiasm of our men." In mid-paragraph he added, "The news just reaches me from the front that the enemy is retreating toward the mountains. I go forward at once to see."

★

For his refusal to obey Pope's misguided orders, General Fitz-John Porter was soon made the scapegoat for the defeat at Second Manassas and court-martialed.

He did go forward, onto the knoll at any rate, and what he saw encouraged him still more. Where bayonets had glittered yesterday along the bed of the unfinished railroad, the goal of so many charges that had broken in blood along its base, today there was stillness and apparent vacancy. Only a few gray riflemen contested the sniping from Federal outposts. Combined with the knowledge of Hood's withdrawal down the turnpike after midnight, this intelligence led Pope to believe that Jackson had pulled out, leaving only a skeleton force to discourage the blue pursuit. Still, anxious though he was to garner the utmost fruits of victory, Pope curbed his tendency toward rashness. In the end, he knew, more would be gained if the chase was conducted in a well-coördinated fashion than if he took off half-cocked and overeager. While he stood there on the headquarters knoll, wreathed in cigar smoke as he chatted with his staff, orders went out prescribing the dispositions for pursuit. McDowell would be in general charge of the two-pronged advance. Porter's corps and two divisions from McDowell's would move directly down the pike; Heintzelman's corps, supported by McDowell's other division, would move up the Hay Market road. With Stonewall's getaway thus contested in both directions, troop commanders were expressly instructed to "press him vigorously during the whole day."

All this took time, but Pope felt he could afford it now that he had a full-scale victory under his belt. Careful preparations, with strict attention to details, would pay dividends in the long run, when the rebels were brought to bay and the mopping-up began. Noon came and went. A heavy silence lay over the heat-shimmered field, broken from time to time by sputters of fire exchanged by the men on outpost. At 2 o'clock, informed that all was in order at last, Pope gave the signal and the pursuit got under way.

★

*D*eliberate though these preparations were, the pursuit itself — or anyhow what Pope conceived as such — was probably the briefest of the war. Jackson was by no means retreating; he had merely withdrawn his troops for some unmolested and hard-earned rest in the woods along the base of Sudley Mountain just in his rear, leaving a thin line to man the works and give the alarm in case the Yankees showed signs of advancing. He doubted that they would do so, after their failures yesterday, but he was perfectly willing to meet them if they tried it. Longstreet — who was very much on hand with all five of his divisions, no matter what evidence Pope had received (or deduced) in denial of the fact — was more than willing; he was downright eager. In fact, now that Porter's corps had been shifted from its threatening position off his flank, he desired nothing in all the world quite so much as that the Federals would launch a full-scale attack across his front, though he too doubted that Fortune's smile could ever be that broad.

Lee, who doubted it most of all, began to be concerned that Pope would get away unsuppressed, having suffered only such punishment as Jackson had managed to inflict while receiving his headlong charges the day before. As the long morning wore away, marked by nothing more eventful than the occasional growl of a battery or the isolated sputter of an argument between pickets, Lee took the opportunity to catch up on his correspondence. "My desire," he wrote the President, "has been to avoid a general engagement, being the weaker force, and by maneuvering to relieve the portion of the country referred to." By this he meant the region along the Rappahannock, whose relief had been accomplished by forcing Pope's retreat on Manassas. Now his mind turned to the possibilities at hand. If Pope would not attack, then he would have to be "maneuvered." About noon, while Lee was working on a plan for moving again around his opponent's right, crossing Bull Run above Sudley Springs in order to threaten his rear, Stuart came to headquarters with an interesting report. He had sent a man up a large walnut tree, Jeb said, and the man had spotted the bluecoats massing in three heavy lines along Jackson's front. Quickly Lee sent couriers to warn of the danger. Jackson alerted his troops but kept them in the woods. He had been observing the Federal activity for some time, but, concluding that nothing would come of it, had remarked to the colonel commanding the Stonewall Brigade: "Well, it looks as if there will be no fight today. . . ."

Shortly before 3 o'clock he found out just how wrong he was. Suddenly, without even the warning preamble of an artillery bombardment, the blue infantry came roaring at him in three separate waves, stretching left and right as far as the eye could see. Buglers along the unfinished railroad gobbled staccato warnings, and the startled troops came running out of the woods to man the line. This was far worse than yesterday. Not only were the attacking forces much heavier; they seemed much more determined, individually and in mass, not to be denied a lodgment. Immediately Jackson began to receive urgent requests for reinforcements all along the front. One officer rode up to report that his brigade commander had been shot down and the survivors were badly shaken. They needed help.

"What brigade, sir?" Jackson asked, not having caught the name.

"The Stonewall Brigade."

"Go back," Jackson told him. "Give my compliments to them, and tell the Stonewall Brigade to maintain her reputation."

For the present, reduced though it was to a ghost of its former self, the brigade managed to do as its old commander asked; but how long it would be able to continue to do so, under the strain, was another question. Rifle barrels grew too hot to handle, and at several points the defenders exhausted their ammunition. At one such critical location, the enemy having penetrated to within ten yards of the embankment, the graybacks beat them back with rocks. All along the two-mile front, the situation was desperate; no sooner was the pres-

---

They came on, running hunched as if into a high wind, charging shoulder to shoulder across fields where long tendrils and sheets of gunsmoke writhed and billowed.

---

sure relieved in one spot than it increased again in another. Broken, then restored, Hill's line wavered like a shaken rope. He was down to his last ounce of strength, he reported, and still the bluecoats came against him, too thick and fast for killing to do more than slow them down. Whereupon Jackson, who had no reserves to send in response to Hill's plea for reinforcements, did something he had never done before. Outnumbered three to one by the attackers, whose bullets he was opposing with flung stones, he appealed to Lee to send him help from Longstreet.

In the Federal ranks there was also a measure of consternation, especially at the brevity of what they had been assured was a "pursuit." Recovering from the shock of this discovery, however, the men fought with redoubled fury, as if glad of a chance to take their resentment of Pope out on the rebels. As usual, McDowell came in for his share of their bitterness — as witness the following exchange between a gray-haired officer and a wounded noncom limping rearward out of the fight:

"Sergeant, how does the battle go?"

"We're holding our own; but McDowell has charge of the left."

"Then God save the left!"

For the better part of an hour they came on, running hunched as if into a high wind, charging shoulder to shoulder across fields where long tendrils and sheets of gunsmoke writhed and billowed, sulphurous and "tinged with a hot coppery hue by the rays of the declining sun." One among them was to remember it so, along with the accompanying distraction of rebel shells "continually screeching over our heads or plowing the gravelly surface with an ugly rasping whirr that makes one's flesh creep." Still they came on. Time after time, they faltered within reach of the flame-stitched crest of the embankment, then time after time came on again, stumbling over the huddled blue forms that marked the limits of their previous advances. They battered thus at Jackson's line as if at a locked gate, beyond which they could see the cool green fields of peace. Determined to swing it ajar or knock it flat, they struck it again and again, flesh against metal, and feeling it tremble and crack at the hinges and hasp, they battered harder.

Longstreet stood on the ridge where his and Jackson's lines were hinged. This not only gave him a panoramic view of the action, it also afforded an excellent position for massing the eighteen guns of a reserve artillery battalion which had arrived at dawn. The batteries were sighted so that they commanded, up to a distance of about 2000 yards to the east and northeast, the open ground across which the Federals were advancing. For the better part of an hour the cannoneers had watched hungrily while the blue waves were breaking against Stonewall's right and center, perpendicular to and well within range of their guns. This was the answer to an artillerist's prayer, but Old Pete was in no hurry. He was saving this for a Sunday punch, to be delivered when the time was right and the final Union reserves had been committed. Then it came: Jackson's appeal for assistance, forwarded by Lee with the recommendation that a division of troops be sent. "Certainly," Longstreet said. He spoke calmly, suppressing the excitement he and all around him felt as they gazed along the troughs and crests of the blue waves rolling northward under the muzzles of his guns. "But before the division can reach him, the attack will be broken by artillery."

So it was. When Longstreet turned at last and gave the signal that unleashed them, the gunners leaped to their pieces and let fly, bowling their shots along the serried rows of Federals who up to now had been unaware of the danger to their flank. The effect was instantaneous. Torn and blasted by this fire, the second and third lines milled aimlessly, bewildered, then retreated in disorder: whereupon the first-line soldiers, looking back over their shoulders to find their supports in flight, also began to waver and give ground. This was that trembling instant when the battle scales of Fortune signal change, one balance pan beginning to rise as the other sinks.

Down on the flat, just after remarking calmly to one of his staff as he watched a line of wagons pass to the front, "I observe that some of those mules are without shoes: I wish you would see to it that all of the animals are shod at once," Lee heard the uproar and divined its meaning. Without a change of expression, he sent word to Longstreet that if he saw any better way to relieve the pressure on Jackson than by sending troops, he should adopt it. Headquarters wigwagged a signal station on the left: "Do you still want reinforcements?" When the answer came back, "No. The enemy are giving way," Lee knew the time had come to accomplish Pope's suppression by launching an all-out counterstroke to compound the blue confusion. An order went at once to Longstreet, directing him to go forward with every man in his command. It was not needed; Old Pete was already in motion, bearing down on the moil of Federals out on the plain. A similar order went to Jackson, together with a warning: "General Longstreet is advancing. Look out for and protect his left flank." But this also was unnecessary. When Stonewall's men saw the bluecoats waver on their front, they too started forward. Right and left, as the widespread jaws began to close, the weird halloo of the rebel yell rang out.

Porter's corps was on the exposed flank, under the general direction of McDowell, and Porter, who had been expressing dark forebodings all along — "I hope Mac is at work, and we will soon get ordered out of this," he had written Burnside the night before — had taken the precaution of stationing two New York regiments, the only volunteer outfits in Sykes' division of regulars, on his left as a shield against disaster. Facing west along the base of a little knoll on which a six-gun battery was posted, these New Yorkers caught the brunt of Longstreet's assault, led by Hood. One regiment, thrown forward as a skirmish line, was quickly overrun. The other — Zouaves, nattily dressed in white spats, tasseled fezzes, short blue jackets, and baggy scarlet trousers — stood on the slope itself, holding firm while the battery flailed the attackers, then finally limbered and got away, permitting the New Yorkers to retire. They did this at a terrible cost, however. Out of 490 present when the assault began, 124 were dead and 223 had been wounded by the time it was over: which amounted to the largest percentage of men killed in any Federal regiment in any single battle of the war. Next morning, one of Hood's men became strangely homesick at the sight of the dead Zouaves strewn about in their gaudy clothes. According to him, they gave the western slope of the little knoll "the appearance of a Texas hillside when carpeted in the spring by wild flowers of many hues and tints."

The respite bought with their blood, however brief, had given Pope time to bring up reinforcements from the right, and they too offered what resistance they could to the long gray line surging eastward along both sides of the pike. This was undulating country, with easy ridges at right angles to the advance, so that to one defender it seemed that the Confederates, silhouetted against the great red ball of the setting sun, "came on like demons emerging from the earth." There was delay as Longstreet's left became exposed to enfilad-

*At Second Ma-
nassas the 5th New
York wore Zouave
uniforms inspired by
the garb of French
colonial troops.*

ing fire from some batteries on Jackson's right, but when these were silenced the advance swept on, tilted battle flags gleaming in the sunset. On Henry Hill, where Stonewall had won his nickname thirteen months ago, Sykes' regulars stood alongside the Pennsylvanians of Reynolds' division — he had been exchanged since his capture near Gaines Mill — and hurled back the disjointed rebel attacks that continued on through twilight into darkness.

There was panic, but it was not of the kind that had characterized the retreat from this same field the year before. The regulars were staunch, now as then, but there was by no means the same difference, in that respect, between them and the volunteers. Sigel's Germans and the men with Reno also managed to form knots of resistance, while the rest withdrew across Stone Bridge in a drizzle of rain. McDowell, seeing the Iron Brigade hold firm along a critical ridge, put Gibbon in charge of the rear guard and gave him instructions to blow up the bridge when his Westerners had crossed over.

After McDowell left, Phil Kearny rode up, empty sleeve flapping, spike whiskers bristling with anger at the sudden reverse the army had suffered. "I suppose you appreciate the condition of affairs here, sir," he cried. "It's another Bull Run, sir. It's another Bull Run!" When Gibbon said he hoped it was not as bad as that, Kearny snapped: "Perhaps not. Reno is keeping up the fight. He is not stampeded; I am not stampeded; you are not stampeded. That is about all, sir. My God, that's about all!"

★

★ ★ ★ *T*wo miles west of there, near Groveton, Lee was composing a dispatch to be telegraphed to Richmond for release by the President:

This army today achieved on the plains of Manassas

a signal victory over combined forces of Generals

McClellan and Pope. . . . We mourn the loss of our

gallant dead in every conflict, yet our gratitude to

Almighty God for his mercies rises higher and higher

each day. To Him and to the valor of our troops a

nation's gratitude is due.

His losses were 1481 killed, 7627 wounded, 89 missing; Pope's were 1724 killed, 8372 wounded, 5958 missing. Lee reported the capture of 7000 prisoners, exclusive of 2000 wounded left by Pope on the field, along with 30 guns and 20,000 small arms, numerous colors, and a vast amount of stores in addition to those consumed or destroyed by Jackson at Manassas Junction two days back.

Nor was that all. A larger triumph was reflected in the contrast between the present overall military situation, here in the East, and that which had existed when Lee assumed command three months ago. McClellan had stood within sight of the spires of Richmond; Jackson had been in flight up the Shenandoah Valley, pursued by superior enemy combinations; West Virginia had been completely in Federal hands, as well as most of coastal North Carolina, with invasion strongly threatened from both directions. Now Richmond had not only been delivered, but the Union host was in full retreat on Washington, with the dome of the Capitol practically in view and government clerks being mustered for a last-ditch defense of the city; the Valley was rapidly being scoured of the blue remnants left behind when Pope assembled his army to cross the Rappahannock; West Virginia was almost cleared of Federals, and the North Carolina coast was safe. Except for the garrisons at Fort Monroe and Norfolk, the only bluecoats within a hundred miles of the southern capital were prisoners of war and men now busy setting fire to U.S. stores and equipment at Aquia Creek, just north of Fredericksburg, preparing for a hasty evacuation.

Nor was that all, either. Beyond all this, there was the transformation effected within the ranks of the Army of Northern Virginia itself: a lifting of morale, based on a knowledge of the growth of its fighting skill. Gone were the clumsy combinations of the Seven Days, the piecemeal attacks launched headlong against positions of the enemy's own choice. Here in the gallant rivalry of Manassas, where Longstreet's soldiers vied with Jackson's for the "suppression" of an opponent they despised, the victory formula had apparently been found; Lee's orders had been carried out instinctively, in some cases even before they were delivered. Tonight at army headquarters, which had been set up in an open field with a campfire of boards to read dispatches by, there was rejoicing and an air of mutual congratulation as officer after officer arrived to report new incidents of triumph. Lee — who had told his wife a month ago, "In the prospect before me I cannot see a single ray of pleasure during this war" — stood in the firelight, gray and handsome, impeccably uniformed, welcoming subordinates with the accustomed grace of a Virginia host.

"General, here is someone who wants to speak to you," a staff captain said.

Lee turned and saw a smoke-grimed cannoneer standing before him, still with a sponge staff in one hand. "Well, my man, what can I do for you?"

"Why, General, don't you know me?" Robert wailed.

There was laughter at this, a further lifting of spirits as troop commanders continued to report of the day's successes. Hood rode up, weary but still elated over what he called "the most beautiful battle scene I have ever beheld." When Lee, adopting the bantering tone he often used in addressing the blond young man, asked what had become of the enemy, Hood replied that his Texans had driven them "almost at a double-quick" across Bull Run. He added that it had been a wonderful sight to see the Confederate battle flags "dancing after the Federals as they ran in full retreat." Lee dropped his jesting manner and said gravely, "God forbid I should ever live to see our colors moving in the opposite direction."

★ ★ ★ While Lee was at Groveton, composing the dispatch to Davis, Pope was at Centreville, composing one to Halleck. All things being considered, the two were by no means as different as might have been expected.

We have had a terrific battle again today. . . . Under all the circumstances, both horses and men having been two days without food, and the enemy greatly outnumbering us, I thought it best to draw back to this place at dark. The movement has been made in perfect order and without loss. The troops are in good heart, and marched off the field without the least hurry or confusion. . . .

Do not be uneasy. We will hold our own here. . . .

P.S. *We have lost nothing; neither guns nor wagons.*

Of the several inaccuracies here involved (one being the comparison of forces; Lee had had 50,000 men engaged, while Pope had had 60,000 — exclusive of Banks, who was guarding his trains) the greatest, perhaps, was the one in which he declared that his troops were "in good heart." It was true that, after the first wild scramble for an exit, they had steadied and retired in column, under cover of the rear-guard action on Henry Hill; but their spirits were in fact so far from being high that they could scarcely have been lower. If Pope did not know the extent of his defeat, his men did. They agreed with the verdict later handed down by one of their corps historians, that Pope "had been kicked, cuffed, hustled about, knocked down, run over, and trodden upon as rarely happens in the history of war. His communications had been cut; his headquarters pillaged; a corps had marched into his rear, and had encamped at its ease upon the railroad by which he received his supplies; he had been beaten or foiled in every attempt he had made to 'bag' those defiant intruders; and, in the end, he was glad to find a refuge in the intrenchments of Washington, whence he had sallied forth, six weeks before, breathing out threatenings and slaughter."

They agreed with this in all its harshness, but just now what they mainly were was sullen. They had fought well and they knew it. Defeat had come, not because they were outfought, but because they were outgeneraled — or misgeneraled. As one of their number put it, "All knew and felt that as soldiers we had not had a fair chance." The fault, they believed, was Pope's; he had "acted like a dunderpate." And McDowell's; he had revived their suspicions by repeating his past performance on this field. "General McDowell was viewed as a traitor by a large majority of the officers and men," one diarist wrote, adding: "Thousands of soldiers firmly believed that their lives would be purposely wasted if they obeyed his orders in the time of the conflict." The story was told that one of his regiments had stepped gingerly up to the firing line, loosed a random volley, then turned and made for the rear, the men shouting over their shoulders as they ran: "You can't play it on us!" Slogging tonight through the drizzle of rain, they saw him sitting his horse beside the pike, identifiable in the murk because of the outlandish silhouette of his canvas helmet. One Massachusetts private nudged another, pointing, and said darkly: "How guilty he looks, with that basket on his head!"

Pope, too, came in for his share of abuse. "Open sneering at General Pope was heard on all sides," one veteran observed. Another, passing the luckless commander by the roadside, hailed him with a quote from Horace Greeley: "Go west, young man! Go west!" Perhaps this had something to do with chang-

Battered and demoralized troops of
Pope's army retreat back across the Stone
Bridge over Bull Run.

ing his mind as to the state of his men's hearts. At any rate, when morning came — Sunday, August 31 — he wired Halleck: "Our troops are . . . much used-up and worn-out," and he spoke of giving the enemy "as desperate a fight as I can force our men to stand up to." Franklin's corps had come up the night before, in time to establish a straggler line in front of Centreville; Sumner too was at hand, giving Pope 20,000 fresh troops with which to oppose the rebels. But his confidence was ebbing. He told Halleck, "I should like to know whether you feel secure about Washington should this army be destroyed. I shall fight it as long as a man will stand up to the work. You must judge what is to be done, having in view the safety of the capital."

No sooner had he sent this, however, than a reply to last night's rosy message bucked him up again. "My Dear General: You have done nobly," Halleck wired. "Don't yield another inch if you can avoid it." Pope thanked him for this "considerate commendation" and passed along the encouraging news that "Ewell is killed. Jackson is badly wounded. . . . The plan of the enemy will undoubtedly be to turn my flank. If he does so he will have his hands full." Meanwhile, Franklin's soldiers mocked and taunted the bedraggled Army of Virginia, jeering along the straggler line at its "new route" to Richmond. Overnight, Pope's confidence took another sickening drop. Three hours after sunrise, September 1, he got off another long dispatch to Halleck. After a bold beginning — "All was quiet yesterday and so far this morning. My men are resting; they need it much. . . . I shall attack again tomorrow if I can; the next day certainly" — he passed at once to darker matters: "I think it my duty to call your attention to the unsoldierly and dangerous conduct of many brigade and some division commanders of the forces sent here from the Peninsula. Every word and act and intention is discouraging, and calculated to break down the spirits of the men and produce disaster." In the light of this, he closed with a recommendation that ran counter to the intention expressed at the outset: "My advice to you — I give it with freedom, as I know you will not misunderstand it — is that, in view of any satisfactory results, you draw back this army to the intrenchments in front of Washington, and set to work in that secure place to reorganize and rearrange it. You may avoid great disaster by doing so."

While waiting to see what would come of this, he found that Jackson (who was no more wounded than Ewell was dead) was in the act of fulfilling his prediction that Lee would try to turn his flank. Stonewall's men had crossed Bull Run at Sudley Springs, then moved north to the Little River Turnpike, which led southeast to Fairfax Courthouse, eight miles in the Union rear. Pope pulled the troops of Phil Kearny and Brigadier General I. I. Stevens, who commanded Burnside's other division under Reno, out

General Philip Kearny, killed on the evening of September 1, was much admired by soldiers of both armies.

of their muddy camps and sent them slogging northward to intercept the rebel column. They did so, late that afternoon. There beside the pike, around a mansion called Chantilly, a wild fight took place during a thunderstorm so violent that it drowned the roar of cannon. Jackson's march had been slow; consequently he was in a grim and savage humor. In the rain-lashed confusion, when one of his colonels requested that his men be withdrawn because their cartridges were too wet to ignite, the reply came back: "My compliments

★

to Colonel Blank, and tell him the enemy's ammunition is just as wet as his."

This spirit was matched on the Federal side by Kearny, who dashed from point to point, his empty sleeve flapping as he rode with the reins clamped in his teeth in order to have his one arm free to gesture with his saber, hoicking his troops up to the firing line and holding them there by showing no more concern for bullets than he did for raindrops. His prescription for success in leading men in battle was a simple one; "You must never be afraid of anything," he had told a young lieutenant two days ago. Stevens followed his example, and between them they made Stonewall call a halt. The firing continued into early darkness, when on A. P. Hill's front the men were surprised to see a Union general come riding full-tilt toward them, suddenly illuminated by a flash of lightning. They called on him to surrender, but he whirled his mount, leaning forward onto its withers with his arm around its neck, and tried to gallop away in the confusion. They fired a volley that unhorsed him, and when they went out to pick him up they found that he was dead, lying one-armed in the mud, the back of his coat and the seat of his trousers torn by bullets. They brought his body into their lines. "Poor Kearny," Hill said, looking down at him. "He deserved a better death than that."

Stevens too was dead by now, shot while leading a charge, and the Federals fell back down the pike and through the woods. They did so more from being disheartened by the loss of their leaders, however, than from being pressed; Jackson did not pursue. Thus ended the Battle of Chantilly, a rain-swept drama with off-stage thunder, vivid flashes of lightning, and an epilogue supplied next morning by Lee, who sent Kearny's body forward under a flag of truce, "thinking that the possession of his remains may be a consolation to his family."

Pope by then was back at Fairfax, within twenty miles of Washington, having received from Halleck the instructions he had sought: "You will bring your forces as best you can within or near the line of fortification." As the army retreated — "by squads, companies, and broken parts of regiments and brigades," according to one enlisted diarist — its commander lost the final vestige of his former boldness. "The straggling is awful in the regiments from the Peninsula," he complained to Halleck. "Unless something can be done to restore tone to this army it will melt away before you know it." This was a new and different Pope, a Pope not unlike a sawdust doll with most of its stuffing leaked away. A surgeon who looked through a headquarters window the previous evening saw him so: "He sat with his chair tipped back against the wall, his hands clasped behind his head, which bent forward, his chin touching his breast — seeming to pay no attention to the generals as they arrived, but to be wholly wrapped in his own gloomy reflections." The doctor wrote long afterward, and being a kind-hearted man, who had dealt with much misery in his life, he added: "I pitied him then. I pity him now."

★

It was perhaps the only pity felt for him by anyone in the whole long weary column slogging its way eastward. Last night's thunderstorm had deepened the mud along the pike, and overhead a scud of clouds obscured the sun, which shed an eerie yellow light upon the sodden fields. In a way, though, the weather was fitting, matching as it did the mood of the retreat. "Everyone you met had an unwashed, sleepy, downcast aspect," one officer observed, "and looked as if he would like to hide his head somewhere from all the world." Now that the immediate danger was past, a still worse reaction of sullenness had set in among the troops, whose mistrust of Pope quite balanced his expressed mistrust of them. As one colonel put it, "No salutary fear kept them in the ranks, and many gave way to the temptation to take a rest. . . . There was everywhere along the road the greatest confusion. Infantry and cavalry, artillery and wagons, all hurried on pell mell, in the midst of rallying cries of officers and calls and oaths of the men."

Banks had come up from Bristoe Station, bringing the army's wagons with him though he had been obliged to put the torch to all the locomotives and freight cars loaded with stores and munitions from Warrenton and other points below the wreckage of Broad Run bridge. His corps, having seen no fighting since Cedar Mountain, was assigned the rear guard duty, which consisted mainly of prodding frazzled stragglers back into motion and gathering up abandoned equipment littered along the roadside. At the head of the column — miles away, for the various units were badly strung out, clotted in places and gapped in others as a result of accordion action — rode Pope and McDowell, attended by their staffs and followed closely by the lead division, formerly King's but now under Brigadier General John P. Hatch, who had succeeded the ailing King. That afternoon the sun came out, but it did little to revive the downcast marchers: least of all Hatch, who had more cause for gloom than most. He had commanded a cavalry brigade, that being the arm of service he preferred, until Pope relieved him for inefficiency and transferred him to the infantry. So Hatch had this to brood over, in addition to the events of the past few days. Then suddenly, up ahead, he saw something that made him forget his and the army's troubles.

Off to one side loomed Munson's Hill, which Joe Johnston had held with a dummy gun last winter. From its crown, Hatch knew, you could see the dome of the Capitol. But what engaged his attention just now was a small group of horsemen coming down the road toward Pope and McDowell: particularly the man in front, who rode a large black horse and wore a vivid yellow sash about his waist. Hatch thought there was something familiar about the trim and dapper way he sat his charger. Then, as the man reined to a halt in front of the two generals, returning their salutes with one of his own which "seemed to carry a little of personal good fellowship to even the humblest private soldier," Hatch knew the unbelievable was true; it was Little Mac. He spurred ahead in time to hear McClellan tell Pope and McDowell he had been authorized to take command of the army. Off to the left rear just then there was a sudden thumping of artillery, dim in the distance. What was that? McClellan asked. Pope said it was probably an attack on Sumner, whose corps was guarding the flank in that direction. Then he inquired if there would be any objection if he and McDowell rode on toward Washington. None at all, McClellan replied; but as for himself, he was riding toward the sound of gunfire.

Before the two could resume their journey, Hatch took advantage of the chance to revenge the wrong he believed had been done when his cavalry brigade was taken from him the month before. Trotting back to the head of his infantry column, within easy hearing distance of Pope and McDowell, he shouted: "Boys, McClellan is in command of the army again! Three cheers!" The result, after an instant of shock while the words sank in, was pandemonium. Caps and knapsacks went sailing high in the air, and men who a moment ago had been too weary and dispirited to do anything more than plant one leaden foot

> *Within seconds every man was on his feet and cheering, raising what one of them called "such a hurrah as the Army of the Potomac had never heard before."*

in front of the other were cheering themselves hoarse, capering about, and slapping each other joyfully on the back. "From an extreme sadness," one Massachusetts volunteer recalled, "we passed in a twinkling to a delirium of delight. A deliverer had come." This was the reaction all down the column as the news traveled back along its length, pausing at the gaps between units, then being taken up again, moving westward like a spark along a ten-mile train of powder.

Such demonstrations were not restricted to green troops, volunteers likely to leap at every rumor. Sykes' regulars, for example, were far back toward the rear and did not learn of the change till after nightfall. They were taking a rest halt, boiling coffee in a roadside field, when an officer on picket duty saw by starlight the familiar figure astride Dan Webster coming down the pike. "Colonel! Colonel!" he hollered, loud enough to be heard all over the area, "General McClellan is here!" Within seconds every man was on his feet and cheering, raising what one of them called "such a hurrah as the Army of the Potomac had never heard before. Shout upon shout went out into the stillness of the night; and as it was taken up along the road and repeated by regiment, brigade, division and corps, we could hear the roar dying away in the distance. The effect of this man's presence upon the Army of the Potomac — in sunshine or rain, in darkness or in daylight, in victory or defeat — was electrical." Hard put for words to account for the delirium thus provoked, he could only add that it was "too wonderful to make it worth while attempting to give a reason for it."

Nor was the enthusiasm limited to veterans of Little Mac's own army, men who had fought under him before. When Gibbon announced the new commander's arrival to the survivors of the Iron Brigade, they too reacted with unrestrained delight, tossing their hats and breaking ranks to jig and whoop, just as the Peninsula boys were doing. Later that night, Gibbon remembered afterward, "the weary, fagged men went into camp cheerful and happy, to talk over their rough experience of the past three weeks and speculate as to what was ahead."

★ ★ ★ It was Lincoln's doing, his alone, and he had done it against the will of a majority of his advisers. Chase believed that the time had come, beyond all doubt, when "either the government or McClellan must go down," and Stanton had prepared and was soliciting cabinet signatures for an ultimatum demanding "the immediate removal of George B. McClellan from any command in the armies of the United States." When Welles protested that such a document showed little consideration for their chief, the War Secretary bristled and said coldly: "I know of no particular obligation I am under to the President. He called me to a difficult position and imposed on me labors and responsibilities which no man could carry." Already he had secured four signatures — his own, Chase's, Bates', and Smith's — and was working hard for more (Welles and Blair were obdurate, and Seward was still out of town) when, on the morning of this same September 2, he came fuming into the room where his colleagues were waiting for Lincoln to arrive and open the meeting. It was a time of strain. Reports of Pope's defeat had caused Stanton to call out the government clerks, order the contents of the arsenal shipped to New York, and forbid the retail sale of spirituous liquors in the city. Now came the climactic blow as he announced, in a choked voice, the rumor that McClellan had been appointed to conduct the defense of Washington.

The effect was stunning: a sort of reversal of what would happen later that day along the blue column plodding east from Fairfax. Just as Chase was declaring that, if true, this would "prove a national calamity," Lincoln came in and confirmed the rumor. That was why he was late for the meeting, he explained. He and Halleck had just come from seeing McClellan and ordering him to assume command of the armies roundabout the capital. Stanton broke in, trembling as he spoke: "No order to that effect has been issued from the War Department." Lincoln turned and faced him. "The order is mine," he said, "and I will be responsible for it to the country."

Four nights ago he had gone to bed confident that the army had won a great victory on the plains of Manassas: a triumph which, according to Pope, would be enlarged when he took up the pursuit of Jackson's fleeing remnant. Overnight, however, word arrived that it was Pope who was in retreat, not Stonewall, and Lincoln came into his secretary's room next morning, long-faced and discouraged. "Well, John, we are whipped again, I am afraid," he said. All day the news got worse as details of the fiasco trickled through the screen of confusion. Halleck was a weak prop to lean on; Lincoln by now had observed that his general in chief was "little more than . . . a first-rate clerk." What was worse, he was apt to break down under pressure; which was presently what happened. Before the night was over, Old Brains appealed to McClellan at Alexandria: "I beg of you to assist me in this crisis with your ability and experience. I am utterly tired out."

Lincoln's mind was also turning in Little Mac's direction, although not without reluctance. Unquestionably, it appeared to him, McClellan had acted badly in regard to Pope. One of his subordinates had even been quoted as saying publicly, "I don't care for John Pope a pinch of owl dung." It seemed to Lincoln that they had wanted Pope to fail, no matter what it cost in the blood of northern soldiers. McClellan, when appealed to for counsel, had advised the President to concentrate all the reserves in the capital intrenchments and "leave Pope to get out of his scrape" as best he could. To Lincoln this seemed particularly callous, if not crazy; his mistrust of the Young Napoleon was increased. But early Tuesday morning, when Pope warned that "unless something can be done to restore tone to this army it will melt away before you know it," he did what he knew he had to do. "We must use what tools we have," he told his secretary. "There is no man in the army who can man these fortifications and lick these troops of ours into shape half as well as [McClellan]. . . . If he can't fight himself, he excels in making others ready to fight."

So he went to him and told him to return to the army whose wounded were already beginning to pour into the city. And that afternoon, despite the howls of the cabinet — Stanton was squelched, but Chase was sputtering, "I cannot but feel that giving command to McClellan is equivalent to giving Washington to the rebels" — Lincoln had Halleck issue the formal order: "Major General McClellan will have command of the fortifications of Washington and of all the troops for the defense of the capital." This left Pope to be disposed of, which was done three days later. "The Armies of the Potomac and Virginia being consolidated," he was told by dispatch, "you will report for orders to the Secretary of War." Reporting as ordered, he found himself assigned to duty against the Sioux, who had lately risen in Minnesota. From his headquarters in St Paul, where he was settled before the month was out, Pope protested vehemently against the injustice of being "banished to a remote and unimportant command." But there he stayed, for the duration.

★　★　★

★

Federals cross over Kentucky's Big Barren River on a bridge that served as one of the vital links in General Buell's Nashville-to-Louisville supply line.

T W O

Invasion West: Richmond, Munfordville

1862 ★ ★ ★ ★ ★ On the day Lee wrecked Pope on the plains of Manassas, driving him headlong across Bull Run to begin his scamper for the Washington intrenchments, Kirby Smith accomplished in Kentucky the nearest thing to a Cannae ever scored by any general, North or South, in the course of the whole war. This slashing blow, the first struck in the two-pronged offensive Bragg had designed to recover for the Confederacy all that had been lost by his predecessors, was delivered in accordance with Smith's precept, announced at the outset, that "brilliant results . . . will be accomplished only with hard fighting."

Accordingly, on August 25, after a week's rest at Barbourville, he had resumed his northward march. There were 21,000 men in his four divisions, but the largest of these — 9000-strong; the others had about 4000 each — remained in front of Cumberland Gap, observing the 9000 Federals who held it, while the rest continued their advance toward the Bluegrass. Meanwhile this was still the barrens, which meant that water was scarce, the going rough, and people in general unfriendly. This last might well have been based on fear, however, for the appearance of the marchers, whether they came as "liberators" or "invaders," struck at least one citizen as anything but prepossessing: "[They were] ragged, greasy, and dirty, and some barefoot, and looked more like the bipeds of pandemonium than beings of this earth. . . . They surrounded our wells like the locusts of Egypt and struggled with each other for the water as if perishing with thirst, and they thronged our kitchen doors and windows, begging for bread like hungry wolves. . . . They tore the loaves and pies into fragments and devoured them. Some even threatened to shoot others if they did not divide with them." ("Notwithstanding such a motley crew," the alarmed observer added with relief, "they abstained from any violence or depredation and appeared exceedingly grateful.") As a supplement to what could be cadged in this manner, they gathered apples and roasting ears from roadside orchards and fields, eating them raw on the march with liberal sprinklings of salt, a large supply of which had been procured at Barbourville. Spirits were high and there was much joking, up and down the column. CSA, they said, stood for "Corn, Salt, and Apples."

No matter how much horseplay went on within the column itself, passing through London on the 27th the men continued to obey their commander's insistence upon "the most perfect decorum of conduct toward the citizens and their property." Two days later, by way of reward for good behavior, they climbed Big Hill, the northern rim of the barrens, and saw spread out before them, like the promised land of old, the lush and lovely region called the Bluegrass. Years afterward, Smith would remember it as it was today, "a long rolling landscape, mellowing under the early autumn rays," and would add that when it "burst upon our sight we were astonished and enchanted." However, there was little time for undisturbed enjoyment of the Pisgah view. Up ahead, near the hamlet of Rogersville, seven miles short of Richmond, the principal settlement this side of the Kentucky River, the cavalry encountered resistance and was driven back upon the infantry. This was a sundown affair, soon ended by darkness. Although he did not know the enemy strength, Smith was not displeased at this development; for it indicated that the Federals would make a stand here in the open, rather than along the natural line of defense afforded by the bluffs of the river eight miles beyond Richmond. Earlier that week he had written Bragg that he would "fight everything that presents itself," and now, having issued instructions for his men to sleep on their arms in line of battle, he prepared to do just that at dawn. After more than a hundred miles of marching, they were about to be required to prove their right to be where they were and — if they won — to penetrate farther into what Smith would call the "long rolling landscape."

The bluecoats slept in line of battle, too, and there were about 7000 of them. They were under William Nelson, whom Buell had sent north two weeks ago, a month after his promotion to major general, to take charge of the defense of his native Kentucky. "The credit of the selection will be mine," Buell had told him. "The honor of success will be yours." Nelson was of a sanguine nature — "ardent, loud-mouthed, and violent," a fellow officer called him — but by now, having completed a tour of inspection of what he had to work with, he was not so sure that either credit or success, let alone honor, was very likely to come his way as a result of the contest he saw looming. Kirby Smith was closing on him with an army of 12,000 hardened veterans, while his own, hastily organized into two small divisions under two ex-civilian brigadiers, was composed almost entirely of green recruits hurried forward by the governors of Ohio and Indiana in response to an urgent call from Washington. Their periods of service ranged in general from three weeks to three days, and for all his arrogant manner, his six feet five inches of height and his three hundred pounds of weight, Nelson was considerably worried as to what they would do when they heard the first shot fired in their direction.

Former naval officer Major General William Nelson was nicknamed Bull because of his impressive stature.

He was not long in finding out. At 2.30 in the morning, August 30, a courier knocked at his bedroom door in Lexington and informed him that the Confederates had come over Big Hill the previous afternoon, approaching Richmond, but that his two brigadiers — Mahlon Manson and Charles Cruft — were on the alert and had intercepted the gray column before it reached the town. This was not at all what Nelson wanted to hear, for he was doubtful that his green men could be maneuvered in open combat, and had intended for them to be pulled back to a better defensive position. Apprehensive, he got dressed and rode forward to see for himself, hearing gunfire as soon as he crossed the Kentucky River. It was well past noon by the time he got to Richmond, however, since he was obliged to travel the byroads to avoid being picked up by rebel horsemen. Arriving at last he found the troops, as he later declared, "in a disorganized retreat or rather rout." With the assistance of Manson and Cruft he got what was left of his army into line on the edge of town, partly under cover of the rock walls and tombstones of a cemetery. Once the rallied men were in position, he walked up and down the firing line, exposing his huge bulk to enemy marksmen and talking all the while to encourage his nervous recruits. "If they can't hit me they can't hit anything!" he roared as he strode back and forth amid the twittering bullets.

In this he was mistaken, as he presently found out. They hit him twice, in fact, both flesh wounds, no less painful for being superficial. But what hurt him worst, apparently, was the conduct of his men, who refused to be encouraged by his example. "Our troops stood about three rounds," he afterwards reported, "when, struck by a panic, they fled in utter disorder. I was left with my staff almost alone." He made his escape, considerably hampered by a bullet in his thigh. So did Cruft; but not Manson, who was pinned under his fallen horse and captured. Nelson listed his casualties as 206 killed, 844 wounded, 4303 captured or missing.

Smith's were 78 killed, 372 wounded, 1 missing out of the approximately 7000 he too had had engaged. After the initial decision to give battle he had left the tactical details to the commander of his lead division, Brigadier General Patrick R. Cleburne, who had charge of the two brigades sent by Bragg from Chattanooga. Cleburne was Irish — about as Irish in fact as possible, having been born in County Cork on St Patrick's Day, thirty-four years ago. As a youth he had done a hitch in the British army, rising to the rank of corporal, then had emigrated to Helena, Arkansas, where he studied and practiced law with the same diligence he applied to his other two prime absorptions, pistol marksmanship and chess. When the war broke out he was elected captain of the local volunteer company, the Yell Rifles. By the time of Shiloh he had attained his present

Another southern capital had returned to what the victors called its true allegiance.

rank and led his brigade of Tennesseans, Mississippians, and Arkansans with conspicuous skill and gallantry through that fight. Today in Kentucky he did likewise, keeping up a slow fire with his guns until the situation was developed, then launching an attack which broke the first of the three lines the bluecoats managed to form between then and sundown. Cleburne himself was not on hand for the breaking of the others, nor for the rounding up of the fugitives in the twilight. While speaking to a wounded colonel, he was struck in the left cheek by a bullet that knocked his teeth out on that side before emerging from his mouth — "which," as one who was with him said, "fortunately happened to be open" — and forced his retirement, speechless, from the field. But the continued application of his tactics against the subsequent two rallies produced the same results, together with the capture of about 4000 prisoners, the entire Union wagon train, substantial army stores, 10,000 small arms, and 9 guns.

"Tomorrow being Sunday," Smith announced in his congratulatory order, "the general desires that the troops shall assemble and, under their several chaplains, shall return thanks to Almighty God, to whose mercy and goodness these victories are due." The day was also spent attending the wounded, burying the dead, and paroling the host of prisoners, after which preparations were made

★

for continuing the advance. September 1, unopposed — three fourths of Nelson's army had been shot or captured; the rest were fugitives, hiding out in the woods and cornfields — the gray marchers crossed the Kentucky River and made camp on the northern bank. Next day they entered Lexington, where large numbers of townspeople turned out to greet them with smiles and cheers, including a delegation of ladies who presented Smith with a flag they had embroidered in his honor. September 3 his troopers rode into Frankfort, to find the governor and the legislature fled to Louisville. Having no suitable Confederate ensign with them, the graybacks raised the colors of the 1st Louisiana Cavalry over the state house. Another southern capital had returned to what the victors called its true allegiance.

Lexington had been the goal announced by Smith when he left Knoxville, and there he made his headquarters throughout September, in virtual control of Central Kentucky, while waiting for Bragg to join or send for him. Back at Cumberland Gap, after holding out through a month of siege, the Federals under George Morgan blew up their magazine, set fire to a warehouse containing 6000 small arms, and made their escape across the barrens, via Manchester and Booneville, to Greenup on the Ohio River, eluding pursuers all two hundred miles of the way. This was a disappointment to Smith, who had counted on capturing his West Point classmate, but at least it permitted his other division to join him at Lexington. Meanwhile he had not been idle. In addition to occupying Frankfort, Cynthiana, Georgetown, and Paris, he sent sizeable detachments of cavalry and infantry to demonstrate against Louisville and Cincinnati, both of which were thrown into turmoil. Summoned to command the defense of the latter city, Lew Wallace decreed martial law, ordered all business activities suspended, and impressed citizens to resume work on the fortifications begun the year before at Covington and Newport, on the opposite bank of the Ohio. "To arms!" the Cincinnati *Gazette* urged its readers. "The time for playing war has passed. The enemy is now approaching our doors!"

Smith was not so much concerned with the reaction of the people of Ohio, however, as he was with the reaction of the people of Kentucky. So far, this had been most gratifying, he informed the Adjutant General on September 6. "It would be impossible for me to exaggerate the enthusiasm of the people here on the entry of our troops. They evidently regarded us as deliverers from oppression and have continued in every way to prove to us that the heart of Kentucky is with the South in this struggle. . . . If Bragg occupies Buell we can have nothing to oppose us but raw levies, and by the blessing of God will always dispose of them as we did on the memorable August 30."

His purpose in seeming to threaten Cincinnati, he added, was "in order to give the people of Kentucky time to organize," and by way of encouragement he broadcast assurances to the citizens in the form of proclamations:

Let no one make you believe we come as invaders, to

coerce your will or to exercise control over your soil.

Far from it. . . . We come to test the truth of what we

believe to be a foul aspersion, that Kentuckians willingly

join the attempt to subjugate us and to deprive us of

our prosperity, our liberty, and our dearest rights. . . .

Are we deceived? Can you treat us as enemies? Our

hearts answer, "No!"

---

*B*ragg too was in Kentucky by now, and he too was issuing proclamations assuring the people that he had come, not to bind them, but to assist them in striking off their chains:

Kentuckians, I have entered your State with the Con-

federate Army of the West, and offer you an opportunity

to free yourselves from the tyranny of a despotic ruler.

We come not as conquerors or as despoilers, but to re-

store to you the liberties of which you have been deprived

by a cruel and relentless foe. We come to guarantee to

all the sanctity of their homes and altars, to punish

with a rod of iron the despoilers of your peace, and to

avenge the cowardly insults to your women. . . . Will

you remain indifferent to our call, or will you rather

vindicate the fair fame of your once free and envied

State? We believe that you will, and that the memory

of your gallant dead who fell at Shiloh, their faces

turned homeward, will rouse you to a manly effort for

yourselves and posterity.

Kentuckians, we have come with joyous hopes. Let us

not depart in sorrow, as we shall if we find you wedded

in your choice to your present lot. If you prefer Federal

rule, show it by your frowns and we shall return whence

we came. If you choose rather to come within the folds

of our brotherhood, then cheer us with the smiles of

your women and lend your willing hands to secure you

in your heritage of liberty.

Dated September 14 at Glasgow, which he had reached the day before, the proclamation was issued during a two-day rest halt, the first he had made in the course of the more than one hundred and fifty miles his army had covered since leaving Chattanooga, seventeen days ago. Despite their exertions, the men were in excellent spirits. Marching over Walden's Ridge, then up the lovely Sequatchie Valley to Pikeville, where they swung east across the Cumberland Plateau — thus passing around Buell's left wing at Decherd — they enjoyed the scenery, the bracing air of the uplands, and the friendly offerings of buttermilk and fried chicken by country people all along the way.

Bragg was happy too, and with cause. Strategically, as events disclosed, the movement had been as sound as it was rapid. He had predicted that Buell would "recede to Nashville before giving us battle," and now his scouts reported that this was just what Buell was doing, as fast as he could: which meant that North Alabama and Chattanooga, along with much of Middle Tennessee, had already been relieved without the firing of a shot. To cap the climax, when he drew near Sparta on September 5, halfway across Tennessee, he received a dispatch from Kirby Smith reporting the destruction of Nelson's army and urging him "to move into Kentucky and, effecting a junction with my command and holding Buell's communications, to give battle to him with superior forces and with certainty of success." Then and there, by way of celebration, Bragg issued a congratulatory address to his soldiers, informing them of Smith's lopsided victory and Buell's hasty withdrawal: "Comrades, our campaign opens most auspiciously and promises complete success. . . . The enemy is in full retreat, with consternation and demoralization devastating his ranks. To secure the full fruits of this condition we must press on vigorously and unceasingly."

Press on they did, and vigorously, for Bragg had now decided on his goal. Finally abandoning any intention to launch an assault on Nashville, where Buell was concentrating his forces and improving the fortifications, he marched hard for Glasgow. Eight days later he arrived and, calling a halt, issued the proclamation announcing his "joyous hopes" that the people of Kentucky would assist him in "punish[ing] with a rod of iron the despoilers of your peace." He was exactly where he wanted to be: squarely between Buell and Kirby Smith, whom he could summon to join him. Or if he chose, he could move on to the Bluegrass and the Ohio, combining there with Smith to capture Louisville or Cincinnati, both of which were nearer to him now than they were to Buell.

★ ★ ★   On the day Bragg issued his proclamation at Glasgow, where his four divisions were taking a hard-earned rest, Buell entered Bowling Green, thirty-five miles to the west. He had five divisions with him and three more back at Nashville under Thomas, who was serving as his second-in-command through the present crisis. His total strength, including a division just arrived from Grant, was 56,000: exactly twice Bragg's, though Buell did not know this, having lately estimated it at 60,000, not including the troops with Kirby Smith.

The past two weeks had been for him in the nature of a nightmare. So much had happened so fast, and nearly all of it unpleasant. Having transferred his headquarters in rapid succession from Stevenson to Decherd to McMinnville, he shifted them once again to Murfreesboro on the day Bragg set out north from Chattanooga. He did this, he told Thomas, by way of preparation for the offensive: "Once concentrated, we may move against the enemy wherever he puts himself if we are strong enough." This sentence, as a later observer remarked, had "an escape clause at both ends," and Buell was not long in giving more weight to them than to the words that lay between. Two days later, while Bragg was passing around his left and Smith was wrecking Nelson up at Richmond, he notified Andrew Johnson, the military governor of Tennessee: "These facts make it plain that I should fall back on Nashville, and I am prepar-

Confederate recruiting posters like this one circulated by Bragg's army as it marched through Kentucky yielded few recruits.

★

ing to do so. I have resisted the reasons which lead to the necessity until it would be criminal to delay any longer."

He arrived September 2 to find the capitol barricaded with cotton bales and bristling with cannon. Inside, Governor Johnson defied the rebels, declaring heatedly that he would defend the citadel with his heart's blood and never be taken alive. Encouraged by this, as well as by the arrival of 10,000 men from Grant, Buell wired Halleck: "I believe Nashville can be held and Kentucky rescued. What I have will be sufficient here with the defenses that are being prepared, and I propose to move with the remainder of the army against the enemy in Kentucky." Two nights ago, swamped by troubles resulting from Nelson's and Pope's simultaneous defeats, Old Brains had thrown up his hands and complained to McClellan that he was "utterly tired out." By now, though, he had recovered enough to send a one-sentence reply to Buell's wire. "Go where you please," he told him, "provided you will find the enemy and fight him."

Buell went nowhere until September 7. Warned then that Bragg was headed for Bowling Green, where a large supply of provisions had been stored for the campaign which had already gone up in smoke, he set out for that point with five of his eight divisions, leaving Thomas to hold Nashville with the others in case the gray invaders doubled back. A week later he got there, only to find that Bragg was at Glasgow, which not only placed him nearer Louisville than the Federals were, but also enabled him to call on Smith for reinforcements. In danger of being attacked (as he thought) by superior numbers, Buell wired for Thomas to hurry north with two divisions, explaining the grounds on which he thus was willing to risk the Tennessee capital: "If Bragg's army is defeated Nashville is safe; if not, it is lost." Another wire went to Halleck. He was "not insensible to the difficulty and embarrassment of the position," Buell declared, and he further assured the harassed general in chief: "I arrived here today . . . and shall commence to move against Bragg's force on the 16th.

★ ★ ★ *T*he day before the one on which Buell had said he would "commence to move," Bragg himself was in motion with his whole army. He moved, however, not toward Buell's main body at Bowling Green, but toward the Green River, twenty miles north, where a 4000-man Federal detachment held a fort on the south bank, opposite Munfordville, guarding the L & N railroad crossing at that point. His original intention had been to hold his ground at Glasgow, receiving attack if Buell turned east, or to lunge forward and strike his flank if he pushed on toward Louisville. What changed his mind was what he later called an "unauthorized and injudicious" action, precipitated two days before by Brigadier General James R. Chalmers.

Chalmers, whose infantry brigade was on outpost and reconnaissance duty at Cave City, ten miles northwest of Glasgow, had made contact on the 13th with one of Kirby Smith's far-ranging cavalry regiments, the colonel of which had sent him word of what he called a rare opportunity. His troopers had cut the railroad north of Munfordville, isolating the south-bank garrison, but his request for its capitulation had been sharply refused. Would Chalmers move up and add the weight of his brigade to the demand? Chalmers would indeed. A youthful and ardent Mississippian, one of the authentic Shiloh heroes, he put his troops in motion at once, without bothering to notify Bragg at Glasgow. Arriving at daylight next morning, he launched an attack on the fort, then drew back and sent a note complimenting the bluecoats on their "gallant defense," pointing out the hopelessness of their position, with Bragg's whole army "a short distance in my rear," and demanding an unconditional surrender "to avoid further bloodshed." The reply, signed by Colonel J. T. Wilder, 17th Indiana Volunteers, was brief and to the point: "Thank you for your compliments. If you wish to avoid further bloodshed keep out of the range of my guns."

AN actual sketch, made on the ... of the Special Artists of Frank Le... trated Newspaper.
Mr. Leslie holds the copyright ... serves the exclusive right of publ...

Concluding from this that the Hoosier colonel had better be left alone, Chalmers gathered up his dead and wounded — which amounted to exactly four times as many as Wilder's: 288, as compared to 72 — and withdrew. Back at Cave City next morning he reported the affair to Bragg, expressing "fear that I may have incurred censure at headquarters by my action in this matter." He was right. Bragg was furious that this first show of combat should be a blot on the record of a campaign which had already yielded such rich fruits without the firing of a shot. Accordingly, being as he said "unwilling to allow the impression of a disaster to rest on the minds of my men," he prepared at once to erase it. All four divisions started that same day for Munfordville.

He was taking no chances. Hardee's wing moved through Cave City that evening, making the direct approach, while Polk's crossed the river a few miles above and circled around to the rear, occupying positions on the bluffs overlooking the fort on the opposite bank. By midafternoon, September 16, the investment was complete. After firing a few rounds to establish ranges, Bragg sent a note informing the Federal commander that he was surrounded by an overwhelming force and repeating the two-day-old demand for an unconditional surrender to avoid "the terrible consequences of an assault." When Wilder asked for proof that such a host was really at hand, Bragg replied: "The only evidence I can give you of my ability to make good my assertion of the

*James Chalmers' Mississippians take
heavy losses during their ill-advised attack on
the Federal garrison at Munfordville.*

presence of a sufficient force to compel your surrender, beyond the statement that it now exceeds 20,000, will be the use of it. . . . You are allowed one hour in which to make known your decision."

Wilder was in something of a quandary. A former Indiana industrialist, he had been thirteen months in service, but nothing so far in his experience had taught him how much credence to give the claims that accompanied such demands for capitulation. Finally he arrived at an unorthodox solution. Knowing that Simon Buckner commanded a division on this side of the river, and knowing moreover that Buckner was a man of honor, he went to him under a flag of truce and asked his advice — as one gentleman to another. If resistance was hopeless,

★

he said, he did not want to sacrifice his men; but neither did he want to be stampeded into surrendering because of his lack of experience in such matters. What should he do? Buckner, taken aback, declined to advise him. Wars were not fought that way, he said. He offered, however, to conduct him on a tour of the position and let him see for himself the odds against him. The colonel took him up on that, despite the fact that it was now past midnight and the truce had expired two hours ago. After counting 46 guns in position on the south bank alone, Wilder was convinced. "I believe I'll surrender," he said sadly.

It was arranged without further delay; Bragg subsequently listed the capture of 4267 prisoners, 10 guns, 5000 rifles, "and a proportionate quantity of ammunition, horses, mules, and military stores." While the bluecoats were being paroled — officers retaining their side arms and the men marching out, as Wilder proudly reported, "with all the honors of war, drums beating and colors flying" — Bragg wired the Adjutant General: "My junction with Kirby Smith is complete. Buell still at Bowling Green."

He had cause for elation. Already astride the Green River, halfway across Kentucky, the western prong of his two-pronged offensive had scored a victory as rich in spoils as the one the eastern prong had scored against Nelson, eighteen days ago at Richmond. In an order issued at Munfordville that same morning, he congratulated his soldiers "on the crowning success of their extraordinary campaign which this day has witnessed," and he told the Adjutant General: "My admiration of and love for my army cannot be expressed. To its patient toil and admirable discipline am I indebted for all the success which has attended this perilous undertaking."

This last sounded more like McClellan than it did like Bragg, and less like Jackson than it did like either: the Jackson of the Valley, that is, whom Bragg had announced as his prototype. And now that he had begun to sound like Little Mac, the terrible-tempered Bragg began to imitate his manner. After telling his men, "A powerful foe is assembling in our front and we must prepare to strike him a sudden and decisive blow," when Buell moved forward to Cave City, still waiting for Thomas to join him, Bragg left Polk's wing north of the Green and maneuvered Buckner's division across Buell's front, attempting to provoke him into attacking the south-bank intrenchments much as Chalmers had done, to his sorrow, five days back. But when Buell refused to be provoked, Bragg pulled Hardee's troops across the river and resumed his northward march, leaving Buell in his rear.

He had his reasons, and gave them later in his report: "With my effective force present, reduced . . . to half that of the enemy, I could not prudently afford to attack him there in his selected position. Should I pursue him farther toward Bowling Green he might fall back to that place and behind his fortifications. Reduced at the end of four days to three days' rations, and in a hostile country, utterly destitute of supplies, a serious engagement brought on any-where in that direction could not fail (whatever its results) to materially cripple me. The loss of a battle would be eminently disastrous. . . . We were therefore compelled to give up the object and seek for subsistence."

So he said. But it seemed to others in his army that there was more to it than this; that the trouble, in fact, was personal; that it lay not within the situation which involved a shortage of rations and a surplus of bluecoats, but somewhere down deep inside Bragg himself. For all the audacity of his concep-tion, for all his boldness through the preliminaries, once the critical instant was at hand he simply could not screw his nerves up to the sticking point. It was strange, this sudden abandonment of Stonewall as his model. It was as if a lesser poet should set out to imitate Shakespeare or Milton. With luck and skill, he might ape the manner, the superficial arrangement of words and even sentences; but the Shakespearian or Miltonic essence would be missing. And so it was with Bragg. He lacked the essence. Earlier he had said that the enemy was to be bro-ken up and beaten in detail, Jackson-style, "by rapid movements and vigorous blows." Now this precept was revised. As he left Munfordville he told a colonel on his staff: "This campaign must be won by marching, not fighting."

★ ★ ★ **W**hen Thomas came up on the 20th, Buell pushed forward and found the rebels gone. Convinced that they were headed for Louisville, he followed at a respectful distance, fearing an ambush but hoping to strike their rear while they were engaged with the troops William Nelson was assembling for the defense of the city. To his surprise, however, less than twenty miles beyond the river Bragg swung east through Hodgenville, over Muldraugh's Hill and across the Rolling Fork to Bardstown, leaving his opponent a clear path to Louisville. Gratefully Buell took it.

He was not the only one who was grateful. Nelson, his flesh wounds healing rapidly since the removal of the bullet from his thigh, had been prepar-ing feverishly, and with a good deal of apprehension based on previous experi-ence, to resist the assault he expected Bragg to launch at his second collection of recruits. When he learned that the gray column had turned off through Lin-coln's birthplace he drew his first easy breath since the early-morning knocking at his bedroom door, almost four weeks ago, first warned him that Kirby Smith's invaders had come over Big Hill and were nearing Richmond. The arrival, Sep-tember 24, of Buell's advance division — 12,000 veterans and half a dozen bat-teries of artillery — produced a surge of confidence within his shaggy breast. He wired department headquarters, Cincinnati: "Louisville is now safe. We can de-stroy Bragg with whatever force he may bring against us. God and liberty."

★ ★ ★

★

Shelby Foote

Confederate dead, just a few of the 5000 from both armies killed at Antietam, lie on the battlefield in front of the shell-damaged Dunker Church.

THREE

Lee, McClellan: Sharpsburg

1862 ★ ★ ★ ★ ★ **A**s Pope's frazzled army faded eastward up the pike toward Washington, and as Lee's — no less frazzled, but considerably lighter-hearted — poked among the wreckage in search of hardtack, the problem for them both was: What next? For the former, the battered and misused conglomeration of troops now under McClellan, who had ridden out to meet them, the question was answered by necessity. They would defend their capital. But for the victors, confronted as usual with a variety of choices, the problem was more complex. Lee's solution, reached before his men's clothes were dry from the rain-lashed skirmish at Chantilly, resulted — two weeks later, and by coincidence on the same date as Wilder's surrender to Bragg at Munfordville — in the bloodiest single day of the whole war.

The solution, arrived at by a narrowing of choices, was invasion. He could not attack the Washington defenses, manned as they were by McClellan's army, already superior in numbers to his own and about to be strengthened, as he heard, by 60,000 replacements newly arrived in response to Lincoln's July call for "300,000 more." Nor could he keep his hungry soldiers in position where they were. The northern counties had been stripped of grain as if by locusts, and his wagon train was inadequate to import enough to feed the horses, let alone the troops. A third alternative would be to fall back into the Valley or south of the Rappahannock. But this not only would be to give up much that had been gained; it would permit a renewal of pressure on the Virginia Central — and eventually on Richmond. By elimination, then, the march would be northward, across the Potomac.

Not that there were no practical arguments against taking such a step. After much strenuous marching on meager rations, the men were bone-weary and Lee knew it. What was more, he wrote Davis on September 3, "The army is not properly equipped for an invasion of an enemy's territory. It lacks much of the material of war, is feeble in transportation, the animals being much reduced, and the men are poorly provided with clothes, and in thousands of instances are destitute of shoes. . . . What occasions me the most concern is the fear of getting out of ammunition." Nevertheless, in Lee's mind the advantages far outweighed the drawbacks. Two successful campaigns within two months, on Virginia soil and against superior numbers, had won for the Confederacy the admiration of the world. A third, launched beyond the Potomac in conjunction with Bragg's two-pronged advance beyond the Cumberland, might win for her the foreign recognition which Davis had known from the start was the one best assurance that this second Revolution, like the first, would be successful. Besides, Maryland was a sister state, not enemy territory. Thousands of her sons were in the Virginia army, and it was believed that thousands more would join the colors once they were planted on her soil. In any event, invasion would draw off the northern armies and permit the Old Dominion farmers, now that the harvest was at hand, to gather their crops unmolested. The one thing Lee could not do was nothing; or as he put it, "We cannot afford to be idle, and though weaker than our opponents in men and military equipments, must endeavor to harass them if we cannot destroy them." Next day, having convinced himself — and hoping, by the usual kid-gloves treatment, to have convinced the President — he wired Davis that he was "fully persuaded of the benefit that will result from an expedition into Maryland, and I shall proceed to make the movement at once, unless you should signify your disapprobation."

Without waiting for a reply — indeed, without allowing time for one — he put the army in motion that same day for White's Ferry, twenty miles south of Frederick, the immediate objective. Approaching the ford on September 6 and 7, the men removed their shoes, those who had them, rolled up their trouser legs, and splashed across the shallows into Maryland. One cavalryman considered it "a magnificent sight as the long column . . . stretched across this beautiful Potomac. The evening sun slanted upon its clear placid waters and burnished them with gold, while the arms of the soldiers glittered and blazed in its radiance." There were for him, in the course of the war, "few moments . . . of excitement more intense, or exhilaration more delightful, than when we ascended the opposite bank to the familiar but now strangely thrilling music of *Maryland, My Maryland*."

Not everyone was so impressed, however, with the beauty of the occasion. A boy who stood on that opposite bank and watched the vermin-infested scarecrows come thronging past him, hairy and sunbaked, with nothing bright about them but their weapons and their teeth, was impressed by them in much the same way as the Kentucky civilian, this same week, had been impressed by their western counterparts. They made him think of wolves. "They were the dirtiest men I ever saw," he afterwards recalled, "a most ragged, lean, and hungry set of wolves." Accustomed to the Federals he had seen marching in compact formations and neat blue uniforms, he added: "Yet there was a dash about them that the northern men lacked. They rode like circus riders. Many of them were from the far South and spoke a dialect I could scarcely understand. They were profane beyond belief and talked incessantly."

Federal pickets (foreground) fire random shots at Lee's invading army as it crosses the Potomac into Maryland on September 4.

Their individuality, which produced the cackling laughter, the end-less chatter, and the circus-rider gyrations, was part of what made them "terri-ble in battle," as the phrase went. But in the present instance it also produced hampering effects: one being that Lee had considerably fewer men in Maryland than he had counted on when he made his decision to move north. Hampton's cavalry brigade, the reserve artillery, and three divisions of infantry under D. H. Hill, Major General Lafayette McLaws, and Brigadier General John G. Walker — 20,000 troops in all — had been forwarded from Richmond and had joined the army on its march to the Potomac. After the deduction of his Manassas casualties, this should have given Lee a total strength of 66,000. The truth was, he had barely more than 50,000 men in Maryland; which meant that close to 15,000 were absent without leave. Some few held back because of con-scientious objections to invasion, but most were stragglers, laggards broken down in body or skulkers broken down in spirit. They would be missed along the thin gray line of battle, invalids and cowards alike, though their defection gave the survivors an added sense of pride and resolution. "None but heroes are left," one wrote home.

Hard-core veterans though they were, they were subject to various ills. Diarrhea was one, the result of subsisting on green corn; "the Confederate disease," it was coming to be called, and the sufferers, trotting white-faced to catch up with the column, joked ruefully about it, offering to bet that they "could hit a dime at seven yards." Another was sore feet; a fourth of the army limped shoeless on the stony Maryland roads. In addition to these ailments, mostly but by no means entirely confined to the ranks, a series of accidents had crippled the army's three ranking generals, beginning with Lee himself. Clad in rubber overalls and a poncho, he had been standing beside his horse on the rainy last day of August when a sudden cry, "Yankee cavalry!" startled the ani-mal. Lee reached for the bridle, tripped in his clumsy clothes, and caught him-self on his hands as he fell forward, with the result that a small bone was broken in one and the other was badly sprained. Both were put in splints, and Lee, un-able to handle a mount, entered Maryland riding in an ambulance. Longstreet too was somewhat incapacitated by a raw blister on his heel; he crossed the river wearing a carpet slipper on his injured foot. Marylanders thus were robbed of the chance to see these two at their robust and energetic best. The third high-ranking casualty was Jackson. Ox-eyed Little Sorrel having been missing for two weeks, the gift of a sinewy gray mare from a group of Confederate sym-pathizers was welcome on the day he crossed the Potomac. Next morning, how-ever, when he mounted and gave her the reins she did not move. He touched her with his spur: whereupon she reared, lost her balance, and toppled back-ward. Stunned, Jackson lay in the dust for half an hour, fussed over by surgeons who feared for a spinal injury, then was transferred, like Lee, to an ambulance.

*Confederates passing through Frederick, Maryland,
halt in one of the town's streets in this photograph
taken from the balcony of a dry-goods store.*

These were partial incapacitations. Two others involving men of rank were unfortunately total, at least for the time being. The charges against Bob Toombs had been dropped in time for him to share in the final hour of victory at Manassas, but no sooner was the battle won than his place in arrest was taken by a general whose services the army could less afford to lose. When Shanks Evans laid claim to some ambulances Hood's Texans had captured, Hood, although outranked, refused to give them up. Evans referred the matter to the wing commander, who ruled in his favor, and when Hood still declined to yield, Longstreet ordered him back to Culpeper to await trial for insubordination. Lee intervened to the extent of allowing Hood to remain with his division, though not to exercise command.

By then the trouble between A. P. Hill and Jackson had come to a head, with the result that another of the army's hardest fighters was in arrest.

★

On the march to the Potomac, Little Powell's division straggled badly. As far as Stonewall could see, Hill was doing little to correct this. What was more, he broke regulations by not calling rest halts at the specified times. Finally Jackson himself halted one brigade: whereupon the red-bearded general came storming back down the column, asking by whose orders the troops were being delayed. The brigadier indicated Stonewall, who sat his horse beside the road. Hill unbuckled his sword and held it out to Jackson. "If you are going to give the orders, you have no need of me," he declared, trembling with rage. Stonewall did not take it. "Consider yourself under arrest for neglect of duty," he said coldly. "You're not fit to be a general," Hill snapped, and turned away.

With his army thus short of equipment and presenting its worst appearance, himself and his two chief lieutenants distracted by injuries, and two of his best division commanders in arrest, Lee busied himself and his staff with the composition, in accordance with instructions received from Davis, of a proclamation addressed "To the People of Maryland":

The people of the Confederate States . . . have seen with profound indignation their sister State deprived of every right and reduced to the condition of a conquered province. . . . [We] have long wished to aid you in throwing off this foreign yoke, to enable you again to enjoy the inalienable rights of freemen. . . . We know no enemies among you, and will protect all, of every opinion. It is for you to decide your destiny freely and without constraint . . . and while the Southern people will rejoice to welcome you to your natural position among them, they will only welcome you when you come of your own free will.

Having thus complied with the President's recommendations, he made some of his own concerning another matter. The time had come, it seemed to him, in view of the present military situation, for the Confederacy to make a peace proposal to the North, based of course on permanent separation. "Such a proposition, coming from us at this time, could in no way be regarded as suing for peace," he wrote Davis; "but, being made when it is in our power to inflict injury upon our adversary, would show conclusively to the world that our sole object is the establishment of our independence and the attainment of an honorable peace. The rejection of this offer would prove to the country that the responsibility of the continuance of the war does not rest upon us, but that the party in power in the United States elect to prosecute it for reasons of their own." This he thought might have an effect upon the pending congressional elections in the North, enabling the voters "to determine . . . whether they will support those who favor a prolongation of the war, or those who wish to bring it to a termination, which can but be productive of good to both parties without affecting the honor of either."

This was perhaps more opportune than he suspected, especially with regard to the effect it might have on foreign opinion, if Davis would act on the advice and Lee could give him time in which to do so. Napoleon III had been friendly all along; but now, stimulated by the offer of one hundred thousand bales of badly needed cotton, as well as by concern for the success of certain machinations already in progress south of the Texas border, he was downright eager. Across the English Channel, meanwhile, the news of Pope's defeat and Lee's entry into Maryland caused Lord Palmerston to write Earl Russell: "The Federals . . . got a very complete smashing. . . . Even Washington or Baltimore may fall into the hands of the Confederates. If this should happen, would it not be time for us to consider whether in such a state of things England and France might not address the contending parties and recommend an arrangement on the basis of separation?" The Foreign Minister replied: "I agree with you that the time is come for offering mediation to the United States Government, with a view to recognition of the independence of the Confederates. I agree further that, in case of failure, we ought ourselves to recognize the Southern States as an independent State." Presently the Prime Minister wrote again: "It is evident that a great conflict is taking place to the northwest of Washington, and its issue may have a great effect on the state of affairs. If the Federals sustain a grave defeat, they may be at once ready for mediation, and the iron should be struck while it is hot. If, on the other hand, they should have the best of it, we may wait a while and see what may follow."

What followed was in a large part up to Lee and his tatterdemalion army, and having given his attention to the question of peace, he turned his mind once more to thoughts of war — in particular to the problem of securing his lines of communication and supply. Once he moved westward, beyond the Catoctins and the trans-Potomac prolongation of the Blue Ridge, these would extend southward up the Shenandoah Valley, through Martinsburg and Winchester. He had expected the Federals to evacuate those places when they found him in their rear, and in the latter case they had done so; but the former still was occupied in strength, as was Harpers Ferry, sixteen miles away. Lee felt obliged to detach part of his army to reduce them before continuing his advance. When he broached this to Longstreet, however, Old Pete argued forcefully against such a division of strength in the enemy's own back yard. Jackson, on the other hand — recovered by now from his fall the day before — was delighted at the prospect, remarking somewhat wistfully that of late he had been entirely too neglectful of his friends in the Valley. Lee thought so too. Dividing the army had worked wonders against Pope; now he would attempt it against McClellan, whose return to command had been announced in the northern papers. Despite Longstreet's objections, Lee began to work out a plan, not only for removing the threat to his supply line, but also for capturing the bluecoats who made it.

The result was Special Orders 191, which called for another of those ambitious simultaneous convergences by widely separated columns upon an assigned objective; in short, a maneuver not unlike the one that had failed, a year ago this week, against Cheat Mountain. In this case, however, since the capture of the Federals could be effected only by cutting off all their avenues of escape, the complication was unavoidable. The basis for it was geography. Low-lying Harpers Ferry, more trap than fortress, was dominated by heights that frowned down from three directions: Bolivar Heights to the west, Maryland Heights across the Potomac, and Loudoun Heights across the Shenandoah. With this in mind, Lee designed a convergence that would occupy all three. Jackson, who had been in command of the Ferry the year before and therefore knew it well, would be in general charge of the operation in its final stage. He would move with his three divisions through Boonsboro to the vicinity of Williamsport, where he would cross the Potomac and descend on Martinsburg, capturing the garrison there or driving it eastward to Harpers Ferry, where he would occupy Bolivar Heights. McLaws, with his own and Anderson's divisions, would move southwest and take position on Maryland Heights. Walker would move south with his two-brigade division, cross the Potomac below Point of Rocks, and occupy Loudoun Heights. The result, with all those guns bearing down on the compact mass of bluecoats, should be something like shooting fish in a rain barrel. Longstreet meanwhile would move westward, beyond the mountains, and occupy Boonsboro with his other four divisions, supported by D. H. Hill. The order was dated September 9; all movements would begin the following morning, with the convergence scheduled for the 12th. After the capitulation, which was expected to be accomplished that same day, or the next day at the latest, Jackson, McLaws, and Walker would rejoin the main body at Boonsboro for a continuation of the campaign through Maryland and into Pennsylvania.

Distribution of the order, which was quite full and gave in detail the disposition of Lee's whole army for the next four days, was to the commanders of the various columns as well as to the commanders of those divisions whose normal assignments were affected. Longstreet took one look at it and, realizing

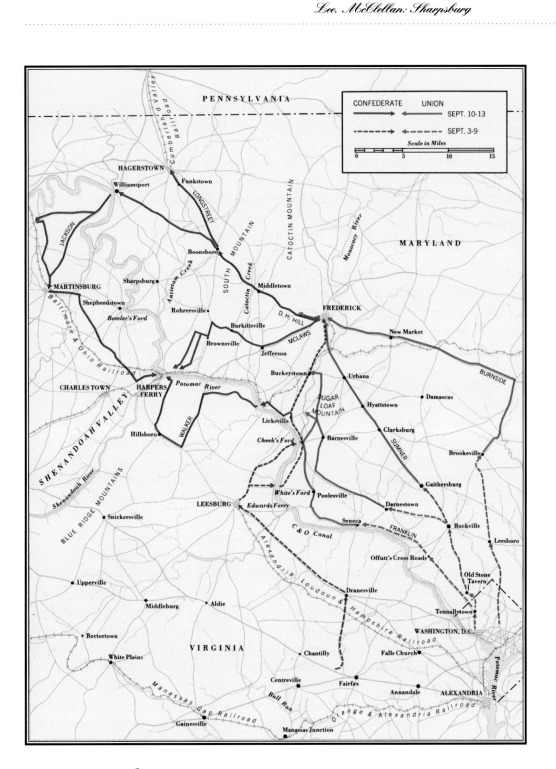

*After the rebels crossed into Maryland, the Federals
moved west in pursuit. Lee briefly divided his army, but
quickly reconsolidated when McClellan closed in.*

the danger if it should fall into unfriendly hands, committed it to memory; after which he tore it up and chewed the pieces into pulp. Jackson, too, hugged it close. Observing, however, that Harvey Hill, who had been attached to his wing for the river crossing, was now assigned to Longstreet, he decided that the best way to let his brother-in-law know that he was aware of the transfer would be to send him a copy of the order. With his usual regard for secrecy, Stonewall himself made the transcript in his spidery handwriting and dispatched it under seal. Hill studied it, then put it carefully away. When the copy arrived from Lee's adjutant, one of Hill's staff officers decided to keep it for a souvenir, but meanwhile used it as a wrapper for three cigars which he carried in his pocket.

Lee knew nothing of this duplication, nor of the menial use to which an important army order was being put. He was doing all he could, however, to make certain that nothing went astray in the intended convergence, as unfortunately had happened every time such a maneuver had been attempted in the past. One precaution he took was to have a personal interview with each of the generals in charge: with Longstreet, who would guard the trains while the others were gone, and with Jackson, McLaws, and Walker, who would be on their own throughout the expedition. In the latter's case this was particularly apt; for Walker, a forty-year-old regular army Missourian, had just come up from the James with his small division — formerly a part of Holmes', in which he had commanded a brigade during the Seven Days — and was therefore unfamiliar with what had since become the army's operational procedure. Lee went over the plan with him, indicating details on the map with his crippled hands. When this was done, he spoke of what he intended to do once his forces were reunited north of the Potomac. If Walker, with his "Show Me" background, had been inclined to suspect that much of the recent praise for the Virginian's audacity was overdone, that doubt was ended now. The sweep and daring of the prospect Lee exposed, speaking quietly here in the fly-buzzed stillness of his tent, widened Walker's eyes and fairly took his breath away.

Sixty air-line miles beyond Hagerstown lay Harrisburg, Pennsylvania, where the Pennsylvania Railroad crossed the Susquehanna River. "That is the objective point of the campaign," Lee explained. Destruction of the bridge there, supplementing the previous seizure of the B & O crossing at Harpers Ferry and the wrecking of the Monocacy aqueduct of the Chesapeake & Ohio Canal — this last would be done by Walker, in accordance with instructions already given him, on the way to Point of Rocks — would isolate the Federal East from the Federal West, preventing the arrival of reinforcements for McClellan except by the slow and circuitous Great Lakes route. "After that," Lee concluded, "I can turn my attention to Philadelphia, Baltimore, or Washington, as may seem best for our interests." The war would be over — won.

Observing Walker's astonishment, Lee said: "You doubtless regard it hazardous to leave McClellan practically on my line of communication, and to march into the heart of the enemy's country?" When the Missourian said he did indeed, Lee asked him: "Are you acquainted with General McClellan?" Walker replied that he had seen little of him since the Mexican War. "He is an able general," Lee said, "but a very cautious one. His enemies among his own people think him too much so. His army is in a very demoralized and chaotic condition, and will not be prepared for offensive operations (or he will not think it so) for three or four weeks. Before that time I hope to be on the Susquehanna."

———————— ⤳ ————————

★ ★ ★   **T**his judgment contained several errors of degree as to the Federal potential, but in none of them was Lee more mistaken than in his estimate of the present condition of the Army of the Potomac, which in fact was less "chaotic" than his own, at least so far as its physical well-being was concerned. Nor was it "demoralized." McClellan was back, along with regular rations, a sense of direction, and a general sweeping up of croakers such as had followed the previous Bull Run fiasco which had brought him on the scene the year before. All this had been the source of much rejoicing, but there were others, no less heartening for being negative. Pope and McDowell, whom the men considered the authors of their woe, were gone — the former to pack his bags for the long ride to Minnesota, the latter to await the outcome of a formal hearing he had demanded in order to clear himself of all the charges brought by rumor — and so was Banks, a sort of junior-grade villain in their eyes, to assume command of the Washington defenses after McClellan marched the field force out the National Road to challenge the invaders up in Maryland.

That too was heartening. After four solid weeks of retreating, some from the malarial bottoms of the Peninsula, some from the blasted fields that bordered the dusty rivers of northern Virginia, and some from both — followed always by eyes that watched from roadside windows, hostile and mocking — not only were they moving forward, against the enemy, but they were doing it through a region that was friendly. "Fine marching weather; a land flowing with milk and honey; a general tone of Union sentiment among the people, who, being little cursed by slavery, had not lost their loyalty; scenery, not grand but picturesque," one young abolition-minded captain wrote, "all contributed to make the march delightful." A Maine veteran recorded that, "like the Israelites of old, we looked upon the land and it was good."

Best of all was Frederick, which they entered after the rebels had withdrawn beyond the Catoctins. "Hundreds of Union banners floated from the roofs and windows," one bluecoat recalled, "and in many a threshold stood the ladies and children of the family, offering food and water to the passing troops, or with tiny flags waving a welcome to their deliverers." Army rations went uneaten, "so sumptuous was the fare of cakes, pies, fruits, milk, dainty biscuit and loaves." A Wisconsin diarist apparently spoke for the whole army in conferring the accolade: "Of all the memories of the war, none are more pleasant than those of our sojourn in the goodly city of Frederick."

    Presently it developed that there was more here for soldiers than an abundance of smiles and tasty food. For two of them, at any rate — three, in fact, if Private B. W. Mitchell and Sergeant J. M. Bloss, Company E, 27th Indiana, decided to share the third with a friend — there were cigars. Or so it seemed at the outset. Saturday morning, September 13, the Hoosier regiment was crossing an open field, a recent Confederate camp site near Frederick, when the men got orders to stack arms and take a break. Soon afterwards Mitchell and Bloss were lounging on the grass, taking it easy, when the former noticed a long thick envelope lying nearby. He picked it up and found the three cigars inside, wrapped in a sheet of official-looking paper. While Bloss was hunting for a

This copy of Lee's Special Orders 191 was written out by Stonewall Jackson for D. H. Hill. The copy found by the Federals was probably an original intended for Hill.

match, Mitchell examined the document. "Headquarters, Army of Northern Virginia, Special Orders 191," it was headed. At the bottom was written, "By command of General R. E. Lee: R. H. Chilton, Assistant Adjutant-General." In between, eight paragraphs bristled with names and place-names: Jackson, Martinsburg, Harpers Ferry; Longstreet, Boonsboro; McLaws, Maryland Heights; Walker, Loudoun Heights. Mitchell showed it to Bloss, and together they took it to the company commander, who conducted them to regimental headquarters, where the colonel examined the handwritten sheet, along with the three cigars — as if they too might have some hidden significance — and left at once for division headquarters, taking all the evidence with him. Mitchell and Bloss returned to their company area and lay down again on the grass, perhaps by now regretting that they had not smoked the lost cigars before taking the rebel paper to the captain. As it turned out, they had sacrificed most of their rest halt, too; for, according to Bloss, "In about three-quarters of an hour we noticed orderlies and staff officers flying in all directions."

McClellan's first considered reaction, after the leap his heart took at his first sight of the document which dispelled in a flash the fog of war and pinpointed the several components of Lee's scattered army, was that it must be spurious, a rebel trick. It was just too good to be true. But a staff officer who had known Chilton before the war identified the writing as unquestionably his. This meant that the order was valid beyond doubt: which in turn meant that McClellan's army, once it crossed the unoccupied Catoctins just ahead, would be closer to the two halves of Lee's army than those halves were to each other. What was more, one of those halves was itself divided into unequal thirds, the segments disposed on naked hilltops on the opposite banks of unfordable rivers. The thing to do, quite obviously, was to descend at once on Boonsboro, where the nearest half was concentrated, overwhelm it, and then turn on the other, destroying it segment by segment. The war would be over — won. At any rate that was how McClellan saw it. Standing there with the documentary thunderbolt in his hand, he said to one of his brigadiers: "Here is a paper with which if I cannot whip Bobby Lee I will be willing to go home."

Partly his elation was a manic reaction to the depression he had been feeling throughout most of the eleven days since Halleck's order, issued in confirmation of Lincoln's verbal instructions, gave him "command of the fortifications of Washington and of all the troops for [its] defense." This had not been supplemented or broadened since. What he did beyond its limitations he did on his own — including the march into Maryland to interpose his army between Lee's and the capital whose defense was his responsibility. Consequently, as he said later, he felt that he was functioning "with a halter around my neck. . . . If the Army of the Potomac had been defeated and I had survived I would, no doubt, have been tried for assuming authority without orders." What the Jacobins wanted, he knew, was his dismissal in disgrace, and he had long since given up the notion that the President would support him in every eventuality. In fact, knowing nothing of Lincoln's defiance of a majority of the cabinet for his sake, he no longer trusted the President to stand for long between him and the political clamor for his removal; and he was right. Back at the White House, after telling Hay, "McClellan is working like a beaver. He seems to be aroused to doing something after the snubbing he got last week," Lincoln added thoughtfully: "I am of the opinion that this public feeling against him will make it expedient to take important command from him . . . but he is too useful just now to sacrifice."

All this while, moreover, Halleck had been giving distractive twitches to the telegraphic lines attached to the halter. Though Banks had three whole corps with which to man the capital fortifications — Heintzelman's, Sigel's, and Porter's, which, together with the regular garrison, gave him a total defensive force of 72,500 men — the general in chief swung first one way, then another, alternately tugging or nudging, urging caution or headlong haste. Four days ago he had wired: "It may be the enemy's object to draw off the mass of our forces, and then attempt to attack us from the Virginia side of the Potomac. Think of this." Two days later he was calmer: "I think the main force of the enemy is in your front. More troops can be spared from here." Today, however, his fears were back, full strength: "Until you know more certainly the enemy forces south of the Potomac you are wrong in thus uncovering the capital." McClellan, his natural caution thus enlarged and played on — he estimated Lee's army at 120,000 men, half again larger than his own — pushed gingerly northwestward up the National Road, which led from Washington to Frederick, forty miles, then on through Hagerstown and Wheeling, out to Ohio.

He averaged about six miles a day, despite the fact that he had reorganized his army into two-corps "wings" in order to march by parallel roads rather than in a single column, which would have left the tail near Washington while the head was approaching Frederick. The right wing, assigned to Burnside, included his own corps, still under Reno, and McDowell's, now under Hooker, who had already won the nickname "Fighting Joe." The center wing was Sumner's and included his own and Banks' old corps, now under the senior division commander, Brigadier General Alpheus Williams. The left wing, Franklin's, included his own corps and the one division so far arrived from Keyes', still down at Yorktown. Porter's corps, which was released to McClellan on the 12th, the day his advance units reached Frederick, was the reserve. Including the troops arrived from West Virginia and thirty-five new regiments distributed throughout the army since its retreat from Manassas, McClellan had seventeen veteran divisions, with an average of eight brigades in each of his seven corps; or 88,000 men in all. Yet he believed himself outnumbered, and he could not forget that the army he faced — that scarecrow multitude of lean,

★

Passing through Frederick on September 12,
McClellan rides his dark bay "Dan Webster" through
a throng of exuberant, pro-Union townspeople.

vociferous, hairy men who reminded even noncombatants of wolves — had two great recent victories to its credit, while his own had just emerged from the confusion and shame of one of the worst drubbings any American army had ever suffered. Nor could he dismiss from his mind the thought of what another defeat would mean, both to himself and to his country. Despised by the leaders of the party in power, mistrusted by Lincoln, badgered by Halleck, he advanced with something of the manner of a man walking on slippery ice through a darkness filled with wolves.

It was at Frederick, that "goodly city," that the gloom began to lift. "I can't describe to you for want of time the enthusiastic reception we met with yesterday in Frederick," he wrote his wife next morning. "I was nearly overwhelmed and pulled to pieces. I enclose with this a little flag that some enthusiastic lady thrust into or upon Dan's bridle. As to flowers — they came in crowds! In truth, I was seldom more affected. . . . Men, women, and children

★

crowded around us, weeping, shouting, and praying." Then, near midday, his fears were abolished and his hopes were crowned. "Now I know what to do," he exclaimed when he read Special Orders 191, and one of the first things he did was share his joy with Lincoln in a wire sent at noon. In his elation he had the sound of a man who could not stop talking:

"I have the whole rebel force in front of me, but am confident, and no time shall be lost. I have a difficult task to perform, but with God's blessing will accomplish it. I think Lee has made a gross mistake, and that he will be severely punished for it. The army is in motion as rapidly as possible. I hope for a great success if the plans of the rebels remain unchanged. We have possession of

---

I have all the plans of the rebels, and will catch them in their own trap if my men are equal to the emergency. I now feel that I can count on them as of old.

— George B. McClellan

Catoctin. I have all the plans of the rebels, and will catch them in their own trap if my men are equal to the emergency. I now feel that I can count on them as of old. . . . My respects to Mrs. Lincoln. Received most enthusiastically by the ladies. Will send you trophies."

He said he would lose no time, and five days ago he had told Halleck, "As soon as I find out where to strike, I will be after them without an hour's delay." But that did not mean he would be precipitate. In fact, now that the once-in-a-lifetime opportunity was at hand, its very magnitude made him determined not to muff it as a result of careless haste. Besides, despite its fullness in regard to the location of the Confederate detachments, the order gave him no information as to their various strengths. For all he knew, Longstreet and Hill had almost any conceivable number of men at Boonsboro, and the nature of the terrain between there and Frederick afforded them excellent positions from which to fight a delaying action while the other half of their army shook itself together and rejoined them — or, worse still, moved northward against his flank. He already had the Catoctins, as he said, but beyond them reared South Mountain, the lofty extension of the Blue Ridge. The National Road crossed this range at Turner's Gap, with Boonsboro just beyond, while six miles south lay Crampton's Gap, pierced by a road leading down to Harpers Ferry from Buckeystown, where Franklin's left wing was posted, six miles south of Frederick. These roads and

★

gaps gave McClellan the answer to his problem. He would force Turner's Gap and descend on Boonsboro with his right and center wings, smashing Longstreet and Hill, while Franklin marched through Crampton's Gap and down to Maryland Heights, where he would strike the rear of Anderson and McLaws, capturing or brushing their men off the mountaintop and thereby opening the back door for the escape of the 12,000 Federals cooped up in Harpers Ferry. That way, too, the flank of the main body would be protected against an attack from the south, in case resistance delayed the forcing of the upper gap.

By late afternoon his plans were complete, and at 6.20 he sent Franklin his instructions. After explaining the situation at some length, he told him: "You will move at daybreak in the morning. . . . Having gained the pass" — Crampton's Gap — "your duty will be first to cut off, destroy, or capture McLaws' command and relieve [Harpers Ferry]." After saying, "My general idea is to cut the enemy in two and beat him in detail," he concluded: "I ask of you, at this important moment, all your intellect and the utmost activity that a general can exercise." Intellect and activity were desirable; haste, apparently, was not. Just as he did not ask it of himself, so he did not ask it of Franklin. Lee's disjointed army lay before him, and the best way to pick up the pieces — as he saw it — was deliberately, without fumbling. The army would get a good night's sleep, then start out fresh and rested "at daybreak in the morning."

And so it was. At sunrise, Franklin's 18,000 — who should indeed have been rested; they had seen no combat since the Seven Days, and not a great deal of it then except for the division that reinforced Porter at Gaines Mill — pushed westward out of Buckeystown, heading for the lower gap, a dozen miles away. The other two wings, 70,000 men under Sumner and Burnside, with Porter bringing up the rear, moved down the western slope of the Catoctins, then across the seven-mile-wide valley toward Turner's Gap, a 400-foot notch in the 1300-foot wall of the mountain, where a fire fight was in progress. They moved in three heavy columns, along and on both sides of the National Road, and to one of the marchers, down in the valley, each of these columns resembled "a monstrous, crawling, blue-black snake, miles long, quilled with the silver slant of muskets at a 'shoulder,' its sluggish tail writhing slowly up over the distant eastern ridge, its bruised head weltering in the roar and smoke upon the crest above, where was being fought the battle of South Mountain."

McClellan was there beside the pike, astride Dan Webster, the central figure in the vast tableau being staged in this natural amphitheater, and the men cheered themselves hoarse at the sight of him. It seemed to one Massachusetts veteran that "an intermission had been declared in order that a reception might be tendered to the general in chief. A great crowd continually surrounded him, and the most extravagant demonstrations were indulged in. Hundreds even hugged the horse's legs and caressed his head and mane." This was perhaps the Young Napoleon's finest hour, aware as he was of all those thousands of pairs of worshipful eyes looking at him, watching for a gesture, and the New England soldier was pleased to note that McClellan did not fail to supply it: "While the troops were thus surging by, the general continually pointed with his finger to the gap in the mountain through which our path lay."

★ ★ ★ *H*arvey Hill was watching him, too, or anyhow he was looking in that direction. Seeing from the notch of Turner's Gap, which he had been ordered to hold with his five-brigade division, the serpentine approach of those four Union corps across the valley — twelve divisions with a total of thirty-two infantry brigades, not including one corps which was still beyond the Catoctins — he said later that "the Hebrew poet whose idea of the awe-inspiring is expressed by the phrase, 'terrible as an army with banners,' [doubtless] had his view from the top of a mountain." He experienced mixed emotions at the sight. Although it was, as he observed, "a grand and glorious spectacle, and it was impossible to look at it without admiration," he added that he had never "experienced a feeling of greater *loneliness*. It seemed as though we were deserted by 'all the world and the rest of mankind.' "

Despite the odds, all too apparent to anyone here on the mountaintop, he had one real advantage in addition to the highly defensible nature of the terrain, and this was that he could see the Federals but they could not see him. Consequently, McClellan knew little of Hill's strength, or lack of it, and nothing at all of his loneliness. He thought that Longstreet, in accordance with Special Orders 191 was there too; whereas he was in fact at Hagerstown, a dozen miles away. Lee had sent him there from Boonsboro, three days ago, to head off a blue column erroneously reported to be advancing from Pennsylvania. After protesting against this further division of force — "General," he said in a bantering tone which only partly covered his real concern, "I wish we could stand still and let the damned Yankees come to us" — Longstreet marched his three divisions northward through the heat and dust. As a result, while McClellan back in Frederick was saying that he intended "to cut the enemy in two," Lee had already obliged him by cutting himself in five:

It was puzzling, this manifest lack of caution on McClellan's part, until late that night a message from Stuart explained the Young Napoleon's apparent change of character. A Maryland citizen of southern sympathies had happened to be at Federal headquarters when the lost order arrived, and he had ridden west at once, beyond the Union outposts, to give the news to Stuart, who passed it promptly on to Lee. So now Lee knew McClellan knew his precarious situation, and now that he knew he knew, he moved to counteract the disadvantage as best he could. He sent for Longstreet and told him to march at daybreak in support of Hill, whose defense of Turner's Gap would keep the Federal main body from circling around South Mountain to relieve the Harpers Ferry garrison by descending on McLaws. Longstreet protested. The march would have his men so blown that they would be in no shape for fighting when they got there, he said, and he urged instead that he and Hill unite at Sharpsburg, twelve miles south of Hagerstown and half that far from Boonsboro; there, near the Potomac, they could organize a position for defense while awaiting the arrival of the rest of the army, or else cross in safety to Virginia in case the troops from Harpers Ferry could not join them in time to meet McClellan's attack. Lee overruled him, however, and Longstreet left to get some sleep. After sending word to McLaws of the danger to his rear and stressing "the necessity of expediting your operations as much as possible," Lee received a note from Longstreet repeating his argument against opposing the Federals at South Mountain. Later the Georgian explained that he had not thought the note would alter Lee's decision, but that the sending of it "relieved my mind and gave me some rest." What effect it had on Lee's rest he did not say. At any rate, he received no reply, and the march for Turner's Gap began at dawn.

As usual, once he got them into motion, Longstreet's veterans marched hard and fast, trailing a long dust cloud in the heat. Shortly after noon they came within earshot of the battle Hill was waging on the mountain. The pace quickened on the upgrade. About 3 o'clock, nearing the crest, Lee pulled off to the side of the road to watch the troops swing past him. Though his hands were still in splints, which made for awkward management of the reins, he was mounted; he could abide the ambulance no longer. Presently the Texas brigade approached. "Hood! Hood!" they yelled when they saw Lee by the roadside. For two weeks Hood had been in arrest, but now that they were going into battle they wanted him at their head. "Give us Hood!" they yelled. Lee raised his hat. "You shall have him, gentlemen," he said.

When the tail of the column came abreast he beckoned to the tall young man with the tawny beard and told him: "General, here I am just on the eve of entering into battle, and with one of my best officers under arrest. If you will merely say that you regret this occurrence" — referring to the clash with Evans over the captured ambulances — "I will release you and restore you to the command of your division," Hood shook his head regretfully and replied that he "could not consistently do so." Lee urged him again, but Hood again declined. "Well," Lee said at last, "I will suspend your arrest till the impending battle is decided." Beaming, Hood saluted and rode off. Presently, from up ahead, loud shouts and cheers told Lee that the Texans had their commander back again.

It was well that they did, for they had need of every man they could muster, whatever his rank. Hill had been fighting his Thermopylae since early morning, and events had shown that the gap was by no means as defensible as it had seemed at first glance. High ridges dominated the notch from both sides, and there were other passes north and south, so that he had had to spread his small force thin in order to meet attacks against them all. Coming up just as Hill was about to be overwhelmed — one brigade had broken badly when its commander Brigadier General Samuel Garland was killed, and others were reduced to fighting Indian-style, scattered among the rocks and trees — Longstreet counterattacked on the left and right and managed to stabilize the situation until darkness ended the battle. McClellan had had about 30,000 men engaged, Lee about half that many. Losses were approximately 1800 killed and wounded on each side, with an additional 800 Confederates taken captive. Among the dead was Jesse Reno, shot from his saddle just after sundown while making a horseback inspection of his corps. Lieutenant Colonel Rutherford B. Hayes of the 23d Ohio, fifteen years away from the Presidency, was wounded. Sergeant William McKinley, another future President from that regiment, was unhurt; the bullet that would get him was almost forty years away.

For Lee it was a night of anxiety. He had saved his trains and perhaps delayed a showdown by holding McClellan east of the mountain, but he had done this at a cost of nearly 3000 of his hard-core veterans. What was more, he knew he could do it no longer: Hill and Longstreet both reported that the gap could not

Both armies lost a general at South Mountain:
Confederate brigadier Samuel Garland (left) and
Union corps commander Jesse Reno.

★

be held past daylight, and defeat here on the mountain would mean annihilation. The only thing to do, Lee saw, was to adopt the plan Old Pete had favored so argumentatively the night before. Gone were his hopes for an invasion of Pennsylvania, the destruction of the Susquehanna bridge, the descent on Philadelphia, Baltimore, or the Union capital. Gone too was his hope of relieving Maryland of what he called her foreign yoke. Outnumbered worse than four to one, this half of the army — which in fact was barely more than a third: fourteen brigades out of the total forty — would have to retreat across the Potomac, and the other half would have to abandon its delayed convergence on Harpers Ferry. For Jackson and Walker this would not be difficult, but McLaws was already in the gravest danger. Soon after nightfall Lee sent him a message admitting defeat: "The day has gone against us and this army will go by Sharpsburg and cross the river. It is necessary for you to abandon your position tonight." McLaws of course would not be able to do this over the Ferry bridge, which was held by the Federal garrison; he would have to cross the Potomac farther upstream. Lee urged him, however, to do this somewhere short of Shepherdstown, which was just in rear of Sharpsburg. He wanted that ford clear for his own command, which would be retreating with McClellan's victorious army hard on its heels.

The evacuation began with Hill, followed by Longstreet; the cavalry brought up the rear. Obliged to abandon his dead and many of his wounded there on the mountain where they had fallen, Lee did not announce that he intended to withdraw across the Potomac, nor did he tell the others that he had instructed McLaws to abandon Maryland Heights. But news that arrived while the retreat was just getting under way confirmed the wisdom, indeed the necessity, of his decision. Crampton's Gap, six miles south, had been lost by the troopers sent to defend it: which not only meant that the Federals were pouring through, directly in rear of McLaws, but also that they were closer to Sharpsburg than Hill and Longstreet were. Unable to count any longer on McClellan's accustomed caution and hesitation, Lee saw that the march would have to be hard and fast, encumbered though he was with all his trains, if he was to get there first. Whereupon, with the situation thus at its worst and his army in graver danger of piecemeal annihilation than ever, Lee displayed for the first time a side to his nature that would become more evident down the years. He was not only no less audacious in retreat than in advance, but he was also considerably more pugnacious, like an old gray wolf wanting nothing more than half a chance to turn on whoever or whatever tried to crowd him as he fell back. And presently he got it.

It came in the form of a message from Jackson, to whom Lee had been sending couriers with information of the latest developments. "Through God's blessing," Stonewall had written at 8.15 p.m. from Bolivar Heights, "the advance, which commenced this evening, has been successful thus far, and I look to Him for complete success tomorrow. . . . Your dispatch respecting the movements of the enemy and the importance of concentration has been received." To Lee this represented a chance to retrieve the situation. By the shortest route, Harpers Ferry was only a dozen miles from Sharpsburg. If the place fell tomorrow, that would mean that a part at least of the besieging force could join him north of the Potomac tomorrow night; for when Jackson said that instructions had been "received," he meant that they would be obeyed. McLaws, too, might give the Federals the slip and march northwest without crossing the river. Accordingly, while Hill and Longstreet pushed on westward unpursued, Lee sent couriers galloping southward through the darkness. Unless the Army of the Potomac got into position for an all-out attack on Sharpsburg tomorrow — which seemed doubtful, despite McClellan's recent transformation; for one thing, there would be no more lost orders — the Army of Northern Virginia would not return to native ground without the shedding of a good deal more blood, Union and Confederate, than had been shed on South Mountain.

★ ★ ★ *M*cLaws was a methodical man, not given to indulging what little imagination he had, and in this case — his present dangers being what they were, with McClellan's left wing coming down on his rear through Crampton's Gap — that was preferable. A forty-one-year-old Georgian, rather burly, with a bushy head of hair and a beard to match, he had been four months a major general, yet except for commanding two brigades under Magruder during the Seven Days had seen no previous service with Lee's army. Now he had ten brigades, his own four and Anderson's six, and he had been given the most critical assignment in the convergence on Harpers Ferry. Maryland Heights was the dominant one of the three. If the place was to be made untenable, it would be his guns that would do most to make it so.

His march from Frederick had been deliberate: so much so that he was a day late in approaching his objective, after which he spent another day brushing Federal detachments off the hilltop and a night cutting a road in order

*N*ot long after Stonewall Jackson's rebels occupied the
heights surrounding Harpers Ferry (right foreground),
the town's Union garrison surrendered.

to manhandle his guns up the side of the mountain. At last, two days late, he
got them into position on the morning of September 14 and opened wigwag
communications with Jackson and Walker, across the way. Northward, up the
long ridge of South Mountain, D. H. Hill's daylong battle rumbled and mut-
tered; but McLaws, having posted three brigades in that direction to protect his

rear, kept his mind on the business of getting his high-perched guns laid in time to open a plunging fire on the Ferry whenever Stonewall, who was a day late and still completing his dispositions, gave the signal. During the afternoon a much nearer racket broke out northward, but whatever qualms McLaws felt at the evidence that his rear guard was under attack were eased by Stuart, who had ridden down from Turner's Gap. The bluecoats in front of Crampton's Gap did not amount to more than a brigade, he said, and McLaws turned back to his guns. Presently, though, as the noise swelled louder, he rode in that direction to see for himself — and arrived to find that he had a first-class panic on his hands. Right, left, and center, his troops had given way and were fleeing in disorder. That was no blue brigade pouring through the abandoned gap, they told him. It was McClellan's entire left wing, a reinforced corps.

Fortunately they had given a good account of themselves before they broke: good enough, at any rate, to instill a measure of caution in their pursuers. McLaws had time to rally the fugitives and bring three more brigades down off the heights, forming a line across the valley less than two miles south of the lost gap. The day was far gone by then, the valley filled with shadows, and Franklin did not press the issue. McClellan had told him to "cut off, destroy, or capture McLaws' command," and apparently he figured that the seizure of Crampton's Gap had fulfilled the first of these alternatives. Also, now that he was in McLaws' rear, he had the worry of knowing that the Confederate main body was in *his*. Anyhow he decided not to be hasty; he had his men bed down for the night in line of battle.

Next morning, as he was about to proceed with his advance, the rebels just ahead began to cheer. One curious bluecoat sprang up on a stone wall and called across to them:

"What the hell are you fellows cheering for?"

"Because Harpers Ferry is gone up, God damn you!"

"I thought that was it," the Federal said, and he jumped back down again.

McLaws had stood fast and Jackson had kept the promise sent by courier to Lee twelve hours before. One hour of plunging fire from the surrounding heights smothered the batteries below. Soon afterwards the white flag went up. Except for two regiments of cavalry that had escaped under cover of darkness — across the Potomac, then northward up the same road old John Brown had come south on, three years ago next month — the whole garrison surrendered, including the men who had marched in from Martinsburg. "Our Heavenly Father blesses us exceedingly," Jackson wrote his wife, enumerating his gains: 12,520 prisoners, 13,000 small arms, 73 cannon, and a goodly haul of quartermaster stores.

According to a northern reporter's O-my-God lay-me-down reaction to his first sight of Stonewall and his men, they had great need of the cap-tured stores — especially the general himself. "He was dressed in the coarsest kind of homespun, seedy and dirty at that; wore an old hat which any northern beggar would consider an insult to have offered him, and in general appearance was in no respect to be distinguished from the mongrel, bare-footed crew who follow his fortunes. I had heard much of the decayed appearance of the rebel soldiers, but such a looking crowd! Ireland in her worst straits could present no parallel, and yet they glory in their shame." The captive Federals (except perhaps the Irish among them) could scarcely argue with this, but they drew a different conclusion. "Boys, he isn't much for looks," one declared, inspecting Jackson, "but if we'd had him we wouldn't have been caught in this trap."

Pleased as he was, the Valley commander took little time for gloat-ing. "Ah," he said to a jubilant companion as they stood looking at the booty, "this is all very well, Major, but we have yet much hard work before us." Though he was unaware of the lost order — "I thought I knew McClellan," he remarked, "but this movement of his puzzles me" — he was aware that Lee was being pressed, and he was eager to move to his support. Five of the six divisions started for Sharpsburg that afternoon and night. The sixth was A. P. Hill's. Like Hood, once combat was at hand, he had burned to pass from the rear to the front of his division on the march to Harpers Ferry, but like Hood he would not compromise his honor with an expression of regret. He simply requested, through a member of the staff, to be released from arrest for the duration of the fighting, after which he would report himself in arrest again. Jackson not only assented; he gave him a prominent part in the operation, and afterwards left him in charge of the place while he himself rode off in the wake of a message he had sent Lee that morning soon after he saw the white flag go up:

> *Through God's blessing, Harpers Ferry and its garrison*
> *are to be surrendered. As Hill's troops have borne*
> *the heaviest part of the engagement, he will be left in*
> *command until the prisoners and public property shall*
> *be disposed of, unless you direct otherwise. The other*
> *forces can move off this evening so soon as they get*
> *their rations.*

"That is indeed good news," Lee said when it reached him at Sharpsburg about noon. "Let it be announced to the troops."

★

★ ★ ★ *M*cClellan's soldiers were feeling good, and so was their commander. For the first time since Williamsburg, back in early May, they were following up a battle with an advance, and as they went forward, past clumps of fallen rebels, they began to observe that their opponents were by no means the supermen they had seemed at times; were in fact, as one New York volunteer recorded, "undersized men mostly . . . with sallow, hatchet faces, and clad in 'butternut,' a color running all the way from a deep, coffee brown up to the whitish brown of ordinary dust." He even found himself feeling sorry for them. "As I looked down on the poor, pinched faces, worn with marching and scant fare, all enmity died out. There was no 'secession' in those rigid forms, nor in those fixed eyes staring blankly at the sky."

They left them where they lay and pushed on down the western slope, following McClellan, whose enthusiasm not even the fall of Harpers Ferry could dampen. Though this deprived him of 12,000 reinforcements which he thought he needed badly, it also vindicated the judgment he had shown in vainly urging the general in chief to order the post evacuated before Jackson rimmed the heights with guns. Moreover, though Old Brains could take no credit for it, his blunder had resulted in the dispersion of Lee's army, and this in turn had made possible yesterday's victory at South Mountain, as well as the larger triumph which now seemed to be within McClellan's grasp. Elated, he passed on this morning to Halleck "perfectly reliable [information] that the enemy is making for Shepherdstown in a perfect panic," and that "Lee last night stated publicly that he must admit they had been shockingly whipped." To old General Scott, in retirement at West Point, went a telegram announcing "a signal victory" and informing him that his fellow Virginian and former protégé had been soundly trounced: "R. E. Lee in command. The rebels routed, and retreating in disorder." Both reactions were encouraging. "Bravo, my dear general! Twice more and it's done," Scott answered, while Lincoln himself replied to the earlier wire: "God bless you and all with you. Destroy the rebel army if possible."

That was precisely what McClellan intended to do, if possible, and that afternoon, five miles southeast of Boonsboro — the scene of another triumphal entry and departure — he came upon a line of hills overlooking a shallow, mile-wide valley through which a rust-brown creek meandered south from its source in Pennsylvania; Antietam Creek, it was called. Beyond it, somewhat lower than the ridge on which he stood with his staff while his army filed in and spread out north and south along the line of hills outcropped with limestone, rose another ridge that masked the town of Sharpsburg, all but its spires and rooftops, and the Potomac, which followed a tortuous southward course, dividing Mary-

On September 17, Lee had his troops deployed north and east of Sharpsburg, while McClellan had brought two of his corps over Antietam Creek to open the battle.

land and Virginia, another mile or so away. What interested him just now, though, was the ridge itself. There were Confederates on it, and Confederate guns, and one reason that they interested him was that they took him under fire. He sent his staff back out of range, dissolving the gaudy clot of horsemen who had drawn the fire in the first place, and went on with his study of the terrain.

A mile to the right of the point where the cluster of spires and gables showed above the ridge, and facing the road that led northward along it to Hagerstown, a squat, whitewashed building was set at the forward edge of a grove of trees wearing their full late-summer foliage; the autumnal equinox was still a week away. The sunlit brick structure, dazzling white against its leafy backdrop, was a church, but it was a Dunker church and therefore had no steeple; the Dunkers believed that steeples represented vanity, and they were as much opposed to vanity as they were to war, including the one that was about to move into their churchyard. On the near side of the road, somewhat farther to the right, was another grove of trees, parklike on the crown of the ridge, and between the two was a forty-acre field of dark green corn, man-tall and ripening for the harvest.

McClellan put his glasses back in their case and retired to do some thinking. Lee had chosen his army's position with care, disposing it along the high ground overlooking the shallow valley so that its flanks were anchored at opposite ends of the four-mile bend of the Potomac. That was his strength; but McClellan thought it might also be his weakness. Once Lee was dislodged from that ridge, with only a single ford in his rear, he might be caught in the coils of the river and cut to pieces. The problem was how to dislodge him, strong as he was. McClellan estimated yesterday's rebel casualties at 15,000 men, but that still left Lee with more than 100,000 according to McClellan, whose total strength — including Franklin, still hovering north of Harpers Ferry — was 87,164. Fortunately, however, there was no hurry; not just yet. The army was still filing in, hot and dusty from its march, and anyhow the day was already too far gone for an attack to succeed before darkness provided cover for a rebel getaway. He decided to work the thing out overnight. Meanwhile the troops could get a hot meal and a good night's rest by way of preparation for whatever bloody work he designed for them to do tomorrow.

Tomorrow came, September 16, but such bloody work as it brought was done by long-range shells from batteries on those ridges east and west of the mile-wide valley with its lazy little copper-colored creek. Wanting another good look at the terrain before completing his attack plan, McClellan rose early and went to the observation post where his staff had set up headquarters. Off to the right of the Boonsboro road and half a mile north of the center of the position, it was an excellent location, just beyond reach of the rebel guns, and there was plenty of equipment there for studying the enemy dispositions, including high-power telescopes strapped to the heads of stakes driven solidly into the ground. Unfortunately, however, these could not penetrate the thick mist that overhung the field until midmorning. By then the sun had burned enough of it away for McClellan to see that the Confederates had made some changes, shifting guns at various points along their line. The time consumed in noting these was well spent, he felt, for he wanted to eliminate snags and thus leave as little to

★

chance as he possibly could. When the blow fell he wanted it to be heavy. Noon came and went, and on both sides men lay drowsing under the press of heat while the cannoneers continued their intermittent argument, jarring the ground and disrupting an occasional card game. By 2 o'clock McClellan had his attack plan: not for today — today, like yesterday, was too far gone — but for tomorrow.

It was based essentially on the presence of three stone bridges that spanned the creek on the left, center, and right. The one on the left was closest to Sharpsburg and the enemy line; in fact it was barely more than its own length away from the latter, since the western ridge came down sharply here, overlooking the bridge and whoever tried to use it. The center bridge, crossed by the Boonsboro road a mile above the first, had some of the same drawbacks, being under observation from the ridge beyond, as well as some of its own growing out of the fact that it debouched onto an uphill plain that was swept by guns clustered thickly along the rebel center. The upper bridge, a mile and a half above the

second, had none of these disadvantages, being well out of range of the batteries across the way. What was more, an upstream crossing would permit an unmolested march to a position astride the Hagerstown road, well north of Lee's left flank, and a southward attack from that direction, if successful, would accomplish exactly what McClellan most desired. It would bowl the Confederates off their ridge and — in conjunction with attacks across the other two bridges, launched when the first was under way with all its attendant confusion — expose them to utter destruction.

In essence that was McClellan's plan, the outgrowth of much poring over the landscape and the map, and now that it had been formulated, all that remained — short, that is, of the execution itself — was for him to assign the various corps their various tasks in the over-all scheme for accomplishing Lee's downfall. Scrapping the previous organization into "wings," he decided that Fighting Joe Hooker was the man to lead the attack down the Hagerstown

Joseph Hooker directed the opening Federal attack only to be knocked out of the battle by a painful foot wound.

road, supported by Brigadier General J. K. F. Mansfield, who had arrived from Washington the day before to take over Banks' corps from Williams. Sumner, too, would come down from that direction, bringing a total of three corps, half of the whole army, to bear on Lee's left flank. If that did not break him, Franklin too could be thrown in there — he had been summoned from Maryland Heights and was expected to arrive tomorrow morning — raising the preponderance to two thirds. Burnside, back in command of his own corps after the death of Reno, was given the job of forcing the lower bridge and launching the direct assault on Sharpsburg, after which he would seize the Shepherdstown ford and thus prevent the escape of even a remnant of the shattered rebel force. Porter, astride the Boonsboro road, in rear of the center bridge, would serve a double function. As the army reserve, his corps could be used to repulse any counterattack Lee might launch in desperation, or it could be committed to give added impetus at whatever point seemed most critical, once success was fully in sight. Or else he could force the middle bridge for an uphill charge that would pierce Lee's center and chop him in two; whereupon Porter could wheel left or right to assist either Burnside or Hooker in wiping out whichever half of the rebel army survived the amputation.

The battle would open at daylight tomorrow, but McClellan — after taking his staff on a fast two-mile ride along his outpost line, drawing fire all the way from the guns across the creek, which permitted his own superior batteries, emplaced along the eastern ridge, to spot and pound them heavily — decided to use what was left of today in getting his men into position to launch the opening attack. Accordingly, about 4 o'clock that afternoon, Hooker's corps began its upstream crossing, the general leading the way on a high-stepping big white charger. The crossing itself was well beyond range of the rebel guns, but the line of march led near the grove of trees northeast of the Dunker Church, with the result that as the flank of the column went past that point it struck sparks, like a file being raked across a grindstone. Hooker drew off; he wanted those woods, but not just yet; and made camp for the night in line of battle astride the Hagerstown road, less than a mile beyond the Confederate left-flank outposts. Poised to strike as soon as there was light enough for him to aim the blow, he was exactly where McClellan wanted him.

So were the others, or anyhow they soon would be. Mansfield was crossing now in the darkness, to be followed by Sumner; Franklin was on the way. Porter was bivouacked in an open field, protected by defilade, just across the Boonsboro road from army headquarters. Farthest south, Burnside had massed his troops in rear of the triple-arched stone bridge which after tomorrow would bear his name. The night was gloomy, with a slow drizzle of rain and occasional sputters of musketry when the outpost men got nervous. For security reasons, the high command had forbidden fires. This was not so bad in itself —

★

for all its dampness, the night was fairly warm — except that it kept the soldiers from boiling water. All along that dark, four-mile arc of blue-clad men, many of whom were going to die tomorrow, those who could not sleep chewed unhappily on dry handfuls of ground coffee.

★ ★ ★   **T**he sun had burned the mist away that morning, but it could not disperse the mental fog which hid from McClellan, whose eye was glued to a telescope even then across the way, the fact that Lee at the time had less than one fifth as many troops as his opponent gave him credit for. He had in fact, along and behind the Sharpsburg ridge, barely 18,000 soldiers under D. H. Hill and Longstreet — fewer than were in Sumner's corps alone — until Jackson arrived at noon with three thin divisions, his own and Ewell's, under Brigadier General J. R. Jones and Lawton, and Walker's, which had crossed the Shenandoah to join him on the march from Harpers Ferry the night before. This brought the total to 26,000 and lowered the odds to three to one. McLaws and Anderson, still on the march, would not arrive before nightfall, and A. P. Hill was still at the Ferry; he might well not arrive at all. Even if he did, so heavy had the straggling been, together with the losses at South Mountain, Lee would not be able to count on putting more than 40,000 men into his line of battle, including the cavalry and artillery, and would still face odds worse than two to one.

Aware of this, Walker expected to find Lee anxious and careworn when he joined him on the outskirts of Sharpsburg, just after noon on the 16th. "Anxious enough, no doubt, he was," Walker observed; "but there was nothing in his look or manner to indicate it. On the contrary, he was calm, dignified, and even cheerful. If he had had a well-equipped army of a hundred thousand veterans at his back, he could not have appeared more composed and confident."

His confidence was doubly based: first, on the troops themselves, the hard-core men who had proved their battle prowess at Manassas and their hardiness by surviving the stony Maryland marches; and, second, on the advantages of the position he had established here on the ridge behind Antietam Creek. "We will make our stand on those hills," he had said as he came within sight of them at dawn of the day before. Unwilling to end his ambitious invasion campaign with the repulse just suffered at South Mountain, he crossed the shallow valley and spread his army north and south along the low western ridge. Longstreet took the right, blocking the near approach, from Sharpsburg down to the heights overlooking the lower bridge; Hill the center, posting his men along a sunken lane that crooked across the northeast quadrant formed by the intersection of the Boonsboro and Hagerstown roads; and Hood the left, occupying the woods beyond the Dunker Church. Next day, when Jackson and Walker came up, Lee sent the former to take charge of the left, joining Hood with his two divisions, while Walker extended Longstreet's right in order to guard the lower fords of the Antietam.

The long odds were somewhat offset by the fact that he would have the interior line, with a good road well below the crest for shifting troops to threatened points along the ridge. In addition, he had the advantage of know-

ing that McClellan could not swing around his flanks, securely anchored as they were near the Potomac in both directions. This last, however, was also the source of some concern. Just as the river afforded the enemy no room for maneuver in his rear, so too it would afford him none in case his army was flung back off the ridge, and what was more there was only a single ford, a mile below the former site of the Shepherdstown bridge, which had been destroyed. He did not expect to be dislodged, but he did take the precaution of covering the ford, from the Virginia side, with such guns as could be spared from the reserve under Brigadier General W. N. Pendleton, his chief of artillery. That completed his preparations. Until McLaws and Anderson came up, Jackson's, Hill's, and Longstreet's 26,000 were all the troops

One of the Confederacy's rising stars, John Bell Hood led a savage early-morning counterattack.

he would have for opposing the blue host whose officers were examining his dispositions from the higher ground across the valley and whose superior guns had already begun the pounding that would make this field "artillery hell" for Confederate cannoneers. "Put them all in, every gun you have, long range and short range," Longstreet said to his battery commanders, but Lee had already cautioned them not to waste their limited ammunition in duels with the heavier Federal pieces. Save it for the infantry, he told them.

Hooker's upstream crossing, and the resultant brush with the Texans in the woods beyond the Dunker Church, gave Lee fair warning that tomorrow's first blow would be aimed at Jackson and Hood. This was not without its comforting aspect, for the men who stood in its path not only were the ones who had held the unfinished railroad against repeated assaults by Pope, but were also the ones who had led the charge that wrecked him; perhaps they would serve Hooker the same way. However, the odds were even longer now, and as night came down Lee's apprehension increased. He had heard nothing from McLaws and Anderson, without whom he had no reserves with which to plug a break in his line or to follow up a Federal repulse. Improvising as best he could, he ordered Stuart out beyond the left, hoping that he would find a position there from which to harass the flank of the attacking column or possibly launch a distracting counterstroke. He also sent a courier to A. P. Hill, seventeen miles away at Harpers Ferry, urging him to join the army with all possible speed. Whether this would get him there in time for a share in tomorrow's battle was highly doubtful, but at least Lee knew that Hill would make the effort.

As Lee was about to retire for the night, conscious that he had drawn his final card in the high-stakes game of showdown he was about to play with McClellan, Hood came to report that his men were near exhaustion, having received only half a ration of beef in the past three days. He requested that they be withdrawn from the line to get some rest and fry some dough and bacon. Distressed though Lee was to hear that his shock brigades were enfeebled, he was obliged to admit that he had no others to put in their place. He told him to see Jackson, and while Lee turned in, the rain murmurous on the canvas, Hood left to do just that.

He found him asleep under a large tree whose exposed roots made a pillow for his head. Hood nudged him awake, and when Stonewall sat up, blinking, told him what he wanted. Jackson had already rearranged his line, shifting troops around to the north and west to meet the attack he knew would come at dawn against those two stretches of woodland and the cornfield in between, but he agreed to spread them thinner in order to give Hood's hungry soldiers a chance to cook their rations, provided they were kept close at hand, ready to come running when he called. Hood agreed, and about midnight his two brigades filed southward to kindle their cookfires in the Dunker churchyard.

Presently a great stillness settled down, broken from time to time by picket firing, the individual shots coming sharp as handclaps through the mist and drizzle. All along the Sharpsburg ridge, while their opposite numbers munched ground coffee in the encircling darkness, men who could not sleep took out their pipes and smoked and thought about tomorrow.

★ ★ ★ *I*t came in gray, with a pearly mist that shrouded the fields and woodlands, and it came with a crash of musketry, backed by the deeper roar of cannonfire that mounted in volume and intensity until it was continuous, jarring the earth beneath the feet of the attackers and defenders. Hooker bore down, his three divisions in line abreast, driving the rebel pickets southward onto the high ground where the road, flanked by what now was called the East Wood and the West Wood, ran past the squat white block of the Dunker Church. That was his immediate objective, barely a thousand yards away, though he was already taking heavy losses. Noting the glint of bayonets and the boil of smoke from the forty-acre cornfield, he called a halt while six of his batteries came up and began to flail the standing grain with shell and canister, their three dozen fieldpieces joined presently by heavier long-range guns pouring in a crossfire from the ridge beyond the creek. Haversacks and splintered muskets began to leap up through the dust and smoke, along with the broad-leafed stalks of corn and the dismembered heads and limbs of men. Hooker said later that "every stalk in the northern and greater part of the field was cut as closely as could have been done with a knife."

Yet when he got his batteries quieted and started his soldiers forward again, the fire seemed no less heavy. Entering the woods on the left and right, and approaching the shattered cornfield in the center, they ran into blinding sheets of flame and the air was quivering with bullets. "Men, I cannot say fell; they were knocked out of ranks by the dozen," one survivor wrote. Still they came on, their battle flags swooping and fluttering, falling and then caught up again. The red flags of the Confederates staggered backward, and still the blue-coats came on, driving them through the blasted corn and through the early morning woods, until at last they broke and fled, their ranks too thin to rally. The Dunker Church lay dead ahead. But just as the Federals saw it within their reach, a butternut column emerged from the woods beyond it and bore down on them, yelling. At point-blank range, the rebels pulled up short, delivered a volley which one receiver said "was like a scythe running through our line," and then came on again, the sunlight glinting and snapping on their bayonets.

It was Hood; Jackson had called for him while his men were preparing their first hot meal in days, and perhaps that had something to do with the violence of their assault. Leaving the half-cooked food in their skillets, they formed ranks and charged the bluecoats who were responsible. Their attack was necessarily unsupported, for Jackson's and Ewell's divisions were shattered. J. R. Jones had been stunned by a shell that exploded directly above his head, and Starke, who resumed command, received three wounds, all mortal, within minutes; command of the Stonewall Division passed to a colonel. Lawton was down, badly wounded, and in his three brigades only two of the fifteen regimental commanders were still on their feet. But Hood took no account of this, nor did his men. Intent on vengeance, they struck the Federals north of the Dunker Church and drove them back through the cornfield, whooping and jeering, calling for them to stand and fight. They did so at the far edge of the field, forming behind their guns, and there the two lines engaged. With only 2400 men in his two brigades, Hood knew that he would not be able to hold on long in the face of those guns, but he was determined to do what he could. When a staff officer arrived to inquire after the situation, Hood said grimly: "Tell General Jackson unless I get reinforcements I must be forced back, but I am going on while I can."

His chances of going on just now were better than he knew; for though the uproar had not slacked perceptibly, Hooker had already shot his bolt. Assailed in front by the demoniacal Texans, on the right by Early's brigade moving east from its position in support of Stuart, whose guns had been tearing the flank of the blue column all along, and on the left by two brigades from D. H. Hill, he was forced back to the line from which he had launched his dawn assault, two hours ago. With 2500 of his men shot down and at least that many more in headlong flight, he was through and he knew it. As

> *That's right, boys — cheer! We're going to whip them today!"*
>
> — Joseph K. Mansfield

he retreated through the shambles of the cornfield, he sent word to Mansfield that he was to bring up his corps and try his hand at completing the destruction so expensively begun.

Mansfield was altogether willing. So far in the war, though he had been in charge of the bloodless occupation of Suffolk, the only real action he had seen was with the coastal batteries that took the *Merrimac* under fire at Hampton Roads. Now he had two divisions of Valley and Manassas veterans, most of them unborn at the time of his West Point graduation forty years before. He liked them and they liked him, even on short acquaintance. "A calm and dignified old gentleman," one called him, while another noted with approval that he had "a proud, martial air and was full of military ardor." This last perhaps was a result of his habit of removing his hat as he rode among them, letting his long white hair and beard stream in the wind. As a performance it was effective, and he did it again this morning, evoking cheers from his troops as they moved forward in response to Hooker's call.

"That's right, boys — cheer!" he cried. "We're going to whip them today!" Doubling the column, he kept waving his hat and repeating his words to regiment after regiment: "Boys, we're going to lick them today!"

They almost did, but not while he was with them. As they approached the East Wood, deploying for action, Hooker rode up on his white horse. "The enemy are breaking through my lines!" he shouted above the roar of guns. "You must hold this wood!" Taken aback, Mansfield watched him gallop off; he had thought Hooker was driving the graybacks handsomely and that his own corps had been summoned to complete the victory. By now his lead regiments had reached a rail fence at the near edge of a field just short of the woods, and he saw to his horror that they had spread along it and were shooting at figures that moved in the shadows of the trees. "You are firing at our own men!" he cried. As soon as he got them stopped he leaped his horse over the fence, intending to ride ahead and see for himself. "Those are rebels, General!" a soldier yelled. Mansfield pulled up, leaning forward to peer into the shadows. "Yes — you're right," he said, and as he spoke his words were confirmed by a volley that came crashing out of the woods, crippling his horse. He dismounted and walked back to the fence, but as he tried to climb over it, moving with the terrific deliberation of an old man among young ones, a bullet struck him in the stomach. He went down, groaning. Three veterans, who saw in the wounded general a one-way ticket out of chaos, took him up and lugged him back to an aid station, where a flustered surgeon half-strangled him with a jolt of whiskey, and presently he died.

Williams resumed command of the corps and sent both divisions forward, swinging one to the right so that its advance swept through the cornfield. Hood's survivors were knocked back, yielding ground and losing a stand of colors for the first time in their brief, furious history. On the bluecoats came, a Massachusetts colonel waving the captured Texas flag. They followed the route

Men of the 1st Texas were compelled to leave this flag in the blood-soaked cornfield after more than a half-dozen colorbearers were shot down.

Hooker's men had taken an hour ago — and, like them, were stopped within reach of the Dunker Church by a two-brigade counterstroke. Jackson had called for reinforcements at the height of the first attack, and Lee had sent Walker's division from the right flank to the left, taking a chance that the Federals would not storm the lower Antietam crossings. These two North Carolina brigades arrived too late to contest the first penetration, but they got there in time to meet the second at its climax. Like Hooker's, Mansfield's men were stopped. However, they did not fall back. They stayed where they were, and Williams sent word to headquarters that if he could be reinforced he would have the battle won.

Reinforcements were already on the way — three divisions of them under Sumner, whose corps was the largest in the army — but they came by a different route: not down the Hagerstown road or parallel to it, but in at an angle through the lower fringes of the East Wood, which had been cleared of all but dead or dying rebels. So far, the close-up fighting had been left to troops formerly under Pope; now McClellan's own were coming in, led by the man who had saved the day at Fair Oaks. Dragoon-style, Sumner rode at the head of his lead division, leaving the others to come along behind. As he emerged from the woods he saw to his right the wreckage of the cornfield and up ahead the Dunker Church, dazzling white through rifts in the smoke boiling up from the line which Mansfield's men were struggling to hold against Walker's counterstroke. As Sumner saw it, the thing to do was get there fast, before that line gave way. With what his corps historian later called "ill-regulated ardor," he kept the lead division in march formation, three brigades close-packed in as many files, moving southwest across the open stretch of ground between the East Wood and the church. It was then that he was struck, two thirds of the way back down the column and squarely on the flank, with results that were sudden and altogether murderous. Too tightly wedged to maneuver as a unit, or even dodge as individuals, men fell in windrows, the long files writhing like wounded snakes. More than two thousand of them were shot down within a quarter of an hour. "My God, we must get out of this!" Sumner cried. His soldiers thought so, too, scrambling frantically for the rear as the graybacks charged.

It was McLaws. When his and Anderson's divisions finally reached Sharpsburg about 7 o'clock that morning — incredibly, they had been delayed at the outset because the paroled Federals, impatient to get home from Harpers Ferry, had clogged the bridge leading northward across the Potomac to the foot of Maryland Heights — more time was lost in a search for Lee, who was away from headquarters inspecting his right and center while Hooker was hammering at his left. When they found him, nearly an hour later, he sent Anderson to reinforce Hill, and McLaws to reinforce Jackson, who by then was receiving the full force of Mansfield's attack. This too had been stopped by the time McLaws got there, but just as he came over the ridge he saw Sumner's lead division emerge from the East Wood, driving straight for the Dunker Church with its flank exposed. He struck it, wrecked it, and took up the pursuit with his four brigades, joined on the left by Walker and Early, who threw Williams into retreat as well. Hooker by now was one of the nearly 7000 casualties the Federals had suffered at this end of the field; he rode northward out of the fight, dripping blood from a wounded foot, and his men followed, along with Mansfield's and Sumner's, to reform beyond the line of guns from which they had taken off at dawn. In rapid sequence, two whole corps and part of a third — six divisions containing 31,000 men — had been shattered and repulsed.

Jackson's losses had been comparable — probably in excess of 5000, which represented a larger percentage of casualties than he had inflicted — but he was strangely elated. Looking out over the shambles of the cornfield, which had just changed hands for the fourth time that morning and which by now was so thickly carpeted with dead men that one witness claimed you could walk in

> *The rebels jeered and hooted at the dark-clothed attackers coming over the rise, silhouetted against the glare of sunlight.*

any direction across it and never touch the ground, his pale blue eyes had a fervent light to them. "God has been very kind to us this day," he said. For the first time since daylight glimmered across the eastern ridge his lines were free of pressure, and so was he himself. Sitting his horse in the yard of the Dunker Church, he ate a peach while his medical director submitted a preliminary casualty report. Stonewall made no comment, except to remark between bites that it was heavy, but when the surgeon expressed the fear that the survivors were too badly shaken to withstand another assault he shook his head, apparently unconcerned, and pointed in the direction of the bluecoats, huddled behind their line of guns a mile to the north. "Dr McGuire, they have done their worst," he said.

He was right, so far as concerned the left; the Federals there had done their worst and best. But Sharpsburg was, in effect, three battles piled one on top of another, and just as the first had ended with the repulse of Sumner's lead division, so did the second open with the repulse of the other two. Recovering his balance in the midst of disaster, the old man rode back through the woods in search of the rest of his corps, which was missing. One division he found had failed to cross the creek on schedule, while the other had lost contact and veered south, coming upon an eroded country lane from which a zigzag line of graybacks loosed a close-up volley that shattered the lead brigade and sent the others scrambling back. The third division, coming up at last, received the same reception and gave ground, but presently rallied and formed a line on which the second rallied, too. And thus, no sooner was Jackson's battle over, than Hill's got under way.

Here along the center the Confederates occupied what amounted to an intrenched position, the only one on the field. For the lane was not only worn below the level of the ground, affording them a considerable measure of protection, but it also ran between snake-rail fences, and they had dismantled the outer fence to make a substantial breastworks of the rails. What was more, the crest of the ridge was just over a hundred yards forward and uphill, so that the bluecoats could not see what they had to face until they were practically upon it, within easy musket range and outlined target-sharp against the eastern sky. This was unnerving, to say the least, and to make matters worse — psychologically, at any rate — the rebels jeered and hooted at the dark-clothed attackers coming over the rise, silhouetted against the glare of sunlight. "Go away, you black devils! Go home!" they yelled as they loosed their volleys. They felt confident and secure, and so did Hill: for a time at least. But as the Federals continued to press their attack with increasing persistency and numbers — Sumner had more than 12,000 men in his remaining two divisions, while Hill himself had less than 7,000, even after Anderson's arrival — the issue began to grow doubtful. Then presently, as a result of two unforeseen mishaps, it grew worse than doubtful. It grew impossible.

The first of these was that Anderson was severely wounded and carried from the field, command of his division passing to the senior brigadier, long-haired Roger Pryor, who by now had proved that his reluctance to fire the first shot at Fort Sumter had not proceeded from a lack of nerve, but whose talents were still primarily oratorical. From that time on, the division no longer functioned as a unit, and in fact went out of existence except as a loose collection of regiments and companies, each one fighting on its own as it saw fit. Which perhaps was just as well, in the end; for that was what happened to Hill's division, too, though its commander emerged unscathed from the experience of having three horses shot from under him in rapid succession.

This second disintegration was a result of the second mishap, which occurred when the brigade on the left, receiving the order to "refuse" its threatened flank, misunderstood the command and pulled out altogether; whereupon the opposing Federals hurried forward, occupied the abandoned portion of the line, and began to lay down an enfilading fire which gave the sunken road the name it bore thereafter: Bloody Lane. What had been a sheltered position, one from which to hoot at charging Yankees and shoot them down when they were so unmissably close that their faces filled the gunsight, became a trap. Quite

*After the battle, Federal burial parties
work to remove some of the scores of bodies
piled up in Bloody Lane.*

suddenly, as if they had tumbled headlong by the hundreds out of the sky, dead
men filled whole stretches of the road to overflowing. Horrified, unit by unit
from left to right, the survivors broke for the rear, and now it was the Yankees
doing the hooting and the shooting.

Faced with the abrupt disintegration of the isolated center, the ex-
ploitation of which would mean the end of Lee's army, Hill did what he could
to rally the fugitives streaming back across the ridge, and though few of them
had a mind for anything but their present dash for safety, he managed to scrape
together a straggler line along the outskirts of Sharpsburg. While these men
were delivering a sporadic fire against the bluecoats, who were massing along
the sunken road, apparently preparing to continue their advance, Hill sent an
urgent call for guns and reinforcements. There were none of the latter to send
him; the right had been stripped and the left had been fought to exhaustion.
But Longstreet had seen the trouble and was already sending every cannon he

★

could lay hands on. He had not wanted to fight this battle in the first place — or for that matter, the odds being what they were, any battle in which there was so little to gain and so very much to lose — but now that it was unavoidably under way, he gave it everything he had. Limping about in carpet slippers and gesturing with an unlighted cigar, he ordered gun crew after gun crew to put their pieces in action along the ridge where Hill was forming his thin new line. As fast as these guns came into the open, the powerful Union batteries took them under fire from across the way, exploding caissons and mangling cannoneers. Observing one section of guns whose fire was weak because there were too few survivors to serve them properly, Old Pete dismounted his staff and improvised two high-ranking gun crews, himself holding their horses and correcting the ranges while they fired.

Hill meanwhile had been watching the bluecoats down in the sunken road. He believed they were about to attack him. Such an attack would surely be successful, weak as he was, and the only way he knew to delay it was to attack them first. However, when he called along his line for volunteers, there was no answer until presently one man said he would go if Hill would lead. Quickly taking him up on that, Hill seized a rifle and started forward with a shout, joined by about two hundred others who were persuaded by his example. The attack was brief; in fact, it was repulsed almost as soon as it began; but Hill believed it served its purpose. Here opposite the denuded Confederate center, the Federals stayed where they were for the rest of the day. According to Hill, this was either because he had frightened them into immobility or else it was an outright miracle.

It was neither, unless it was something of both. What it really was was Sumner — and McClellan. Franklin had come up by now, and though he had left one division on Maryland Heights, he still brought more than 8000 soldiers onto the field. One brigade had shared in the fight on the right, and now he wanted to use the other five in an assault on the gray line beyond the sunken road. But Sumner stopped him. The old man's corps had lost 5100 men today, more than Hooker's and Mansfield's combined; apparently he had seen enough of killing north of the Dunker Church and here in front of Bloody Lane. The thirty-nine-year-old Franklin tried to argue, but Sumner, who not only outranked him but was also nearly twice his age, kept insisting that the army was on the verge of disintegration and that another repulse would mean catastrophe. Presently a courier arrived from McClellan, bringing a suggestion that the attack be pressed by both commands if possible. Sumner — to whom, except for his long, pointed nose, old age had given the glaring look of a death's head — turned on him and cried hotly: "Go back, young man, and tell General McClellan I have no command! Tell him my command, Banks' command, and Hooker's command are all cut up and demoralized. Tell him General Franklin has the only organized command on this part of the field!"

When McClellan received this message he came down off the hill and crossed the creek to see for himself the situation in the center. Sumner and Franklin presented their arguments, and now that he had a close-up view of the carnage, McClellan sided with the senior. He told them both to hold what had been won; then he rode back across the creek. It was now about 2 o'clock, and the second battle, which like the first had lasted about four hours, was over. The third was about to begin.

★ ★ ★ *I*n a broader sense, it had already been going on for as long as the other two combined. That is, the opponents had been exchanging shots across the lower reaches of the creek since dawn. But, so far, all that had come of this was the maiming of a few hundred soldiers, most of them in blue. Despite McClellan's repeated orders — including one sent at 9 o'clock, directing that the crossing be effected "at all hazards" — not a man out of the nearly 14,000 enrolled in Burnside's four divisions had reached the west bank of the Antietam by the time the sun swung past the overhead. "McClellan appears to think I am not trying my best to carry this bridge," the ruff-whiskered general said testily to a staff colonel his friend the army commander sent to prod him. "You are the third or fourth one who has been to me this morning with similar orders."

As he spoke he sat his horse beside a battery on a hilltop, looking down at the narrow, triple-arched stone span below. He watched it with a fascination amounting to downright prescience, as if he knew already that it was to bear his name and be in fact his chief monument, no matter what ornate shafts of marble or bronze a grateful nation might raise elsewhere in his honor. So complete was his absorption by the bridge itself, he apparently never considered testing the depth of the water that flowed sluggishly beneath it. If he had, he would have discovered that the little copper-colored stream, less than fifty feet in width, could have been waded at almost any point without wetting the armpits of the shortest man in his corps. However, except for sending one division downstream in search of a local guide to point out a ford that was rumored to exist in that direction, he remained intent on effecting a dry-shod crossing.

Admittedly this was no easy matter. The road came up from the southeast, paralleling the creek for a couple of hundred yards, and then turned sharply west across the bridge, where it swung north again to curve around the heights on the opposite bank. Just now those heights were occupied by rebels — many of them highly skilled as marksmen, though at that range skill was practically superfluous — which meant that whoever exposed himself along that road, in the shadow of those heights, was likely to catch a faceful of bullets. Nevertheless, this was the only route Burnside could see, and he kept sending men along it, regiment by regiment, intermittently all morning, with predictable results.

Observing from across the way the ease with which this lower threat was being contested, Lee all this time had been stripping his right of troops in order to strengthen his hard-pressed left and center. By noon he was down to an irreducible skeleton force; so that presently, when he learned that Hill had lost the sunken road and was calling in desperation for reinforcements, he had none to send him. Like Hill in this extremity, knowing that he probably could not withstand an assault, he decided that his only recourse was to deliver one — preferably on the left, which had been free of heavy pressure for two hours. Accordingly, he sent word for Jackson to attack the Federal right, if possible, swinging it back against the river. Stonewall was delighted at the prospect, and set out at once to reconnoiter the ground in that direction. "We'll drive McClellan into the Potomac," he said fervently. Back at Sharpsburg, meanwhile, Lee was doing what little he could to make this possible. When the captain of a shattered Virginia battery reported with his few surviving men, he instructed him to join Jackson for the proposed diversion. One of the smoke-grimed cannoneers spoke up: "General, are you going to send us in again?" Lee saw then that it was Robert. "Yes, my son," he told him. "You all must do what you can to help drive these people back." The battery left, heading northward; but no such attack was delivered. Reconnoitering, Stonewall found the Union flank securely anchored to the east bank of the river and well protected by massed artillery. He had to abandon his hopes for a counterstroke. "It is a great pity," he said regretfully. "We should have driven McClellan into the Potomac."

By the time Lee learned that the proposed attack could not be delivered, that no diversion to relieve the pressure against the sagging center would be made, the urgent need for it had passed. Hill's thin line — along which, in accordance with his instructions now that his feeble two-hundred-man charge had been repulsed, the colorbearers flourished their tattered battle flags, hiding his weakness behind gestures of defiance — went unchallenged by the bluecoats massed along the sunken road. But Lee was not allowed even a breathing space in which to enjoy the relaxation of tension. Catastrophe, it seemed, was still with him; had in fact merely withdrawn in order to loom up elsewhere. Immediately on the heels of the news that the Federal advance had stalled in front of the center, word came from the right that the contingency most feared had come to pass. Burnside was across the bridge at last.

Robert Toombs was in command there, holding the heights with three slim Georgia regiments against four Federal divisions. Lately, just as previously he had wearied of his cabinet post, he had been feeling disenchanted with the military life. Exasperated, now as then, by the obtuseness of those around him, he had decided to resign his commission, but not before he had distinguished himself in some great battle. "The day after such an event," he wrote his wife, "I will retire if I live through it." Such an event was now at hand, and he had been in his glory all that morning, successfully challenging with 550 men the advance of more than twenty times their number. At 1 o'clock, after seven hours of fitful and ineffectual probing, Burnside at last sent two regiments pounding straight downhill for the bridge, avoiding the suicidal two-hundred-yard gauntlet-run along the creek bank. They got across in a rush, joined presently by others, until the west-bank strength had increased to a full division at that point. Meanwhile the downstream division had finally located the ford and splashed across it, the men scarcely wetting their legs above the knees. About to be swamped from the front and flank, Toombs reported the double crossing and received permission to avoid capture by withdrawing from the heights. He did so in good order, proud of himself and his weary handful of fellow Georgians, whom he put in line along the rearward ridge. There on the outskirts of Sharpsburg with the rest of Longstreet's troops — not over 2500 in all, so ruthlessly had Lee thinned their ranks in his need for reinforcements on the left and center — they prepared to resist the advance of Burnside's four divisions.

What came just then, however, was a lull. After forming ranks for a forward push, the commander of the lead blue division found that his men had burnt up most of their ammunition banging away all morning at the snipers on the heights. Informed of this, Burnside decided to replace them with another division instead of taking time to bring up cartridges. This too took time though. It was nearly 3 o'clock before the new division started forward. Off to the left, after crossing the ford and floundering in the bottoms, the other division at last recovered its sense of direction and joined the attack. Few though the rebels seemed to be, they were laying down a mass of fire out of all proportion to their numbers. A New York soldier, whose regiment was pinned down by what he termed "the hiss of bullets and the hurtle of grapeshot," later recalled that "there burst forth from it the most vehement, terrible swearing I have ever heard." When the order came to rise and charge, he observed another phenomenon: "The mental strain was so great that I saw at that moment the singular effect mentioned, I think, in the life of Goethe on a similar occasion — the whole landscape for an instant turned slightly red."

Across this reddened landscape they came charging, presenting a two-division front that overlapped the Confederate flank and piled up against the center. Down at his headquarters, beyond the town (the lull had been welcome, but he could only use it to rest his men, not to bring up others; he had no others, and would have none until — and if — A. P. Hill arrived from Harpers Ferry) Lee heard the uproar drawing nearer across the eastern hills, and presently the evidences of Federal success were visual as well. The Sharpsburg streets were crowded with fugitives, their demoralization increased by shells that burst against the walls and roofs of houses, startling flocks of pigeons into bewildered flight, round and round in the smoke. Blue flags began to appear at vari-

Burnside Bridge is seen here from the high, wooded bluff on the west side of Antietam Creek that was defended by Robert Toombs' Georgians.

ous points along the ridge above. The men who bore them had advanced almost a mile beyond the bridge; another mile would put them astride the Shepherdstown road, which led west to the only crossing of the Potomac.

Observing a column moving up from the southeast along the ridge line, Lee called to an artillery lieutenant on the way to the front with a section of guns: "What troops are those?" The lieutenant offered him his telescope. "Can't use it," Lee said, holding up a bandaged hand. The lieutenant trained

*During the battle's final phase, a North Carolina
artillery lieutenant using this telescope confirmed for Lee
the arrival of A. P. Hill's relief column.*

and focused the telescope. "They are flying the United States flag," he reported. Lee pointed to the right, where another distant column was approaching from the southwest, nearly perpendicular to the first, and repeated the question. The lieutenant swung the glass in that direction, peered intently, and announced: "They are flying the Virginia and Confederate flags." Lee suppressed his elation, although the words fulfilled his one hope for deliverance from defeat. "It is A. P. Hill from Harpers Ferry," he said calmly.

It was indeed. Receiving Lee's summons at 6.30 that morning, Little Powell had left one brigade to complete the work at the Ferry, and put the other five on the road within the hour. Seventeen roundabout miles away, the crash and rumble of gunfire spurred him on — particularly when he drew near enough for the sound to be intensified by the clatter of musketry. Forgotten were Stonewall's march regulations, which called for periodic rest halts; Hill's main concern was to get to Sharpsburg fast, however bedraggled, not to get there after sundown with a column that arrived well-closed and too late for a share in the fighting. Jacket off because of the heat, he rode in his bright red battle shirt alongside the panting troops, prodding laggards with the point of his saber. Beyond this, he had no dealings with stragglers, but left them winded by the roadside, depending on them to catch up in time if they could. Not many could, apparently; for he began the march with about 5000 men, and ended it with barely 3000. But with these, as was his custom, he struck hard.

In his path, here on the Federal left, was an outsized Connecticut regiment, 900-strong. That was a good many more soldiers than Hill had in any one of his brigades, but they were grass green, three weeks in service, and already considerably shaken by what they had seen of their first battle. To add to their confusion, a large proportion of the rebels bearing down on them wore new blue uniforms captured at Harpers Ferry. The first thing they received by way of positive identification was a close-up volley that dropped about four hundred of them and broke and scattered the rest. A Rhode Island outfit, coming up just then, was likewise confused, as were two Ohio regiments which arrived to find bluecoats fleeing from bluecoats and held their fire until they too were knocked sprawling. With that, the Union left gave way in a backward surge, pursued by Hill, whose

★

men came after it, screaming their rebel yell. The panic spread northward to the outskirts of Sharpsburg, where several blue companies, meeting little resistance, had already entered the eastern streets of the town; Burnside's whole line came unpinned, and presently the retreat was general. Toombs' Georgians, along with the rest of Longstreet's men, took up the pursuit and chased the Northerners back onto the heights they had spent the morning trying to seize.

And now in the sunset, here on the right, as previously on the left and along the center, the conflict ended; except that this time it was for good. Twilight came down and the landscape was dotted with burning haystacks, set afire by bursting shells. For a time the cries of wounded men of both armies came from these; they had crawled up into the hay for shelter, but now, bled too weak to crawl back out again, were roasted. Lee's line was intact along the Sharpsburg ridge. McClellan had failed to break it; or, breaking it, had failed in all three cases, left and center and right, to supply the extra push that would keep it broken.

———— ⌒⌒⌒ ————

★ ★ ★ T here were those in the Federal ranks who had been urging him to do just that all afternoon. Nor did he lack the means. The greater part of four divisions — two under Franklin, two under Porter: no less than 20,000 men, a solid fourth of his effective force — had stood idle while the battle raged through climax after climax, each of which offered McClellan the chance to wreck his adversary. But he could not dismiss the notion that somewhere behind that opposite ridge, or off beyond the flanks, Lee was massing enormous reserves for a knockout blow. The very thinness of the gray line, which was advanced as an argument for assaulting it, seemed to him to prove that the balance of those more than 100,000 rebels were being withheld for some such purpose, and when it came he wanted to have something with which to meet it.

"At this critical juncture," he afterwards reported, "I should have had a narrow view of the condition of the country had I been willing to hazard another battle with less than an absolute assurance of success. At that moment — Virginia lost, Washington menaced, Maryland invaded — the national cause could afford no risks of defeat. Lee's army might then have marched as it pleased on Washington, Baltimore, Philadelphia, or New York . . . and nowhere east of the Alleghenies was there another organized force able to arrest its march."

It never occurred to him, apparently, to look at the reverse of the coin: to consider that Lee's army, like his own, was the only organized force that blocked the path to its capital. But it did occur to Sykes, who appealed to him, late in the day and in the presence of Porter, to be allowed to strike at the rebel

★

129

center with his regulars. Part of one of his brigades had been up close to the western ridge, serving as a link between Sumner's left and Burnside's right, and its officers had seen that D. H. Hill was about to buckle — indeed, had buckled already, if someone would only take advantage of the fact. Let him launch an attack against that point, Sykes said, supported by Porter's other division and one from Franklin, and he would cut Lee's line in two, thereby exposing the severed halves to destruction.

At first McClellan seemed about to approve; but in the moment of hesitation he looked at Porter, and Porter slowly shook his head. "Remember, General," one witness later quoted him as saying, "I command the last reserve of the last army of the republic." That cinched it. The attack was not made. Porter and Franklin, who between them lost only 548 of today's more than 12,000 casualties, remained in reserve.

As night came down, the two armies disengaged, and when the torches of the haystack pyres went out, darkness filled the valley of the Antietam, broken only by the lanterns of the medics combing the woods and cornfields for the injured who were near enough to be brought within the lines. Lee remained at his headquarters, west of Sharpsburg, greeting his generals as they rode up. Jackson, the two Hills, McLaws and Walker, Hood and Early, all had heavy losses to report. The gray commander spoke with each, but he seemed unshaken by the fact that more than a fourth of his army lay dead or wounded on the field. Nor did he mention the word that was in all their minds: retreat. "Where is Longstreet?" he asked, after he had talked with all the others. Presently Old Pete arrived, still limping in carpet slippers and still chewing on the unlighted cigar; he had stopped in the town to help some ladies whose house was on fire. Lee stepped forward to greet him. "Ah," he said, placing his crippled hands on the burly Georgian's shoulders. "Here is Longstreet. Here is my old warhorse."

This last report was as gloomy as the others. The army was bled white and near exhaustion, with all its divisions on the firing line. Aside from a trickle of stragglers coming in, Lee's only reserve, and in fact the only reserve in all northern Virginia, was the one brigade A. P. Hill had left to complete the salvage work at Harpers Ferry. All the generals here informally assembled were agreed that another day like today would drive the surviving remnant headlong into the Potomac. All, that is, but Lee. When he had heard his lieutenants out, he told them to return to their men, make such tactical readjustments as would strengthen their defenses, and see that rations were cooked and distributed along the present line of battle. If McClellan wanted another fight, he would give him one tomorrow.

McClellan, it seemed, wanted no such thing. Despite an early morning telegram to Halleck: "The battle will probably be renewed today. Send all the troops you can by the most expeditious route," and a letter in which he told his wife: "[Yesterday's battle] was a success, but whether a decided victory de-

Union and Confederate officers shake hands near the Dunker Church during a truce arranged on September 18 for the collection of the dead and wounded.

pends on what occurs today," he soon took stock and found the portents far from favorable. Reno and Mansfield were dead, along with eight other general officers; Hooker was out of action, wounded; Sumner was despondent; Burnside was even doubtful whether his troops could hold the little they had gained the day before. After what he called "a careful and anxious survey of the condition of my command, and my knowledge of the enemy's force and position," Mc-Clellan decided to wait for reinforcements, including two divisions on the way from Maryland Heights and Frederick. As a result, the armies lay face to face all day, like sated lions, and between them, there on the slopes of Sharpsburg ridge and in the valley of the Antietam, the dead began to fester in the heat and the cries of the wounded faded to a mewling.

There were a great many of both, the effluvium of this bloodiest day of the war. Nearly 11,000 Confederates and more than 12,000 Federals had fallen along that ridge and in that valley, including a total on both sides of about 5000 dead. Losses at South Mountain raised these doleful numbers to 13,609 and 14,756 respectively, the latter being increased to 27,276 by the surrender of the Harpers Ferry garrison. Lee had suffered only half as many casualties as he had inflicted in the course of the campaign; but even this was more than he could afford. "Where is your division?" someone asked Hood at the close of the battle, and Hood replied, "Dead on the field." After entering the fight with 854 men, the Texas brigade came out with less than three hundred, and these figures were approximated in other veteran units, particularly in Jackson's command. The troops Lee lost were the best he had — the best he could ever hope to have in the long war that lay ahead, now that his try for an early ending by invasion had been turned back.

★

★ ★ ★   *O*rders for the retirement were issued that afternoon, and at nightfall, in accordance with those orders, fires were kindled along the ridge to curtain the retreat across the Potomac. Longstreet went first, forming in support of Pendleton's guns on the opposite bank. Two brigades of cavalry followed, then moved upstream, prepared to recross and harry the enemy flank in case the withdrawal was contested. Walker's division was the last to cross. At sunup, as Walker followed the tail of his column into the waist-deep water of the ford, he saw Lee sitting his gray horse in midstream. Apparently he had been there all night. When Walker reported all of his troops safely across the river except some wagonloads of wounded and a battery of artillery, which were close at hand, Lee showed for the first time the strain he had been under. "Thank God," he said.

That was in fact the general reaction, though in most cases it was expressed with considerably less reverence. Crossing northward two weeks ago, the bands had played "My Maryland" and the men had gaily swelled the chorus; but now, as one of the round-trip marchers remarked, "all was quiet on that point. Occasionally some fellow would strike up that tune, and you would then hear the echo, 'Damn my Maryland.' " Another recorded his belief that "the confounded Yankees" could shoot straighter on their home ground. Nor was this aversion restricted to the ranks. "I have heard but one feeling expressed about [Maryland]," one brigadier informed his wife, "and that is a regret at our having gone there." A youthful major on Lee's own staff wrote home to his sister: "Don't let any of your friends sing 'My Maryland' — not 'My Western Maryland' anyhow."

Presently there was apparent cause for greater regret than ever. Leaving Pendleton with forty-four guns and two slim brigades of infantry to discourage pursuit by holding the Shepherdstown ford, Lee moved the rest of his army into bivouac on the hills back from the river, then lay down under an apple tree to get some badly needed sleep himself. Not long after midnight he woke to find Pendleton bending over him. The former Episcopal rector was shaken and bewildered, and as he spoke Lee found out why. McClellan had brought up his heavy guns for counterbattery work, Pendleton explained, and then at the height of the bombardment had suddenly thrown Porter's corps across the Potomac, driving off the six hundred rear-guard infantry and the startled cannoneers. All the guns of the Confederate reserve artillery had been captured.

"All?" Lee said, brought upright.

"Yes, General, I fear all."

Unwilling to attempt a counterattack in the dark with his weary troops, Lee decided to wait for daylight. But when Jackson heard the news he was too upset to wait for anything. He had A. P. Hill's men turn out at once and put them in motion for the ford, arriving soon after sunrise to find that things were by no means as bad as the artillery chief had reported. A subordinate had brought off all but four of the guns, and only a portion of Porter's two divisions had crossed the river. "With the blessing of Providence," Stonewall informed Lee, "they will soon be driven back." They were. Hill launched another of his savage attacks: one of those in which, as he reported, "each man felt that the fate of the army was centered in himself." Something over 250 Federals were shot or drowned in their rush to regain the Maryland bank, and when it was over, all who remained in Virginia were captives. Hill drew back to rejoin the main body, unpursued.

What at first had been taken for a disaster turned out in the end to be a tonic — a sort of upbeat coda, after the crash and thunder of what had gone before. The army moved on to Martinsburg, where by September 22 enough stragglers had returned to bring its infantry strength to 36,418. A week later, with all ten divisions — or at any rate what was left of them — resting between Mill Creek and Lick River, Lee wrote Davis: "History records but few examples of a greater amount of labor and fighting than has been done by this army during the present campaign. . . . There is nothing to report, but I desire to keep you always advised of the condition of the army, its proceedings, and prospects."

He had occupied his present position near Winchester, he told the President, "in order to be prepared for any flank movement the enemy might attempt." It soon developed, however, that he had no grounds for worry on that score. McClellan was not contemplating a flank movement. In point of fact, despite renewed pressure from Washington, McClellan was not contemplating any immediate movement at all. After completing the grisly and unaccustomed work of cleaning up the battlefield, he reoccupied Harpers Ferry with Sumner's corps and spread the others along the north bank of the Potomac, guarding the fords. The main problem just now, as he saw it, was the old one he had always been so good at: reorganizing, drilling, and resupplying his 93,149 effectives. Lee's strength — precisely tabulated at 97,445 — forbade an advance, even if the Federal army had been in any condition to make one, which McClellan did not believe to be the case.

As he went about the familiar task of preparing his men for what lay ahead, he looked back with increasing pride on what had gone before. Originally he had been guarded in his pronouncements as to the outcome of the battle on the 17th. "The general result was in our favor," he wrote his wife next morning; "that is to say, we gained a great deal of ground and held it." But now that he had had time to consider the overall picture, he said, "I feel that I have done all that can be asked in twice saving the country." He felt, too, "that this last short campaign is a sufficient legacy for our child, so far as honor is concerned." And he added, rather wistfully: "Those in whose judgment I rely tell me that I fought the battle splendidly and that it is a masterpiece of art."

★ ★ ★

★

Shelby Foote

FOUR

The Emancipation Proclamation

1862 ★ ★ ★ ★ ★ ★ For Lincoln it was something less, and also something more. The battle had been fought on a Wednesday. At noon Monday, September 22, he assembled at the White House all the members of his cabinet, and after reading them an excerpt from a collection of humorous sketches by Artemus Ward, got down to the business at hand. "When the rebel army was at Frederick," he told them, "I determined, as soon as it should be driven out of Maryland, to issue a proclamation of emancipation, such as I thought most likely to be useful. I said nothing to anyone; but I made the promise to myself and" — hesitating slightly — "to my Maker. The rebel army is now driven out, and I am going to fulfill that promise." And with that he began to read from a manuscript which was the second draft of the document he had laid aside, two months ago today, on Seward's advice that to have issued it then would have been to give it the sound of "our last *shriek* on the retreat" down the Peninsula. Second Bull Run had been even worse, particularly from this point of view. But now had come Antietam, and though it was scarcely a "masterpiece," or even a clear-cut victory, Lincoln thought it would serve as the occasion for his purpose.

It was highly characteristic, and even fitting, that he opened this solemn conclave with a reading of the slapstick monologue, "High Handed

★

Outrage at Utica," not only because he himself enjoyed it, along with most of his ministers — all except Stanton, who sat glumly through the dialect performance, and Chase, who maintained his reputation for never laughing at anything at all — but also because it was in line with the delaying tactics and the attitude he had adopted toward the question during these past two months. With the first draft of the proclamation tucked away in his desk, only awaiting a favorable turn of military events to launch it upon an unsuspecting world, he had seemed to talk against such a measure to the very people who came urging its promulgation. Presumably he did this in order to judge their reaction, as well as to prevent a diminution of the thunderclap effect which he foresaw. At any rate, he had not even hesitated to use sarcasm, particularly against the most earnest of these callers.

One day, for example, a Quaker woman came to request an audience, and Lincoln said curtly: "I will hear the Friend." She told him she had been sent by the Lord to inform him that he was the minister appointed to do the work of abolishing slavery. Then she fell silent. "Has the Friend finished?" Lincoln asked. She said she had, and he replied: "I have neither the time nor disposition to enter into discussion with the Friend, and end this occasion by suggesting for her consideration the question whether, if it be true that the Lord has appointed me to do the work she has indicated, it is not probable he would have communicated knowledge of the fact to me as well as to her?"

Similarly, on the day before the Battle of South Mountain, when a delegation of Chicago ministers called to urge presidential action on the matter, he inquired: "What good would a proclamation of emancipation from me do, especially as we are now situated? I do not want to issue a document that the whole world will see must necessarily be inoperative, like the Pope's bull against the comet. Would my word free the slaves, when I cannot even enforce the Constitution in the rebel states? Is there a single court or magistrate or individual that would be influenced by it there? . . . I will mention another thing, though it meet only your scorn and contempt. There are fifty thousand bayonets in the Union armies from the border slave states. It would be a serious matter if, in consequence of a proclamation such as you desire, they should go over to the rebels." In parting, however, he dropped a hint. "Do not misunderstand me because I have mentioned these objections. They indicate the difficulties that have thus far prevented action in some such way as you desire. I have not decided against a proclamation of liberty to the slaves, but hold the matter under advisement. . . . I can assure you that the subject is on my mind, by day and night, more than any other. Whatever shall appear to be God's will, I will do."

Sadly the Illinois ministers filed out; but one, encouraged by the closing words, remained behind to register a plea in that direction. "What you have said to us, Mr President, compels me to say to you in reply, that it is a mes-

*A*bolitionist
Horace Greeley
used his news-
paper, the New
York Tribune, to
both scourge and
extol the Lincoln
administration.

sage to you from our Divine Master, through me, commanding you, sir, to open the doors of bondage that the slaves may go free." Lincoln gave him a long look, not unlike the one he had given the Quaker woman. "That may be, sir," he admitted, "for I have studied this question by night and by day, for weeks and for months. But if it is, as you say, a message from your Divine Master, is it not odd that the only channel he could send it by was the roundabout route by way of that awful wicked city of Chicago?"

These remarks were in any case supplementary to those he had made already in reply to Horace Greeley, who published in the August 20 *Tribune* an open letter to the President, titled "The Prayer of Twenty Millions," in which he charged at some length that Lincoln had been "strangely and disastrously remiss in the discharge of your official and imperative duty." The first such duty, as Greeley saw it, was to announce to the army, the nation, and the world that this war was primarily a struggle to put an end to slavery. Lincoln, having heard that the New Yorker was preparing to attack him, had asked a mutual friend, "What is he wrathy about? Why does he not come down here and have a talk with me?" The friend replied that Greeley had said he would not allow the President of the United States to act as advisory editor of the *Tribune*. "I have no such desire," Lincoln said. "I certainly have enough on my hands to satisfy any man's ambition." But now that the journalist had aired his grievance publicly, Lincoln answered two days later with a public letter of his own, headed "Executive Mansion" and addressed to Greeley:

As to the policy I "seem to be pursuing," as you say, I have not meant to leave anyone in doubt.

I would save the Union. I would save it the shortest way under the Constitution. The sooner the national authority can be restored, the nearer the Union will be "the Union as it was." If there be those who would not save the Union unless they could at the same time save slavery, I do not agree with them. If there be those who would not save the Union unless they could at the same time destroy slavery, I do not agree with them. My paramount object in this struggle is to save the Union, and is not either to save or destroy slavery. If I could save the Union without freeing any slave, I would do it; and if I could save it by freeing all the slaves, I would do it; and if I could save it by freeing some and leaving others alone, I would also do that. What I do about slavery and the colored race, I do because I believe it helps to save the Union; and what I forbear, I forbear because I do not believe it would help to save the Union. I shall do less whenever I shall believe what I am doing hurts the cause, and I shall do more whenever I shall believe doing more will help the cause. I shall try to correct errors when shown to be errors, and I shall adopt new views so fast as they shall appear to be true views.

I have here stated my purpose according to my view of official duty; and I intend no modification of my oft-expressed personal wish that all men everywhere could be free.

And having thus to some extent forestalled his anticipated critics — particularly the conservatives, whose arguments he advanced as his own while pointing out the expediency of acting counter to them — he read to the cabinet this latest draft of what he called a Preliminary Emancipation Proclamation. Two opening paragraphs emphasized that the paper was being issued by him as Commander in Chief, upon military necessity; that reunion, not abolition, was still the primary object of the war; that compensated emancipation was still his goal for loyal owners, and that voluntary colonization of freedmen, "upon this continent or elsewhere," would still be encouraged. In the third paragraph he got down to the core of the edict, declaring "That on the first day of January, in the year of our Lord one thousand eight hundred and sixty-three, all persons held as slaves within any State or designated part of a State the people whereof shall then be in rebellion against the United States, shall be then, thenceforward, and forever free." He closed, after quoting from congressional measures prohibiting the return of fugitive slaves to disloyal masters, with the promise that, on restoration of the Union, he would recommend that loyal citizens of all areas "be compensated for all losses by acts of the United States, including the loss of slaves."

In this form, after adopting some minor emendations suggested by Seward and Chase, Lincoln gave the document to the world next morning. *Return to the Union within one hundred days,* he was telling the rebels, *and you can keep your slaves — or anyhow be compensated for them, when and if (as I propose) the law takes them away. Otherwise, if you lose the war, you lose your human property as well.* It was in essence counterrevolutionary, a military edict prompted by expediency. Whoever attacked him for it, whatever the point of contention, would have to attack him on his own ground.

This the South was quick to do. Recalling his inaugural statement, "I have no purpose, directly or indirectly, to interfere with the institution of slavery in the states where it exists. I believe I have no lawful right to do so, and I have no inclination to do so," southern spokesmen cried that Lincoln at last had dropped the mask. They quoted with outright horror a passage from the very core of the proclamation which seemed to them to incite the slaves to riot and massacre: "The Executive Government of the United States, including the military and naval authority thereof . . . will do no act or acts to repress such persons, or any of them, in any efforts they may make for their actual freedom." What was this, they asked, if not an invitation to the Negroes to murder them in their beds? Bestial, they called Lincoln, for here he had touched the quick of their deepest fear, and the Richmond *Examiner* charged that the proclamation was "an act of malice towards the master, rather than one of mercy to the slave." Abroad, the London *Spectator* reinforced this view of the author's cynicism: "The principle is not that a human being cannot justly own another, but that he cannot own him unless he is loyal to the United States." Jefferson Davis, while he deplored that such a paper could be issued by the head of a government of which he himself had once been part, declared that it would inspire the South to new determination; for "a restitution of the Union has been rendered forever impossible by the adoption of a measure which . . . neither admits of retraction nor can coexist with union."

In the North, too, there were critics, some of whom protested that the proclamation went too far, while others claimed that it did not go far enough. Some, in fact, maintained that it went nowhere, since it proclaimed freedom only for those unfortunates now firmly under Confederate control. One such critic was the New York *World,* whose editor pointed out that "the President has purposely made the proclamation inoperative in all places where we have gained a military footing which makes the slaves accessible. He has proclaimed emancipation only where he has notoriously no power to execute it." Not only were the loyal or semiloyal slave states of Delaware and Maryland, Kentucky and Missouri omitted from the terms to be applied, but so was the whole rebel state of Tennessee, as well as those parts of Virginia and Louisiana under Federal occupation. This was a matter of considerable alarm to the abolitionists. For if emancipation was not to be extended to those regions a hundred days from now, they asked, when would it ever be extended to them? What manner of document was this anyhow?

Yet these objections were raised only by those who read it critically. Most people did not read it so. They took it for more than it was, or anyhow for more than it said; the container was greater than the thing contained, and Lincoln became at once what he would remain for them, "the man who freed the slaves." He would go down to posterity, not primarily as the Preserver of the Republic — which he was — but as the Great Emancipator, which he was not. "A poor *document,* but a mighty *act,*" the governor of Massachusetts privately called the proclamation, and Lincoln himself said of it in a letter to Vice-President Hamlin, six days later: "The time for its effect southward has not come; but northward the effect should be instantaneous." Whatever truth there was in Davis's claim that it would further unite the South in opposition, Lincoln knew that it had already done much to heal the split in his own party; which was not the least of his reasons for having released it.

Seward understood such things. Asked by a friend why the cabinet had done "so useless and mischievous a thing as to issue the proclamation," he told a story. Up in New York State, he said, when the news came that the Revolutionary War had been won and American independence at last established, an old patriot could not rest until he had put up a liberty pole. When his neighbors asked him why he had gone to so much trouble — wasn't he just as free without it?—the patriot replied, "What is liberty without a pole?" So it was with the present case, Seward remarked between puffs on his cigar: "What is war without a proclamation?"

Something more it had done, or was doing, which was also included

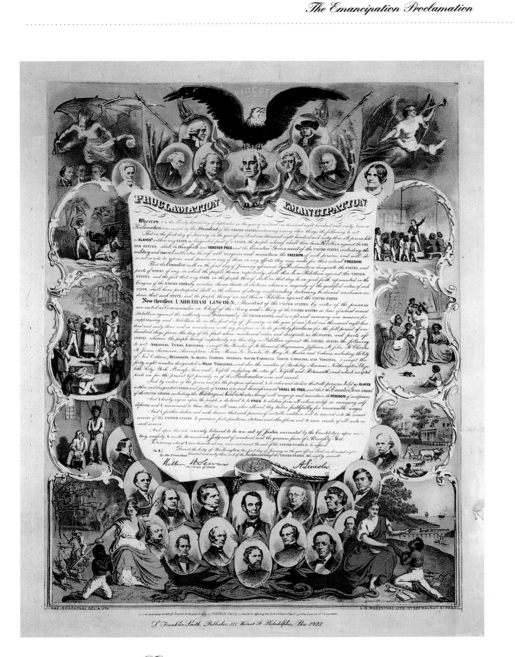

*Commemorative copies of the Emancipation
Proclamation, like this decorative version,
were produced by the thousands.*

in Lincoln's calculations. Abroad, as at home, a bedrock impact had been felt. In London, like the pro-Confederate *Spectator,* the *Times* might call the proclamation "A very sad document," which the South would "answer with a hiss of scorn"; a distinguished Member of Parliament might refer to it as "a hideous outburst of weak yet demoniacal spite" and "the most unparalleled last card ever played by a reckless gambler"; Earl Russell himself might point out to his colleagues that it was "of a very strange nature" and contained "no declaration of a principle adverse to slavery." Yet behind these organs of opinion, below these men of influence, stood the people. In their minds, now that Lincoln had spoken out — regardless of what he actually said or left unsaid — support for the South was support for slavery, and they would not have it so. From this point on, the editors might favor and the heads of state might ponder ways and means of extending recognition to the Confederacy, but to do this they would have to run counter to the feelings and demands of the mass of their subscribers and electors. Not even the nearly half-million textile workers already idle as a result of the first pinch of the cotton famine were willing to have the blockade broken on such terms. And the same was true in France. With this one blow — though few could see it yet: least of all the leader most concerned — Lincoln had shattered the main pillar of what had been the southern President's chief hope from the start. Europe would not be coming into this war.

Another change the document had wrought, though this one was uncalculated, occurring within the man himself. Sixteen years ago, back in Illinois, when an election opponent charged that he was an infidel, Lincoln refuted it with an open letter to the voters; but this was mainly a denial that he was a "scoffer," and not even then did he make any claim to being truly religious. Herndon, who saw him almost daily through that period, as well as before and after, later declared that he had never heard his partner mention the name of Jesus "but to confute the idea that he was the Christ." The fact remains that in a time when even professional soldiers called upon God in their battle reports, Lincoln seemed not to be a praying man and he never joined a church. Concerned as he had always been with logic, he had not yet reached a stage of being able to believe in what he could not comprehend. But now, in this second autumn of the war, a change began to show. In late September, when an elderly Quaker woman came to the White House to thank him for having issued the Emancipation Proclamation, Lincoln replied in a tone quite different from the one with which he had addressed her fellow Quaker the month before.

"I am glad of this interview," he told her, "and glad to know that I have your sympathy and prayers. We are indeed going through a great trial — a fiery trial. In the very responsible position in which I happen to be placed, being a humble instrument in the hands of our Heavenly Father, as I am, and as we all are, to work out his great purposes, I have desired that all my works and acts may be according to his will; and that it might be so, I have sought his aid. But if, after endeavoring to do my best in the light which he affords me, I find my efforts fail, I must believe that for some purpose unknown to me, he wills it otherwise. If I had had my way, this war would never have been commenced. If I had been allowed my way, this war would have been ended before this. But we find it still continues, and we must believe that he permits it for some wise purpose of his own, mysterious and unknown to us; and though with our limited understandings we may not be able to comprehend it, yet we cannot but believe that he who made the world still governs it."

This was a theme that would bear developing. In the proclamation itself he had omitted any reference to the Deity, and it was at the suggestion of Chase that he invoked, in the body of a later draft, "the gracious favor of Almighty God." But now, out of the midnight trials of his spirit, out of his concern for a race in bondage, out of his knowledge of the death of men in battle, something new had come to birth in Lincoln, and through him into the war. After this, as Davis said, there could be no turning back; Lincoln had sounded forth a trumpet that would never call retreat. And having sounded it, he turned in these final days of September to the inscrutable theme he had touched when he thanked the second Quaker woman for her prayers. His secretary found on the presidential desk a sheet of paper containing a single paragraph, a "Meditation on the Divine Will," which Lincoln had written with no thought of publication. Hay copied and preserved it:

The will of God prevails. In great contests each party claims to act in accordance with the will of God. Both may be, and one must be, wrong. God cannot be for and against the same thing at the same time. In the present civil war it is quite possible that God's purpose is something different from the purpose of either party; and yet the human instrumentalities, working just as they do, are of the best adaptation to effect his purpose. I am almost ready to say that this is probably true; that God wills this contest, and wills that it shall not end yet. By his mere great power on the minds of the now contestants, he could have either saved or destroyed the Union without a human contest. Yet the contest began. And, having begun, he could give the final victory to either side any day. Yet the contest proceeds.

★　★　★

*Federal soldiers survey the
Confederate dead on the battlefield
at Corinth, Mississippi, where
Earl Van Dorn's rebels suffered
a bloody repulse.*

Corinth, Perryville; Bragg Retreats

1862 ★ ★ ★ ★ ★ Whatever else it was or might become, whatever reactions it produced within the minds and hearts of men — including Lincoln's — the proclamation was first of all a military measure; which meant that, so far, its force was merely potential. Its application dependent on the armies of the Union, its effect would be in direct ratio to their success, 1) in driving back the Confederate invaders, and 2) in resuming the southward movement whose flow had been reversed, East and West, by the advances of Lee and Bragg into Maryland and Kentucky. The nearer of these two penetrating spearheads had been encysted and repelled by McClellan, and for this Lincoln was grateful, though he would have preferred something more in the way of pursuit than an ineffectual bloodying of the waters at Shepherdstown ford. Even this, however, was better than what he saw when he looked westward in the direction of his native state. The other spearhead was not only still deeply embedded in the vitals of Kentucky, but to Lincoln's acute distress it seemed likely to remain so. After winning by default the race for Louisville, Buell appeared to be concerned only with taking time to catch his breath; with the result that, near the end of September, Lincoln's thin-stretched patience snapped. He ordered Buell's removal from command.

His distress no doubt would have been less acute if he had known

★

that, with or without pressure from Buell, Bragg was already considering a withdrawal. At the outset the North Carolinian had announced that he would make the "Abolition demagogues and demons . . . taste the bitters of invasion," but now he found his own teeth set on edge. From Bardstown, which he had reached three days before, he reported to Richmond on September 25 that his troops were resting from "the long, arduous, and exhausting march" over Muldraugh's Hill. "It is a source of deep regret that this move was necessary," he declared, "as it has enabled Buell to reach Louisville, where a very large force is now concentrated." Then he got down to the bedrock cause of his discontent: "I regret to say we are sadly disappointed at the want of action by our friends in Kentucky. We have so far received no accession to this army. General Smith has secured about a brigade — not half our losses by casualties of different kinds. We have 15,000 stand of arms and no one to use them. Unless a change occurs soon we must abandon the garden spot of Kentucky to its cupidity. The love of ease and fear of pecuniary loss are the fruitful sources of this evil."

In saying this he took his cue from Smith, who — though privately he admitted, "I can understand their fears and hesitancy; they have so much to lose" — had written him from Lexington the week before: "The Kentuckians are slow and backward in rallying to our standard. Their hearts are evidently with us, but their blue-grass and fat cattle are against us." The day after Bragg reached Bardstown — with Buell still moving northward, more or less across his flank and rear — Smith told him that he regarded "the defeat of Buell before he effects a junction with the force at Louisville as a military necessity, for Buell's army has always been the great bugbear to these people, and until [it is] defeated we cannot hope for much addition to our ranks." In other words, before the citizens would risk their lives and property in open support of the Confederates, they wanted to be assured that they would *stay* there. But to Bragg it seemed that this was putting the cart before the horse. He later explained his reluctance in a letter to his wife: "Why should I stay with my handful of brave Southern men to fight for cowards who skulked about in the dark to say to us, 'We are with you. Only whip these fellows out of our country and let us see you can protect us, and we will join you'?"

And so for a time the two Confederate commanders, both flushed with recent victories, remained precisely where they were, Smith at Lexington and Bragg at Bardstown, fifty air-line miles apart, gathering supplies and issuing recruiting appeals which largely went unanswered. The former kept urging the latter to pounce on Buell, claiming that he could whip him unassisted, while he himself continued to load his wagons and round up herds of cattle. Bragg was unwilling to move on Louisville alone, and yet he was also unwilling to ask Smith to abandon the heart of the Bluegrass region by moving westward to join him. Between the two, they had arrived at a sort of impasse of indecision, behind which both were intent on the fruitful harvest they were gleaning against the day when they would retrace their steps across the barrens. What had been announced as a full-scale offensive, designed to establish and maintain the northern boundary of the Confederacy along the Ohio River, had degenerated into a giant raid.

This did not mean that Bragg abandoned all his hopes. Unwilling though he was to risk a pitched battle while Buell hugged the Louisville intrenchments, he thought there still might be a bloodless way to encourage prospective bluegrass volunteers by replacing the Unionist state government, which had fled its capital, with one that was friendly to the South. Moreover, he had the means at hand. In November of the previous year, an irregular convention had met at Russellville to declare the independence of Kentucky, establish a provisional government, and petition the Confederacy for admission. All this it did, and was accepted; Kentucky had representatives in the Confederate Congress and a star in the Confederate flag. Presently, however, when Albert Sidney Johnston's long line came unhinged at Donelson, the men who followed that star were in exile — including Provisional Governor George W. Johnson, who fell at Shiloh and was succeeded by the lieutenant governor, Richard Hawes. Hawes was now on his way north from Chattanooga, and it was Bragg's intention to inaugurate him at Frankfort. With a pro-Confederate occupying the governor's chair in the capitol, supported by a *de facto* government of Confederate sympathies, the entire political outlook would be changed; or so Bragg thought. At any rate, he considered it so thoroughly worth the effort that he decided to see it done himself, lending his personal dignity to the occasion.

Accordingly, leaving Polk in charge of the army around Bardstown, he set out for Lexington on September 28 to confer with Smith before proceeding to Frankfort. Joined by Hawes and his party two days later at Danville, he wrote Polk: "The country and the people grow better as we get into the one and arouse the other." October 1, he reached Lexington, where he arranged for Smith to move his whole army up to Frankfort for the inaugural ceremonies, two or three days later. By now, however, though he still expected much from the current political maneuver, his reaction to what he had seen during his ride through the Bluegrass was mixed. "Enthusiasm is unbounded, but recruiting at a discount," he wired Polk. "Even the women are giving reasons why individuals cannot go."

★ ★ ★ *B*ragg was not the only army commander displaying symptoms of discouragement at this stage of the far-flung campaign. A Cincinnati journalist, watching Buell ride north through Elizabethtown at the head of his retrograding column on September 24, was unfavorably impressed: "His dress was that of a brigadier instead of a major general. He wore a shabby straw hat, dusty coat, and had neither belt, sash or sword about him. . . . Though accompanied by his staff, he was not engaged in conversation with any of them, but rode silently and slowly along, noticing nothing that transpired around him. . . . Buell is, certainly, the most reserved, distant and unsociable of all the generals in the army. He never has a word of cheer for his men or his officers, and in turn his subordinates care little for him save to obey his orders, as machinery works in response to the bidding of the mechanic." The reporter believed that this lack of cheer and sociability on the part of the commander was the cause of the army's present gloom. McClellan, for example, had "an unaccountable something, that keeps this machinery constantly oiled and easy-running; but Buell's unsympathetic nature makes it 'squeak' like the drag wheels of a wagon."

More than the past was fretting Buell; more, even, than the present. After the lost opportunities down along the Tennessee River, after the long hot weary trudge back north to the Ohio, he was confronted with the prospect of having to fight two opponents who, inured by and rested from their recent victories, could now combine to move against him. Nor was this all. Near the end of his 250-mile withdrawal — aware that his superiors were hostile, ready to let fall the Damoclean sword of dismissal, and that his subordinates were edgy, ready to leap at his own and each other's throats — he was also suffering forebodings: forebodings which were presently borne out all too abruptly. Passing through Elizabethtown, he reached Louisville next day. Within another three days he had his whole army there. On the day after that, September 29, in the midst of a general reorganization, he was struck two knee-buckling blows, both of which fell before he had even had time to digest his breakfast.

The first was that, in a time when aggressiveness was at a considerable premium, he lost William Nelson, the most aggressive of his several major generals. He lost him because the Indiana brigadier Jefferson Davis, home from the Transmississippi on a sick leave, had come down to Louisville to assist Nelson in preparing to hold the city against Smith. Nelson was overbearing, Davis touchy; the result was a personality clash, at the climax of which the former ordered the latter out of his department. Davis went, but presently he returned, bringing the governor of Indiana with him. This was Oliver P. Morton, who also had a bone to pick with Nelson over his alleged mishandling of Hoosier volunteers during the fiasco staged at Richmond a month ago tomorrow. They accosted him in the lobby of the Galt House, Buell's Louisville headquarters, just after early breakfast. In the flare-up that ensued, Davis demanded satisfaction for last week's rudeness, and when Nelson called him an "insolent puppy," flipped a wadded calling-card in his face; whereupon Nelson laid the back of a ham-sized hand across his jaw. Davis fell back, and the burly Kentuckian turned on Morton, asking if he too had come there to insult him. Morton said he had not. Nelson started up the staircase, heading for Buell's room on the second floor. "Did you hear that damned insolent scoundrel insult me, sir?" he demanded of

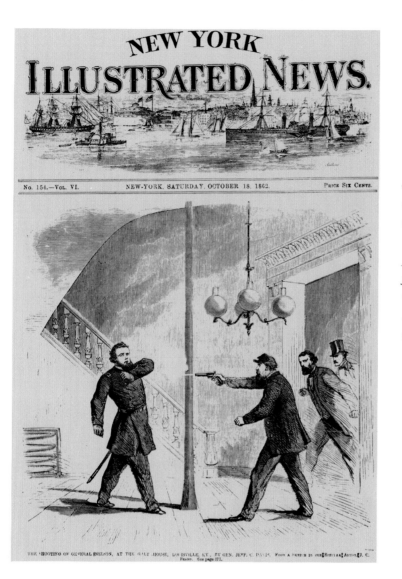

NEW YORK
ILLUSTRATED NEWS.

No. 154.—VOL. VI.   NEW-YORK, SATURDAY, OCTOBER 18, 1862.   PRICE SIX CENTS.

THE SHOOTING OF GENERAL NELSON, AT THE GALT HOUSE, LOUISVILLE, KY., BY GEN. JEFF. C. DAVIS. FROM A SKETCH BY OUR SPECIAL ARTIST, J. C. BEARD. See page 571.

Shortly after exchanging barbs over breakfast, Union general Jefferson C. Davis fatally wounds General William Nelson with a borrowed pistol.

an acquaintance coming down. "I suppose he don't know me, sir. I'll teach him a lesson, sir." He went on up the stairs, then down the hall, and just as he reached the door of Buell's room he heard someone behind him call his name. Turning, he saw Davis standing at the head of the stairs with a pistol in his hand.

Davis had not come armed to the encounter, but after staggering back from the slap he had gone around the lobby asking bystanders for a weapon. At last he came to a certain Captain Gibson. "I always carry the article," Gibson said, producing a pistol from under his coat. Davis took it, and as he started up the stairs Gibson called after him, "It's a tranter trigger. Work light." So when Nelson turned from Buell's door and started toward him, Davis knew what to do. "Not another step farther!" he cried; and then, at a range of about eight feet,

★

shot the big man in the chest. Nelson stopped, turned back toward Buell's door, but fell before he got there. "Send for a clergyman; I wish to be baptized," he told the men who came running at the sound of the shot. Gathering around him, they managed to lift the 300-pound giant onto a bed in a nearby room. "I have been basely murdered," he said. Half an hour later he was dead.

Buell had Davis placed in arrest, intending to try him for murder, but before he could appoint a court or even prepare to conduct an investigation — indeed, before Nelson's blood had time to dry on the rug outside his door — he found that he no longer had any authority in the matter. The second blow had landed: Halleck's order for Buell's removal, issued at Lincoln's insistence, was delivered by special courier that morning. The courier, a colonel aide of Halleck's, acting under instructions similar to the ones given in Frémont's case the year before — that is, the order was not to be delivered if Buell had fought or was about to fight a battle — had left Washington on the 24th, before Lincoln or Halleck knew the outcome of the race for Louisville. Three days later, learning that Buell had reached the Ohio ahead of Bragg, Halleck wired the colonel: "Await further orders before acting." But it was too late. At noon of the 29th the reply came back: "The dispatches are delivered. I think it is fortunate that I obeyed instructions. Much dissatisfaction with General Buell." On its heels came a wire from Buell himself: "I have received your orders . . . and in further obedience . . . I shall repair to Indianapolis."

The government thus was put in the position of having sacked the man who, in some quarters at least, was being hailed as the savior of Louisville and his home state of Ohio. The reaction was prompt. Three congressmen and a senator from the region wired that the double catastrophe of Nelson's death and Buell's supersession had produced "great regret and something of dismay. . . . In our judgment the removal of General Buell will do great injury to the service in Kentucky." However, the courier had carried not one message, but three: a brief note informing Buell that he was relieved, a War Department order appointing George Thomas to succeed him, and a letter warning the new commander that the general-in-chief expected "energetic operations." Thomas answered without delay: "General Buell's preparations have been completed to move against the enemy, and I therefore respectfully ask that he may be retained in command. My position is very embarrassing." Halleck replied: "You may consider the order as suspended until I can lay your dispatch before the Government and get instructions." This was a way out, and Lincoln took it; the order changing commanders was suspended, "by order of the President." Whatever doubt there was that Buell would be willing to turn the other cheek and expose himself to another buffeting was removed by the acknowledgment he sent the following day: "Out of sense of public duty I shall continue to discharge the duties of my command to the best of my ability until otherwise ordered."

That was the last day of September. By then he had completed the reorganization, incorporating the green men with the seasoned men — seasoned, that is, by marching, if not by fighting; his army still had never fought a battle on its own — for a total of better than 75,000 effectives. This was half again more than were with Bragg and Smith, he knew, but he was also aware that, except for the few recruits they had managed to attract in the Bluegrass, their troops were veterans to a man, whereas no less than a third of his own had barely progressed beyond the manual of arms. Whatever qualms proceeded from this, on the first day of October he moved out. Too busy to concern himself with Nelson's slayer or spare the officers for a court to try him, he recommended that Halleck appoint a commission to look into the case. But nothing came of this, not even the filing of charges. Later that month a Louisville grand jury indicted Davis for manslaughter, but nothing came of this either; he was admitted to bail and released. Presently he was back on duty, having acquired a reputation as a man whom it was advisable not to provoke.

Buell had ten divisions, nine of them distributed equally among three corps led by major generals, with Thomas as second in command of the whole. The march was southeast, out of Louisville toward Bardstown, and the army made it in three columns, a corps in each, commanded (left to right) by Alexander McCook, T. L. Crittenden, and Charles Gilbert. Bragg was in that direction, Smith at Frankfort. Buell figured his chances were good if he could keep them divided and thus encounter them one at a time; less good — in fact, not good at all — if he had to face them both at once. So he feinted toward the latter place with a division detached from McCook, supported by the large 15,000-man tenth division, composed almost entirely of recruits under Brigadier General Ebenezer Dumont. That way, Buell would not only cover Louisville; but also, by confusing his opponents as to his true objective, he might keep them from combining against him in the battle he was seeking at last. After four months of building and repairing roads and railroads, tediously advancing and hastily backtracking, enduring constant prodding from above, he was about to fight.

———————

★ ★ ★ *D*own in Mississippi all this while, Van Dorn and Price had been pursuing separate courses, neither of which had produced anything substantial even in the way of a diversion. Not only were they independent of each other; Van Dorn was also independent of Bragg, and now that he (and Isaac Brown) had accomplished the salvation of Vicksburg, the diminutive Mississippian had larger things in mind than keeping Grant amused along the lower Tennessee border while Bragg got all the glory in Kentucky. After the loss of the *Arkansas* and Breckinridge's repulse at Baton Rouge, Van Dorn had abandoned his "Ho! for New Orleans" notion and shifted his gaze upriver, reverting to his earlier slogan: "St Louis, then huzza!" His plan was to swing through West Tennessee, skirting Memphis to pounce on Paducah, from which point he would move "wherever circumstances might dictate." So when Price, mindful of Bragg's instructions to harry the Federals in North Mississippi, called on his former chief for aid, Van Dorn replied that he would rather have Price join *him*. Price declined. Nettled, Van Dorn invoked his seniority and appealed directly to the Secretary of War: "I ought to have command of the movements of Price, that there may be concert of action. . . . Bragg is out of reach; I refer to you." Davis himself wired back: "Your rank makes you the commander, and such I supposed were the instructions of General Bragg."

Van Dorn had what he wanted. But Price had already moved on his own, striking for Iuka, twenty-odd miles down the Memphis & Charleston Railroad from Corinth, the fortified eastern anchor of Grant's contracted line. September 14, as Price's nearly 15,000 troops approached, the badly outnumbered Union garrison retreated in haste, leaving a quantity of confiscated cotton and army stores behind. Price burned the one and appropriated the other. It was now his intention to march on Middle Tennessee, to which Bragg informed him the Federals were retiring; but finding that this was not entirely the case — that Grant, though he had sent three of his five left-flank divisions to Buell, still had the other two near Iuka under Rosecrans — he hesitated to leave such a substantial force in his rear. While he was pondering this dilemma and distributing the captured stores, the problem was solved by the arrival of a courier from Van Dorn's headquarters at Holly Springs, sixty miles west of Corinth, informing Price that the President had authorized his fellow Mississippian to order a junction of the two armies, under his command, for whatever "concert of action" he had in mind.

The Missourian's intention was to stay in Iuka until he heard from Van Dorn just what it was he wanted him to do; then he would move out, more or less at his leisure, in whatever direction Van Dorn advised in order to combine the two commands for a resumption of the offensive. However, this was overlooking Grant's plans in the matter — and Grant intended not only to interrupt Price's leisure, but also to destroy him. In fact, he said later, "It looked to me that, if Price would remain in Iuka until we could get there, his annihilation was inevitable."

By "we" he meant himself and Rosecrans, whose two divisions contained about 9000 effectives, and he also meant Ord, who would advance from Corinth with another two divisions, leaving a strong garrison to man the fortifications in case Van Dorn pushed east from Holly Springs for an assault while he was gone. Price had 15,000 men; Rosecrans and Ord had 17,000 between them.

★

This in itself was by no means enough of a preponderance to assure the annihilation Grant expected, but he had designed a tactical convergence to accomplish that result. Ord would swing north and descend on Iuka from that direction, while Rosecrans came up from the south. Once Price had his attention thoroughly fixed on the former, the latter would fall on his rear; so that the rebels, demoralized and cut off from all avenues of escape, would have to choose between death and capitulation. Advised of the plan, both of Grant's subordinate commanders were as optimistic as their chief, though Rosecrans warned: "Price is an old woodpecker," meaning that he would be hard to take by surprise.

Accordingly, on September 17 (while Lee, with his back to the Potomac, was defending Sharpsburg against McClellan, and Wilder, with his back to the Green, was surrendering Munfordville to Bragg) Ord moved twelve miles down the Memphis & Charleston to Burnsville, where Grant established headquarters, having instructed Rosecrans to concentrate at Jacinto, eight miles south. From these two points, the four divisions were to push on to within striking distance of Iuka the following day in order to deliver their sequential north-south attacks soon after dawn of the 19th. But that was not

General Earl Van Dorn, called "elegant," was also accused of "negligence, whoring, and drunkenness."

to be. Rosecrans reported that one of his divisions had been so badly delayed that he could not be in position before midafternoon of the appointed day. Ord moved up on schedule, however, establishing contact with the Confederate cavalry outposts, and Grant used the waiting time to engage in a bit of psychological warfare.

Last night he had received from the telegraph superintendent at Cairo a dispatch concerning the Battle of Antietam. According to this gentleman, the news was very good indeed: "Both sides engaged until 4 p.m. at which time Hooker gained position, flanked rebels, and threw them into disorder. Longstreet and his entire division prisoners. General Hill killed. Entire rebel army of Virginia destroyed, Burnside having reoccupied Harpers Ferry and cut off retreat. . . . Latest advices say entire rebel army must be captured or killed, as Potomac is rising and our forces pressing the enemy continually." Grant sent the message forward to Ord, who passed it on to the Confederates this morning under a flag of truce. "I think this battle decides the war finally," he explained in a covering note, "and that upon being satisfied of its truth General Price or whoever commands here will avoid useless bloodshed and lay down his arms. There is not the slightest doubt of the truth of the dispatch in my hand." The reply was prompt. Formally employing the third person, Price said flatly that he did not believe the report was true, but "that if the facts were as stated in those dispatches they would only move him and his soldiers to greater exertions in behalf of their country, and that neither he nor they will ever lay down their arms — as humanely suggested by General Ord — until the independence of the Confederate States shall have been acknowledged by the United States."

Psychological warfare having failed to produce the desired result, Grant told Ord to go ahead with the opening phase, diverting Price's attention northward, though he warned: "[Rosecrans] is behind where we expected. Do not be too rapid in your advance . . . unless it should be found that the enemy are evacuating." Ord moved forward, encountering light resistance, but since there still was no word that the southward escape route was blocked, Grant told him to halt within four miles of the town "and there await sounds of an engagement between Rosecrans and the enemy before engaging the latter." Ord did so, and the afternoon wore on. About 6 o'clock he received a message written two hours before by the commander of his lead division: "For the last twenty minutes there has been a dense smoke arising from the direction of Iuka. I conclude that the enemy are evacuating and destroying the stores." Ord pushed forward tentatively, but still hearing no sound of conflict from the south, halted his troops in line of battle, and there they remained through twilight into darkness, a northwest wind blowing hard against their backs. His total loss for the day, in both divisions, was 1 man wounded.

The smoke had been beyond, not in the town, and it came from Price's guns, not his stores. Just as Grant had intended, the "old woodpecker" had concentrated northward against Ord; but about 2 o'clock, learning that another Union column was approaching from the south, he shifted one brigade in that direction and presently followed it with another. Soon afterwards, since Ord seemed disinclined to press the issue, he called for a third. Before it got there, the fight with Rosecrans had begun. Seeing the lead blue division waver, Price ordered a charge that drove the Federals back on their supports and captured nine of their guns. Upwind, Ord heard nothing. Grant, in fact, did not suspect that his other column was at hand until next morning, when he received a note Rosecrans had written the night before. Headed "Two miles south of Iuka," it reported that he had "met the enemy in force just above this point. . . . The ground is horrid, unknown to us, and no room for development. . . . Push on into them until we can have time to do something." The convergence, though delayed, had worked exactly as Grant planned it; but instead of producing a victory, as expected, had resulted in a repulse which, though it cost him nine guns and nearly 800 soldiers, gained him nothing.

An ill wind had blown no good, but now at least he knew he had both of his columns in position north and south of the town, ready to put the squeeze on Price, who was boxed in. Or so Grant thought when he told Ord at 8.35 that morning, "Get your troops up and attack as soon as possible." Ord did so, banging away with his guns as he advanced, and so did Rosecrans: only to find that they were converging on emptiness. Price — whose wagons had been packed for the move before the Federals appeared — had evacuated Iuka during the night, taking a southeast road which Rosecrans left unguarded. At Grant's insistence, the latter took up the pursuit, hoping at least to recapture the stores being hauled away, but abandoned it when he ran into an ambush eight miles out. All Grant's strategic pains had netted him was an empty town and the task of burying the dead of both armies. Rosecrans had lost 790 men, Price 535, and the latter had gotten away with all his spoils.

Ord meanwhile was hurrying back west by rail, in case Van Dorn had left Holly Springs and crossed the Hatchie River for a leap at Corinth. The prospect of this held no dismay for Rosecrans. In fact, he welcomed it. Whatever blunders he had committed against Price, he looked forward to a contest with Van Dorn. They had been classmates, West Point '56; he had finished fourth from the top, the Southerner fourth from the bottom, and Rosecrans was eager to extend this proof of his superiority beyond the academic. Back at Jacinto that night, he wired Grant: "If you can let me know that there is a good opportunity to cross the railroad and march on Holly Springs to cut off the forces of Buck Van Dorn I will be in readiness to take everything. If we could get them across the Hatchie they would be clean up the spout."

★ ★ ★ *H*e was about to be accommodated in his desire for **a bloody reunion east of the Hatchie,** although not in the manner he imagined, since it would involve a change of roles. Instead of the hunter, he would be the hunted.

Van Dorn had set aside the elaborate scheme for a march on Paducah, which would expose both of his flanks to attack by superior numbers, and had decided to precede it with a much simpler, though in its way no less daring, operation. He was planning a direct assault on Corinth. That place, he saw now, was the linchpin of the Federal defenses in North Mississippi. Once it was cracked and unseated, he could move at will on Memphis or he could revert to his earlier plan for a march on St Louis, gobbling up blue detachments as he went. "We may take them in detail if they are not wary," he explained in a dispatch that reached Price the day before the Battle of Iuka; "but once combined we will make a successful campaign, clear out West Tennessee, and then —— "

His new plan, outlined in this and other messages written after Price's hairbreadth escape from Iuka with the aid of a friendly wind, was for their two commands to unite at Ripley, just west of the Hatchie, then move north, up that bank of the river, as if against Bolivar. However, this would only be a feint, serving to immobilize Grant's reserve force under Hurlbut at that point. When they reached the Memphis & Charleston at Pocahontas, they would turn sharp right and drive for Corinth, twenty miles away, blocking the path of reinforcements from the northwest and striking before Rosecrans had time to bring in troops from the east for its defense. Combined, Van Dorn and Price had 22,000 men, while in Corinth, the former explained, there were no more than 15,000, the rest — about 8000 — being posted out toward Burnsville and Jacinto, guarding against attack from that direction. These odds, he said, gave him "a reasonable hope of success" in driving the defenders from their guns and intrenchments and capturing the lot, together with the supplies being collected for an advance.

Price, who had been associated with the Mississippian in a similar venture against Curtis seven months before in the wilds of Arkansas — with results barely short of disastrous — was not so sure; but at any rate, after eight weeks of being hamstrung by conflicting orders and exposed to ridicule, he was glad to be doing *some*thing. Back in his home state, the 290-pound Missourian had been nicknamed "Old Skedad" by Unionist editors, one of whom remarked that "as a racer he has seen few equals for his weight." To cap the climax, rumors had been spread that he was a West Pointer. After these and other such vexations (although the educational slander was promptly refuted by a friendly correspondent who assured the public that Price "owes his success to practical good sense and hard fighting. He never attended a military school in his life") he was glad of a chance to move against the enemy, even though Van Dorn himself, sanguine as he was by nature, characterized their "hope of success" as no more than "reasonable."

Accordingly, both commands reached Ripley on September 28: Van Dorn's one division under Mansfield Lovell — who, like his chief, was out to redeem misfortune, New Orleans bulking even larger in this respect than Elkhorn Tavern — and Price's two under Brigadier Generals Dabney Maury and Louis Hébert. Lovell began the northward march that afternoon, followed by Maury and Hébert the next morning. They had fifty miles to go, thirty up to Pocahontas, then twenty down to Corinth, all along a single narrow road through densely wooded country, bone-dry after the summer-long drouth. The final lap would be the hardest, not only because it called for speed and accurate timing to achieve concerted action and surprise, but also because, after they crossed the Hatchie, there would be no water until they reached Corinth, where they would have to fight for it and win or else go thirsty. Nevertheless, according to Van Dorn, "the troops were in fine spirits, and the whole Army of West Tennessee" — so he called it, anticipating the movement which would follow

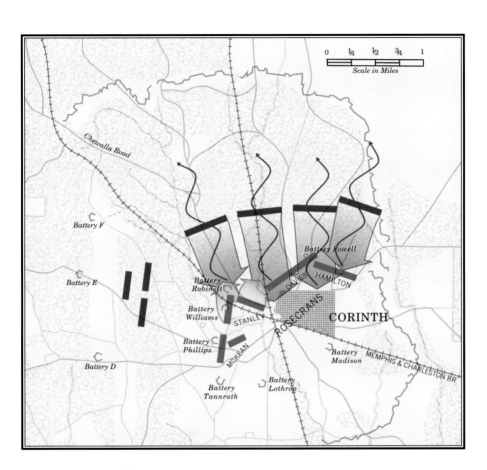

*For two days, Van Dorn hurled attacks at Rosecrans'
defensive lines around Corinth, but the Confederates
failed to achieve a decisive breakthrough.*

victory — "seemed eager to emulate the armies of the Potomac and of Kentucky." Like their leaders, the soldiers were out to undo past reverses. Van Dorn
himself reported: "No army ever marched to battle with prouder steps, more
hopeful countenances, or with more courage."

October 1 the van approached Pocahontas and, ending the feint at
Bolivar, swung east. Encountering cavalry here and infantry the following day at
Chewalla, ten miles short of Corinth, Van Dorn knew that whatever the element
of secrecy could accomplish was behind him. From here on in, Rosecrans was
forewarned. The Confederates pressed on, skirmishing as they advanced, and
next morning, October 3, two miles short of their objective, came upon a heavy
line of Federal infantry occupying the intrenchments Beauregard — and, incidentally, Van Dorn himself — had dug along the crescent ridge to hold off Halleck,

★

back in May. Unlike Halleck, the Mississippian put his troops into assault formation and sent them forward without delay: Lovell on the right, astride the Memphis & Charleston, and Maury and Hébert beyond him, reaching over to the
Mobile & Ohio, so that as they moved east and south the three divisions would
converge on the crossing. Whooping, the graybacks started up the ridge after the
bluecoats firing down at them from the crest, and that was the beginning of what
turned out to be a two-day battle which was one of the most violent of the war.

   The reason it stretched to two days, despite its having been designed
as a slashing attack that would crumple in a matter of hours whatever stood in its
path, was that Rosecrans was not only braced for the shock but actually outnumbered his assailants. For the wrong reasons, he had done the right things; and
what was more he had done them mostly on his own. Grant, following the post-
Donelson pattern — the Shiloh pattern, too, for that matter — had gone off to
St Louis to confer with Curtis about the possibility of bringing reinforcements
across the river from Helena, and, failing in this, had not returned to his headquarters at Jackson, Tennessee, until Van Dorn and Price had already begun their
northward march out of Ripley. Supposing — as Van Dorn intended for him to
suppose — that the rebels were moving against Hurlbut at Bolivar, Rosecrans
reacted in a fashion which his opponent had not foreseen. That is, he called in his
troops from Burnsville and Jacinto, two full divisions of them, and prepared to
go to Hurlbut's assistance; so that when the Confederates swung east at Pocahontas, ending their feint and driving hard in his direction, the Corinth commander was ready for them. Instead of catching 15,000 Federals unaware, Van
Dorn and his 22,000 were moving against an army which had not only been consolidated, but also in fact outnumbered his own by more than a thousand men.

   As if this was not advantage enough, Rosecrans had his four divisions posted behind a formidable double line of intrenchments. Three were
thrust forward along the northward ridge, where Beauregard had done their
digging for them, and one was held in reserve to man the works recently constructed along the northern and western perimeter of the town itself. Van Dorn
and Price struck hard. Advancing with thirsty desperation, the Confederates
threw the defenders off the outer ridge soon after midday, taking several pieces
of artillery in the process. But the Federals were stubborn. Yielding each to only
the heaviest pressure, they took up four separate positions between the two
fortified lines. The sun was near the land line and the attackers were near
exhaustion by the time they came within musket range of the gun-bristled
outskirts of Corinth. Regretfully, while his men dispersed to draw water from
the captured Union wells, Van Dorn deferred the coup de grâce — or anyhow
what he conceived as such — till morning.

   Losses on both sides had been heavy. Rosecrans (though he was later
to claim, like Van Dorn, that another hour of daylight would have meant victory

on the first day of battle) was thankful for the respite. That morning, with the graybacks bearing down on him, he had complained to Grant at Jackson: "Our men did not act or fight well." Now, though, he felt better. "If they fight us tomorrow," he wired Grant half an hour before midnight, "I think we shall whip them." Then, bethinking himself of the unpredictable nature of his classmate Buck Van Dorn, he added: "If they go to attack you we shall advance upon them."

Van Dorn, however, was through with trickery, double envelopments and the like — at least for the present. His blood was up; it was Rosecrans he was after, and he was after him in the harshest, most straightforward way imaginable. Today he would depend not on deception to complete the destruction begun the day before, but on the rapid point-blank fire of his guns and the naked valor of his infantry. Before dawn, October 4, his artillery opened on the Federal inner line, which was prompt in reply. "It was grand," one Union brigadier declared. "The different calibers, metals, shapes, and distances of the guns caused the sounds to resemble the chimes of old Rome when all her bells rang out." This continued until after sunrise, when a long lull succeeded the uproar, punctuated by sharpshooters banging away at whatever showed a head. Rosecrans was curious but cautious, wondering what was afoot out there beyond the screen of trees. "Feel them," he told one regimental commander, "but don't get into their fingers." "I'll feel them!" the colonel said, and led a sally. Entering the woods, the regiment was received with a crash of musketry and fell back, badly cut up, its colonel having been shot through the neck and captured. All that Rosecrans learned from this was that Van Dorn was still there, in strength.

Shortly after 10 o'clock he received even more emphatic proof that this was the case; for at that hour Van Dorn launched his all-or-nothing assault. Price's two divisions began it, surging forward in echelon, to be met with a blast of cannonfire. The left elements suffered a sudden and bloody repulse, but three regiments in the center achieved a breakthrough when the Union cannoneers fell back from their guns in a panic that spread to the supporting infantry. Yelling men in butternut burst into the streets of Corinth, driving snipers out of houses by firing through the windows, swept past Rosecrans' deserted headquarters, then on to the depot beyond the railroad crossing. At that point, however, finding their advance unsupported and the Federals standing firm, they turned and fought their way back out again. On the far right, pinned down by heavy fire from a ridge to its immediate front, Lovell's division gained no ground at all. The day was hot, 94° in the shade; panting and thirsty, the attackers hugged what cover they could find. From time to time they would rise and charge, urged on by their officers, but after the original short-lived penetration they had no luck at all. The bluecoats stood firm. "Our lines melted under their fire like snow in thaw," one Confederate afterwards recalled. Perhaps the hardest fighting of the day occurred in front of Battery Robinette, just north of the

During the climax of the second day's fight, the colonel of the 2d Texas, carrying the regimental flag, is shot down just as he gains the parapet of one of the Union strong points.

Memphis & Charleston Railroad, a three-gun redan protected by a five-foot ditch which overflowed with dead and dying Texans and Arkansans within two hours. By then it was noon and Van Dorn knew his long-shot gamble had failed. "Exhausted from loss of sleep, wearied from hard marching and fighting, companies and regiments without officers," he later reported, "our troops — let no one censure them — gave way. The day was lost."

How lost it was he would not know until he counted the casualties he had suffered, and weighed them against the number he had inflicted: 4233 Confederates, as compared to 2520 Federals, with well over one third of the former listed as "missing." Price wept as he watched his thinned ranks withdraw, the men's faces sullen with the knowledge that hard fighting had won them nothing more than the right to stitch the name of another defeat on their battle flags. By 1 o'clock they were in full retreat — unpursued. Instead of pressing their rear, Rosecrans was riding along his battered line to deny in person a rumor that he had been slain. "Old Rosy," his men called him, a red-faced man in his middle forties, with the profile of a Roman orator. At Battery Robinette

he drew rein, dismounted, bared his head, and told his soldiers, most of whom were Ohioans like himself: "I stand in the presence of brave men, and I take my hat off to you." Van Dorn meanwhile had stopped for the night at Chewalla, from which he had launched his first attack the day before. Next morning, finding the Hatchie crossing blocked by 8000 fresh troops sent down from Bolivar, he fought a holding action in which about 600 men fell on each side, then turned back south and crossed by a road leading west out of Corinth, which Rosecrans — as at Iuka — had left open. Stung into vigor, Old Rosy at last took up the pursuit, complaining bitterly when Grant called him off. Van Dorn returned to Holly Springs by way of Ripley, accompanied by Price.

     The brief, vicious campaign was over. What had been intended as a third prong in the South's late-summer early-fall offensive had snapped off short as soon as it was launched. Including the holding action on the Hatchie, it had gained the Confederacy nothing except the infliction of just over 3000 casualties on the Federals in North Mississippi, and for this Van Dorn had paid with nearly 5000 of his own. A cry went up that the nation could no longer afford to pay in blood for the failure of his thick-skulled fights and harebrained maneuvers. Nor were the protests limited in reference to his military judgment. The man himself was under fire. "He is regarded as the source of all our woes," a senator from his native state complained, "and disaster, it is prophesied, will attend us so long as he is connected with this army. The atmosphere is dense with horrid narratives of his negligence, whoring, and drunkenness, for the truth of which I cannot vouch; but it is so fastened in the public belief that an acquittal by a court-martial of angels would not relieve him of the charge." These and other allegations — specifically, that he had been drunk on duty at Corinth, that he had neglected his wounded on the retreat, and that he had failed to provide himself with a map of the country — resulted in a court of inquiry, called for by the accused himself. The court, by a unanimous decision, cleared him of all blame, adding that the charges "are not only not proved, but they are disproved."

Thus were Van Dorn's critics officially answered and rebuked. However, the best answer, although unofficial, had already been made for him on the field of battle itself, shortly after his departure. Near Battery Robinette, having bared his head "in the presence of brave men," Rosecrans came upon an Arkansas lieutenant, shot through the foot and propped against a tree. He offered him a drink of water. "Thank you, General; one of your men just gave me some," the Confederate replied. When the Federal commander, glancing around at the heaped and scattered corpses in their butternut rags, remarked that there had been "pretty hot fighting here," the rebel Westerner agreed. "Yes, General, you licked us good," he said. "But we gave you the best we had in the ranch."

★ ★ ★ The best they had was not enough; but even if it had served the Mississippi general's purpose, it would have been of small help to Bragg, three hundred air-line miles northeastward in Kentucky. At the same hour of the same day that Van Dorn broke off the fight at Corinth and retreated — 1 p.m. October 4 — the boom of Union guns lobbing shells into the outskirts of Frankfort disrupted the inaugural ceremonies and ended in midsentence the address being delivered by Confederate Governor Hawes, who had been sworn in at high noon and whose *de facto* tenure of office thus was brief.

Despite a shortage of cavalry for outpost work and scouting — Forrest had been sent back to Middle Tennessee to raise another new brigade, and John Morgan was off chasing his Federal namesake across the barrens — Bragg was not entirely surprised at this development. Nor was he in any sense dismayed. In fact, having been forewarned, he had expressed the hope that Buell would attempt just such a maneuver. Informed two days before, October 2, that a blue column was moving east from Louisville toward Shelbyville and Frankfort, he passed the word along to Polk, whom he had left in command of the four divisions around Bardstown while he himself joined Kirby Smith to attend the inauguration at the capital. "It may be a reconnaissance," he added, "but should it be a real attack we have them. . . . With Smith in front and our gallant army on the flank I see no hope for Buell if he is rash enough to come out. I only fear it is not true. . . . Hold yourself informed by scouts toward Shelbyville, and if you discover a heavy force that has moved on Frankfort strike without further orders." A few hours later, more positive evidence was at hand, and Bragg followed this first message with a second: "The enemy is certainly advancing on Frankfort. Put your whole available force in motion . . . and strike him in flank and rear. If we can combine our movements he is certainly lost."

Couriers taking these messages to Bardstown — Pennsylvania's Stephen Foster's Old Kentucky Home — passed en route a courier bringing a dispatch Polk had written that same morning. He too was being advanced on, he declared: not by a single Federal column, but by three, all moving southeast out of Louisville on as many different roads. His original instructions, in the event that he was menaced by a superior force, had been to fall back eastward. Accordingly, he told Bragg, "I shall keep the enemy well under observation, and my action shall be governed by the circumstances which shall be developed. If an opportunity presents itself I will strike. If it shall be clearly inexpedient to do that I will, according to your suggestion, fall back on Harrodsburg and Danville on the roads indicated by you, with a view to a concentration [of both armies]." Pointedly, he observed in closing: "It seems to me we are too much scattered."

Next morning, October 3, having received Bragg's two messages of the day before, instructing him to strike the flank and rear of the column moving against Frankfort, he replied: "The last twenty-four hours have developed a condition of things on my front and left flank which I shadowed forth in my last note to you, which makes compliance with this order not only eminently inexpedient but impractical. I have called a conference of wing and division commanders to whom I have submitted the matter, and find that they unanimously indorse my views of what is demanded. I shall therefore pursue a different course, assured that when facts are submitted to you you will justify my decision." Reverting to his original instructions to fall back eastward, he added: "The head of my column will move this evening."

Bragg concurred: at least for the time being. Receiving Polk's dispatch at Frankfort during the early hours of inauguration day, he replied: "Concentrate your force in front of Harrodsburg. . . . Smith's whole force is concentrating here and we will strike the enemy just as soon as we can concentrate." Mindful of the effect the retrograde movement might have on the troops, he admonished the bishop-general: "Keep the men in heart by assuring them it is not a retreat, but a concentration for a fight. We can and must defeat them." Near midday he followed this with further assurance: "We shall put our governor in power soon and then I propose to seek the enemy." Just then, however, the ceremony was interrupted by the boom of guns. The enemy, it appeared, had sought *him*. So Bragg tacked a postscript on the message: "1.30 p.m. Enemy in heavy force advancing on us; only 12 miles out. Shall destroy bridges and retire on Harrodsburg for concentration and then strike. Reach that point as soon as possible."

Throughout the greater part of this exchange, despite the sudden and apparently unpremeditated changes of decision and direction — which came full circle and brought him back to the start before the finish — Bragg had given an effective imitation of a man who not only knew where he was going, but also knew what he was going to do when he got there; "concentrate" and "strike" were the predominant verbs, especially the former. But the truth was, he was badly confused, whether he knew it or not. Buell's feint toward Frank-

---

Bragg had given an effective imitation of a man who not only knew where he was going, but also knew what he was going to do when he got there.

---

fort, led by Brigadier General Joshua Sill's division and supported by the oversized division of green men under Dumont, succeeded admirably: Bragg, being directly confronted, considered this the major Federal effort and, discounting Polk's specific warning to the contrary, underrated the strength of the three-corps column moving down toward Bardstown.

Not that Buell himself had no problems. Though his army was large — 55,000 soldiers in one column, 22,000 in the other; the former alone was larger than Bragg's and Smith's, even if they had been combined, which they had not — size also had its drawbacks, particularly on the march, as he was rapidly finding out. Besides, at least one third of this 77,000-man collection were recruits, so-called Squirrel Hunters, rallied to the call of startled governors who had suddenly found the war approaching their Ohio River doorsteps. A gloomy-minded general, and Buell was certainly that, would be inclined to suppose that such troops had established their all-time pattern of behavior at the Battle of Richmond, five short weeks ago: in which case, panic being highly contagious in combat, they were likely to prove more of a liability than an asset. Nor was this inexperience limited to the ranks. The corps commanders themselves, raised to their present positions during the hasty reorganization at Louisville the week before, were doubtful quantities at best, untested by the pressure of command responsibility in battle. Crittenden had dignity, but according to a correspondent who knew and respected him, his talents were mainly those of a country lawyer. In his favor was a fervid devotion to the Union, no doubt intensified by the fact that his brother had chosen the opposite side. McCook, on the other hand, was "an overgrown schoolboy" according to the same reporter. Barely thirty-one, he had a rollicking manner and was something of a wag, and as such he irritated more often than he cheered. By all odds, however, the strangest of the three, at least in the method by which he had arrived at his present eminence, was Gilbert. A regular army captain of infantry, he had happened to be in Louisville when Bragg started north, and the department commander at Cincinnati, alarmed and badly in need of professional help, issued the order: "Captain C. C. Gilbert, First Infantry, U.S. Army, is hereby appointed a major general of volunteers, subject to the approval of the President of the United States." Lincoln in time appointed him a brigadier, subject to confirmation by Congress — which decided after some debate that he was only a captain after all. For the present, though, he was apparently a bona fide major general, and as such he received the corps command to which his rank entitled him.

These, then, were the troops with which Buell was expected to fling Bragg's and Smith's veterans out of Kentucky, and these were the ranking officers on whom he depended for execution of his orders. In partial compensation, there was Thomas; but Old Pap, as he was coming to be called, had never been one to offer unsolicited advice. Officially designated as second in command of the whole army, for the present he was riding with Crittenden's column as a sort of super corps commander. This arrangement not only placed Buell's most competent subordinate in a superfluous position and beyond his immediate reach, but what was more it led in time to trouble.

The Confederates having evacuated Bardstown on the 4th, the Federals entered or by-passed the place that evening and slogged on down the dusty roads toward Mackville, Springfield, and Lebanon, encountering only rebel horsemen who faded back whenever contact was established. This was satisfactory, but there was a disturbing lack of coördination between the three columns with which Buell was groping for Bragg as if with widespread fingers. On the left, McCook wrote Thomas, who was with Crittenden on the right, twenty miles away: "Please keep me advised of your movements, so that I can coöperate. I am in blissful ignorance." Another lack was more immediately painful, at least to the marchers themselves. One Illinois volunteer later recalled that after the summer-long drouth, which had stretched into fall, creeks and even rivers were "either totally dry or shrunken into little, heated, tired-looking threads of water, brackish and disagreeable to taste and smell." Brackish or not, water was much on the men's minds, as well as on the minds of their commanders.

Pushing on through Springfield, Buell ordered a concentration near Perryville on the 7th. There was water there — in Doctor's Creek, a tributary of Chaplin River, which in turn was a tributary of the Salt. There were also rebels there, or so he heard, in strength. After four hard months of marching hundreds of miles, sneered and sniped at by the authorities much of the time, the Army of the Ohio was about to come to grips with the gray-clad authors of its woes.

They did come to grips that evening, or nearly to grips — part of them at any rate. McCook, coming down through Mackville, was delayed by a bad road and went into camp eight miles short of his objective. Crittenden, coming up from Lebanon, was delayed by a detour Thomas authorized him to make in search of water; he too had to stop for the night, ten miles short of the designated point of concentration. Only Gilbert's central column, trudging east from Springfield by the direct route, reached the field on schedule. His troops marched in near sundown, tired and thirsty, but found Doctor's Creek defended by snipers on a ridge across the way. Sorely in need of the water standing in pools along the creek bed, the bluecoats launched a vigorous downhill attack. Repulsed, they fell back toward the sunset, re-formed, and tried again, this time by the light of a full moon rising beyond the ridge where enemy riflemen lay concealed to catch them in their sights. Again they were repulsed. Exhausted by these added exertions, and thirstier than ever, they made a dry camp in the woods, tantalized by the thought of water gleaming silver in the moonlight just ahead.

It was an inauspicious beginning. What was more, Buell himself was indisposed, having been lamed and badly shaken up as a result of being thrown by a fractious horse that afternoon. But he was not discouraged. He had suffered and sweltered too much and too long, all through the long summer into fall, to be anything but relieved by the thought that he had Bragg's whole army at last within reach of the widespread fingers now being clenched into a fist. The feint at Frankfort having served its purpose, Sill was on the way south to rejoin McCook, who himself had only a short way left to come. Off to the southwest, Crittenden too was within easy marching distance. To make certain that his army was concentrated without further delay, Buell had his chief of staff send a message to Thomas, urging him to be on the road by 3 a.m. Bragg had been brought to bay at Perryville, he told him, adding: "We expect to attack and carry the place tomorrow."

★ ★ ★ **B**uell's estimate of the enemy situation, particularly in regard to the strength of the force which had denied his men a drink from Doctor's Creek, was considerably mistaken. Bragg's whole army was not there on the opposite ridge; only a part of it was — so far only half, in fact — which in turn was the result of a mistake in the opposite direction. Still confused by the feint at Frankfort, Bragg assumed that only a part of Buell's army was approaching Perryville. And thus was achieved a

Author of a work on infantry tactics, William J. Hardee was beloved by his troops because of his "kind and considerate" disposition.

curious balance of error: Buell thought he was facing Bragg's whole army, whereas it was only a part, and Bragg thought he was facing only a part of Buell's army, whereas it was (or soon would be) the whole. This compound misconception not only accounted for much of the confusion that ensued, but it was also the result of much confusion in the immediate past.

At Harrodsburg that morning Bragg had issued a confidential circular, calling for a concentration of both armies near Versailles, south of Frankfort, west of Lexington, and east of the Kentucky River. Polk was to move his two divisions there at once, joining Kirby Smith, while Hardee followed, delaying the enemy column as he fell back. It was all quite carefully worked out; each commander was told just what to do. But no sooner was it completed than Bragg received a dispatch Polk had written late the night before, reporting that he had told Hardee "to ascertain, if possible, the strength of the enemy which may be covered by his advance. I cannot think it large." Polk meant by this that he did not think the Federal covering force, or advance guard, was large; but Bragg took him to mean the main body. Accordingly, he decided to have Hardee give the enemy column a rap that would slow it down and afford him the leisure he needed to cross the Salt and Kentucky Rivers and effect the concentration. Polk was instructed to have one of his divisions continue its march to join Smith beyond the river, but to return to Perryville with the other in order to reinforce Hardee for this purpose. "Give the enemy battle immediately," Bragg wrote. "Rout him, and then move to our support at Versailles."

This was written at sundown, just as the Federals began their fight for the water west of Perryville. A copy of it reached Hardee, together with the confidential circular, just after the second repulse. The *Tactics* author read them both, and while he approved of the circular, finding it militarily sound, he was horrified by the instructions given Polk to divide his wing and precipitate a battle in which Bragg would employ only three of the four divisions of one of the armies moving toward a proper concentration. So horrified was Hardee, in fact, by this violation of the principles he had outlined in his book on infantry tactics, that he retired at once to his tent and wrote the commanding general a personal letter of advice:

Permit me, from the friendly relations so long existing between us, to write you plainly. Do not scatter your forces. There is one rule in our profession which should never be forgotten; it is to throw the masses of your troops on the fractions of the enemy. The movement last proposed will divide your army and each may be defeated, whereas by keeping them united success is certain. If it be your policy to strike the enemy at Versailles, take your whole force with you and make the blow effective; if, on the contrary, you should decide to strike the army in front of me, first let that be done with a force which will make success certain. Strike with your whole strength first to the right then to the left. I could not sleep quietly tonight without giving expression to these views. Whatever you decide to do will meet my hearty co-operation.

He signed it, "Your sincere friend," then added a postscript: "If you wish my opinion, it is that in view of the position of your depots you ought to strike this force first," and gave it to an officer courier for immediate delivery.

Three hours would suffice to bring an answer, but there was none: except that Polk arrived in the night with one division, which in itself was a sort of negative answer, and assumed command by virtue of his rank. The Confederate over-all strength was 16,000 men. What the Federal strength was, neither Polk nor Hardee knew, though they suspected that it was considerably larger than their own. At earliest dawn, while they were discussing whether to attack as Bragg had ordered, Buell solved the problem for them by attacking first.

Once more it was a dash for water, and this time it succeeded. Where other units had failed the night before, Brigadier General Philip H. Sheridan, commanding a division under Gilbert, went forward with one of his brigades in the gray twilight before sunrise, October 8, and seized not only a stretch of the creek itself, with several of its precious pools of water, but also the dominant heights beyond, throwing the rebel snipers back and posting his own men along the ridge to prevent their return. A thirty-one-year-old bandy-legged Ohioan with heavy, crescent-shaped eyebrows, cropped hair, and a head as round as a pot, he looked more like a Mongolian than like the Irishman he was. Less than ten years out of West Point, he had received his star two weeks ago and had been a division commander just nine days, previous to which time he had been a commissary captain under Halleck for six months until by a fluke he secured a promotion to colonel and command of a Michigan cavalry regiment which he led with such dash, in pursuit of Beauregard after the Corinth evacuation, that in late July five of his superiors, including Rosecrans, recommended his promotion with the indorsement: "He is worth his weight in gold."

Now in Kentucky, having received his star, he was out to prove the validity of their claim, as well as his right to further advancement. Other inducements there were, too. The son of immigrant parents — born in County Cavan, some said, or en route in mid-Atlantic, according to others, though Sheridan himself denied this: not only because he was strenuously American and preferred to think of himself as having sprung from native soil, but also because he learned in time that no person who drew his first breath outside its limits could ever become President of the United States — he had an intense dislike of Southerners, particularly those with aristocratic pretensions, and had suffered a year's suspension from the Academy for threatening with a bayonet a Virginia upperclassman whose tone he found offensive on the drill field. He was a man in a hurry. In addition to other provocations, real or imaginary, he felt that the South owed him repayment, preferably in blood, for the year he had lost; and this morning he began to collect in earnest. However, the fury of his attack across Doctor's Creek was apparently about as alarming to his own corps commander as it had been to the Confederates. Gilbert kept wigwagging messages forward, imploring the young enthusiast not to bring on a general engagement contrary to Buell's wishes. Sheridan, who was up where he could see what was going on, later wrote that he "replied to each message that I was not bringing on an engagement, but that the enemy evidently intended to do so, and that I believed I should shortly be attacked."

Attacked as he predicted, he brought up his other brigades and held his ground; after which a long lull ensued. Gilbert, taking heart at this, sent the other two divisions forward to take position along the ridge and astride the Springfield road, which crossed it on the way to Perryville, just under two miles

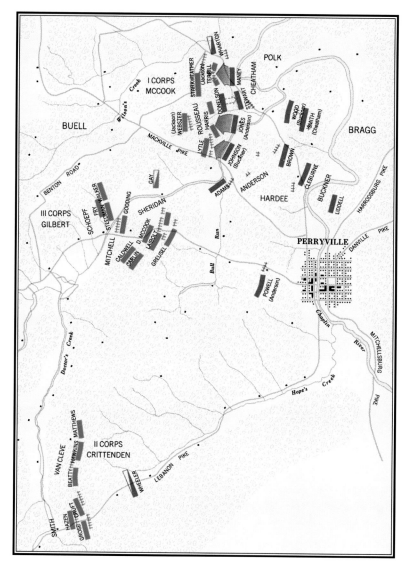

Most of the fighting at the Battle of Perryville took place northwest of the town, where Bragg assailed the Federal left. The attacks eventually stalled due to heavy losses and the Confederates were finally compelled to retire.

ahead. This done, he went to report his success to army headquarters, three miles back down the road. He got there about 12.30 to find that McCook had just arrived. Much to Buell's relief, his two divisions were filing in on the Mackville road to take position on Gilbert's left, separated from it by a quarter-mile-wide valley cradling a bend of Doctor's Creek. Within another half hour, more good news was received: Crittenden too was at hand, entering by the Lebanon road and preparing to move northward up the ridge beyond the creek, taking position on Gilbert's right and thus extending the line of battle.

    During these early afternoon hours everything was falling into place, as if the pieces of an enormous jigsaw puzzle had suddenly interlocked of their

own accord: a common enough phenomenon, but one that never failed to exhil-
arate and amaze. Except for Sill's division, which was on the way from Frankfort, and the green division under Dumont, which was continuing the feint,
Buell at last had all his troops collected. Eight divisions, with an over-all
strength of 55,000 men, were posted along a six-mile front. His latest information was that Hardee was definitely at Perryville with two divisions. What else
might be there he did not know, but for the present all was suspiciously quiet in
that direction. At any rate, the Federal fist was clenched and ready to strike.

This time, though, it was Buell's turn to be beaten to the punch —
with results a good deal more costly than the loss of a few spare pools of brackish water. What would be lost now was blood.

Bragg had waited at Harrodsburg through the early morning hours,
cocking an ear to catch the steady roar of guns ten miles southwest, which
would signify that the attack he had ordered was under way; but, hearing nothing, had ridden down to Perryville to see for himself the reason for delay. Arriving about 10 o'clock, he found Polk reconnoitering the high ground near the
confluence of Doctor's Creek and Chaplin River. The three divisions were in
line: from right to left, Buckner, Patton Anderson, and Cheatham, the latter
posted near the town itself, while Wheeler's cavalry was off to the south, making
a show of strength in that direction. Except for the occasional pop of an outpost
rifle, a heavy silence overhung the field. Confronted by Bragg, who wanted to
know why his orders to "give the enemy battle immediately" had not been carried out, Polk explained that he was convinced that most of Buell's entire army
was gathering in his front. What was more, the Yankees had struck first. Consequently, he had called another council of war, and "in view of the great disparity
of our forces," he and Hardee had decided "to adopt the defensive-offensive, to
await the movements of the enemy, and to be guided by events as they were
developed." In short, he "did not regard [last night's] letter of instructions as
a peremptory order to attack at all hazards, but that . . . I should carry the
instructions into execution as judiciously and promptly as a willing mind and
sound discretion would allow."

So he said, then and later. However, he added that he had observed
signs of activity here on the Federal left and had decided to switch Cheatham's
division to this flank in order to guard against being overlapped in this direction.
If Bragg approved, he would convert this into an offensive as soon as the men
were in position. Bragg did approve, emphatically, and Polk began to make his
dispositions accordingly, massing Cheatham's and Buckner's divisions under
cover of the woods beyond the confluence of the creek and river. They would
be supported by two brigades from Anderson, whose remaining two brigades
would make a simultaneous holding attack to the south and west, thereby discouraging any weakening of the enemy right to bolster the left when it was

assailed. By 1 o'clock, apparently without Federal detection of what was going on behind the screen of trees, the butternut troops were in assault formation, supported rank on rank by heavy concentrations of artillery. Soon afterward, Polk passed the word for both divisions to move forward.

The attack could scarcely have come at a more propitious time: propitious for the Confederates, that is. The bluecoats Polk had spotted late that morning on the Federal left were members of McCook's advance elements, reconnoitering for occupation of the position by his two divisions shortly after noon. While they were filing in, McCook himself rode back to report to Buell at army headquarters, having explained to the commander of his lead division, Brigadier General J. S. Jackson, that he was to form a line of battle along the near bank of Chaplin River. Jackson was glad to hear this, for his men were thirsty after their dusty march. So was his senior brigade commander, Brigadier General William Terrill, whom he told to advance his skirmishers to the river bank as soon as he had his troops in attack formation. "I'll do it, and that's my water," Terrill said. He was a Union-loyal Virginian. In fact, he was the former cadet Sheridan had lunged at with a bayonet, ten years ago at the Academy. Since then, they had shaken hands and agreed to forget their grievance. Sheridan was thankful ever afterwards that they had staged this reconciliation; for Terrill was dead within an hour of his arrival on the field.

Cheatham and Buckner struck with tremendous force and all the added impact of surprise, emerging suddenly from the drowsy-looking woods in a roaring charge. Terrill's men were mostly green, and being taken thus while they were advancing toward their baptism of fire, they heard in the rebel yell the fulfillment of their dry-mouthed apprehensions. Jackson, who was with them when the blow fell, was killed by one of the first volleys. They wavered, then broke completely when a bullet cut down Terrill. Behind them, the other deploying brigades were also taken unawares. Some of the men fled at once under the shock. Others stood and fought, sometimes hand to hand. Steadily, though, they were thrown back, the massed Confederate batteries knocking down the stone walls and fences behind which the retreating Federals had sought refuge. A mile or more they were driven, losing fifteen guns in the process. By the time McCook returned from the rear he found his two divisions near demoralization and utter ruin staring him in the face. In this extremity he called across the way for help from Gilbert.

That general also had his hands full, however. Or anyhow he thought so. He had repulsed Anderson's attack down the south bank of the creek, but he did not know how soon another would be launched or in what strength. Sheridan, from his advanced position on the left, could look across the intervening valley and see the graybacks sweeping westward, driving McCook's troops before them. All he could do for the present was turn his guns in that direction, heaving shells into the flank of the gray columns as they crossed his line of fire. This threw them into considerable confusion and encouraged Gilbert to detach first one brigade, then another, to go to McCook's assistance. When they had left, he counterattacked with his right-flank brigade and drove Anderson back on Perryville, capturing a fifteen-wagon ammunition train. But this was late in the day. Having advanced so far, the brigade commander put his

A Virginian loyal to the Union, William Terrill was mortally wounded while trying to rally his brigade.

batteries in position west of the town and, firing his shells across the rooftops, engaged some rebel guns on the opposite side until darkness put an end to the duel and relieved the terror of the civilians, who had crouched in their cellars and heard the projectiles arching overhead with a flutter as of wings.

Such was Gilbert's contribution, and such was the contribution of his 20,000 men, who faced barely 2500 Confederates while McCook and his 12,500 were being mauled by nearly equal numbers, just beyond easy musket range on the left. Crittenden, on the right with 22,500 men, contributed even less; in fact he contributed nothing at all, being bluffed into immobility by Joe Wheeler's 1200 horsemen and two guns. Thus it was that 16,000 rebels could successfully challenge 55,000 bluecoats, not more than half of whom were seriously engaged. In partial extenuation, because of unusual atmospheric and topographical factors reminiscent of Grant's experience with the ill wind at Iuka, the clatter of musketry did not carry far today; so that in this respect the six-mile-long scene of action (or nonaction) was compartmented, each sector being sealed off from the others as if by soundproof walls. One Union staff officer, riding the field, later made the incredible statement that "at one bound my horse carried me from stillness into the uproar of battle." Partially, too, this explained the lack of over-all control which should have remedied the drawback of temporary deafness. Buell, nursing yesterday's bruises back at headquarters, not only did not know what had hit him today; it was after 4 o'clock before he even knew he had been struck.

By that time the battle was more than two hours old, and the Confederates too had been thrown into considerable confusion. This was accomplished partly by Sheridan's gunners, bowling shells across the narrow valley to crush the flank of the advancing files, toppling men like tenpins — including Pat

Cleburne, who had recovered from the face wound he had suffered at Richmond in time to receive a leg wound here when his horse was shot from under him by one of the fast-firing guns across the way — and partly by the disorganization incident to the rapid advance itself. Units had intermingled, not only gray and gray, but also blue and gray, as some stood fast and others retreated. On both sides there was much anguished crying of "*Friends!* You are firing into friends!" However, this too was not without its advantages to the attackers: particularly in one instance. When the commander of one of the brigades Gilbert had sent to reinforce McCook approached an imposing-looking officer to ask for instructions as to the posting of his troops — "I have come to your assistance with my brigade!" the Federal shouted above the uproar — the gentleman calmly sitting his horse in the midst of carnage turned out to be Polk, who was wearing a dark-gray uniform. Polk asked the designation of the newly arrived command, and upon being told raised his eyebrows in surprise. For all his churchly faith in miracles, he could scarcely believe his ears. "There must be some mistake about this," he said. "You are my prisoner."

Fighting without its commander, the brigade gave an excellent account of itself. Joined presently by the other brigade sent over from the center, it did much to stiffen the resistance being offered by the remnants of McCook's two divisions. Sundown came before the rebels could complete the rout begun four hours ago, and now in the dusk it was Polk's turn to play a befuddled role in another comic incident of confused identity. He saw in the fading light a body of men whom he took to be Confederates firing obliquely

This period watercolor depicts General Polk in a stern, overbearing pose familiar to many men who served under him.

into the flank of one of his engaged brigades. "Dear me," he said to himself. "This is very sad and must be stopped." None of his staff being with him at the time, he rode over to attend to the matter in person. When he came up to the erring commander and demanded in angry tones what he meant by shooting his own friends, the colonel replied with surprise:

"I don't think there can be any mistake about it. I am sure they are the enemy."

"Enemy!" Polk exclaimed, taken aback by this apparent insubordination. "Why, I have only just left them myself. Cease firing, sir! What is your name, sir?"

"Colonel Shryock, of the 87th Indiana," the Federal said. "And pray, sir, who are you?"

The bishop-general, learning thus for the first time that the man was a Yankee and that he was in rear of a whole regiment of Yankees, determined to brazen out the situation by taking further advantage of the fact that his dark-gray blouse looked blue-black in the twilight. He rode closer and shook his fist in the colonel's face, shouting angrily: "I'll soon show you who I am, sir! Cease firing, sir, at once!" Then he turned his horse and, calling in an authoritative manner for the bluecoats to cease firing, slowly rode back toward his own lines. He was afraid to ride fast, he later explained, because haste might give his identity away; yet "at the same time I experienced a disagreeable sensation, like screwing up my back, and calculated how many bullets would be between my shoulders every moment."

Screened at last by a small copse, he put the spurs to his horse and galloped back to the proper side of the irregular firing line. But the fighting was practically over by now. Two of his brigades had been withdrawn to meet Gilbert's threat to the left rear, ending all chance for a farther advance, even if Bragg had been willing to risk a night engagement. Presently even the guns east and west of Perryville ceased their high-angle quarrel across the rooftops. . . . Buell had fought his first battle, and fought it badly, having been assaulted and outdone by an army less than a third the size of his own. More than 7600 men had fallen: 4211 Federals, 3396 Confederates. The former had had 845 killed, 2851 wounded, and 515 captured or missing, while the latter had lost 510, 2635, and 251 in those same categories. Buell consoled himself for this disparity by predicting that the conflict would "stand conspicuous for its severity in the history of the rebellion." Bragg agreed, later reporting that "for the time engaged, it was the severest and most desperately contested engagement within my knowledge."

The moon being only just past the full, the night was nearly as bright as day, and there were those in the Union army who were in favor of launching an immediate full-scale counterattack. Buell himself had tried to get such a movement under way on the right as soon as he discovered he had a battle on his hands; but the messenger, who set out at 4.15 with a verbal order for Thomas to have Crittenden move forward, got lost in the tricky bottoms of Doctor's Creek and did not find him till past sunset. Thomas, who was convinced that the rebels were in heavy strength to his front, sent back word that it was too late for an attack today, but that he would "advance in the morning with the first sound of action on the left." Dissatisfied with this dependence on his shattered left, which he knew was in no condition for more fighting, Buell replied that Thomas was to tell Crittenden "to press his command forward as much as possible [tonight] and be prepared to attack at daylight in the morning." The Virginian then rode back to army headquarters, where Buell repeated these instructions after midnight. Thomas passed them along to Crittenden at 1.30: "Have your different divisions ready to attack at daylight. Issue orders at once." Crittenden replied: "I am all ready. My post will be to the rear of the center of the line."

Morning came, October 9, but with it there came to headquarters no sound of conflict on the right. Buell waited, then waited some more. At 8 o'clock, three hours past dawn, he had his chief of staff send Crittenden the message: "Have you commenced the advance? What delays your attack?" Crittenden replied that he had received no orders to attack; he had been told, rather, to have his troops "ready to attack," and that was precisely what he had done. If they wanted him to go forward, let them say so. Exasperated, Buell told him to get moving, and he did. But Bragg was gone.

★ ★ ★ The Confederates had pulled out after midnight. Convinced at last that he had most of Buell's army to his front, and moreover having accomplished what he had intended when he told Polk to "rout him" and thus gain time for a concentration to the east, Bragg ordered a prompt junction with Kirby Smith, whom he instructed to move forward from Versailles to Harrodsburg for that purpose. Two miles short of the latter place, having crossed the Salt and burned the bridges behind him, Polk halted and formed a line of battle in the rain, the long drouth apparently having been broken by the booming of heavy guns the day before. Receiving word from Wheeler, who had charge of the rear-guard cavalry, that the Federals had not ventured beyond Perryville today, Polk rode with Chaplain C. T. Quintard — afterwards a bishop like himself — to an Episcopal church in Harrodsburg, where the Tennessee chaplain donned his surplice and stole and entered the sanctuary. While Polk knelt at the altar, Quintard read the litany and pronounced the benediction, accompanied by the murmur of rain against the stained-glass windows. Overcome by emotion as he contrasted the peace of the present interlude with what he had seen yesterday in one of the

★

great battles of that fratricidal war, the gray-clad bishop bowed his head and wept.

Kirby Smith arrived next morning, several hours before Buell at last came up. Bragg now had all his available troops consolidated, and that night the two armies lay face to face outside the town, each waiting to see what the other was going to do. "Fifty thousand effectives" was Buell's estimate of the Confederate strength, and though he himself had sixty thousand — including Sill, who had promised to join him "*without fail* tomorrow, I think" — he could not forget that Bragg, with less than a third his present number of men, had wrecked one wing of the Federal army when it had been nearly as large as it was now. So Buell did nothing, waiting for Bragg to show his hand. And Bragg did nothing either.

"For God's sake, General," Smith exclaimed, "let us fight Buell here."

"I will do it, sir," Bragg replied.

But he did not. Whatever it was that had come over him three weeks ago at Munfordville, when he stood aside while Buell passed around his flank and on to Louisville, came over him again. What was more, disheartening news from North Mississippi informed him that Van Dorn and Price had failed at Corinth, just as Lee had failed in Maryland; Bragg's was the only one of the three intended invasion barbs still stuck in the enemy's hide. Besides, unable to see that he had much to gain from a victory — whereas a defeat might cost him not only the bountiful supply of goods and foodstuffs he had collected, but also his army — he had already decided to withdraw. As he put it in the letter to his wife, "With the whole southwest thus in the enemy's possession, my crime would have been unpardonable had I kept my noble little army to be ice-bound in a northern clime, without tents or shoes, and obliged to forage daily for bread, etc."

Evincing what one observer called "a perplexity and vacillation which had now become simply appalling to Smith, to Hardee, and to Polk," Bragg ordered a retreat toward Bryantsville that night. At dawn, when Buell found the southern army gone again, he could scarcely believe that it was not maneuvering for a better position in which to fight the battle which he, and indeed practically everyone else in both armies except Bragg, believed was about to be fought. He followed warily through Harrodsburg, waiting for Bragg to make a stand or else come flailing back at him, guns booming. Beyond Dick's (or Dix) River, the Confederates again formed line of battle near Camp Dick Robinson, but Buell once more found the position too strong for him to risk attacking it. For a full day Bragg stayed there; then on the following day, October 13, when Buell sidled around toward the south, threatening his line of retreat, he got under way in earnest for Cumberland Gap. As long ago as September 29, anticipating withdrawal from Kentucky ten days before the Battle of Perryville, he had ordered 100,000 rations collected there, as well as another 200,000 at London, half way between the present position of his army and the gap.

The retreat — though Bragg did not call it that; he called it a with-

*During the war, the Federals transformed
Nashville's railroad depot into the central
hub of the Union's rail network in Tennessee.*

drawal, the successful completion of a giant raid — was in two columns, Polk and
Hardee marching by way of Lancaster and Crab Orchard, Kirby Smith by way of
Big Hill, accompanying the heavy-laden trains. It was, as a later observer remarked,
"a dismal but picturesque affair." Cavalry fanned out front and rear and flankwards
to protect the enormous droves of hogs, sheep, and beef cattle, herded by cowboys
recruited from Texas regiments. Conspicuous among the motley aggregation of ve-
hicles in the creaking train, which included carriages, omnibuses, and stagecoaches
pressed into service to remove the mountain of supplies, were the 400 bright new
wagons, each with "US" stenciled on its canvas, which had been captured nearby
from Nelson in late August. Approaching Big Hill from the opposite direction,

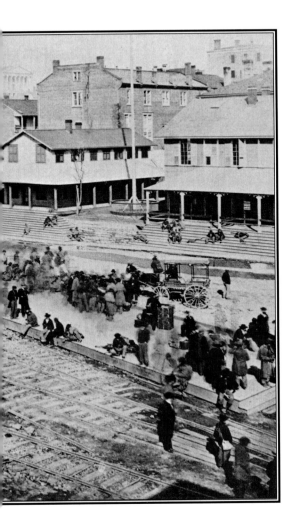

Smith was feeling none of the elation he had experienced then, with victory still before him, not behind. "My command from loss of sleep for five nights, is completely exhausted," he reported during the early morning hours of October 14. "The straggling has been unusually great. The rear of the column will not reach here before daybreak. I have no hope of saving the whole of my train, as I shall be obliged to double teams in going up Big Hill, and will necessarily be delayed there two or three days."

His near-despair was based on an overrating of Buell, who he thought would press him hard, and an underrating of his own troops, particularly those in the rear guard under Wheeler. These horsemen fought no less than twenty-six separate engagements during the first five days and nights of the march — one for each year of their youthful colonel's life — beating off Feder-

al attempts to hack at the long, slow-moving line of wagons. By dawn of the second day, however, Smith's gloom had deepened. Still at Big Hill, he notified Bragg: "I have little hope of saving any of the train, and fear much of the artillery will be lost." But here again he was unduly pessimistic. While Stevenson's division held a line beyond range of the hill, Heth's men lined the difficult slope from foot to summit and, as one of them later wrote, when "starved and tired mules faltered and fell, seized the wagons and lifted them by sheer force over the worst places." All day, all night, until noon of the following day, October 16, "the trains, in one unbroken stream, continued to pour over Big Hill, and then the troops followed." Smith felt considerably better now, having broken into the clear. Even the fact that this was hostile country had its advantages, since it encouraged stragglers to keep up. Beyond Mount Vernon next day at Big Rockcastle River, he appealed to Polk, who had already crossed: "Cannot we unite and end this disastrous retreat by a glorious victory?"

But even if Bragg had been willing — which he was not — it was too late. Hearing from Nashville this same day that a Confederate force was "rapidly concentrating" against that place, Buell broke contact just beyond London, abandoned the pursuit, and turned west. "I have no apprehension," the Nashville commander had assured him; but Buell more than made up for this lack. He was apprehensive not only for the safety of the Tennessee capital but also for the safety of his army, which by now had entered the barrens. He wired Halleck: "The enemy has been driven into the heart of this desert and must go on, for he cannot exist in it. For the same reason we cannot pursue in it with any hope of overtaking him, for while he is moving back on his supplies and as he goes consuming what the country affords we must bring ours forward. . . . I deem it useless and inexpedient to continue the pursuit, but propose to direct the main force under my command rapidly upon Nashville, which General Negley reported to me as already being invested by a considerable force and toward which I have no doubt Bragg will move the main part of his army."

In thus abandoning the pursuit, which in the end might have taken him into East Tennessee — the one region Lincoln most wanted "delivered" — Buell knew that he was fanning the wrath of his superiors, who had removed him from command once already and had restored him only under political pressure after his successor had declined the post. Anticipating what would follow, he told Halleck: "While I shall proceed with these dispositions, deeming them to be proper for the public interest, it is but meet that I should say that the present time is perhaps as convenient as any for making any change that may be thought proper in the command of this army." And having thus invited his dismissal, he said of the army he had led: "It has not accomplished all that I had hoped or all that faction might demand; yet, composed as it is, one half of perfectly new troops, it has defeated a powerful and thoroughly disciplined army in one battle and has driven it away baffled and dispirited at least, and as much demoralized as an army can be under such discipline as Bragg maintains over all troops that he commands."

Bragg would have appreciated the closing compliment, dealing as it did with the quality on which he placed the strongest emphasis, but just now he was satisfied with being allowed to continue his withdrawal unmolested. He pressed on through Barbourville, leaving Kirby Smith to bring up the rear. That general, much disgusted, formally resumed command of the Department of East Tennessee on October 20, as soon as he reached Flat Lick, Kentucky. Approaching Cumberland Gap two days later, he was astounded and enraged to receive from Bragg, already in Knoxville, orders for him to leave 3000 men at that strategic point and prepare the remainder for another joint incursion — this time into Middle Tennessee. His troops were "worn down," he replied, "much in want of shoes, clothing, and blankets," and reduced by straggling to about 6000 effectives. "Having resumed the command of my department," he added pointedly, "I am directly responsible to the Government for the condition and safety of my army." It was in effect a bill of divorcement. He wanted no more joint campaigns, not with Bragg at any rate, and doubtless he was relieved to find the North Carolinian gone from Knoxville when he himself arrived October 24, so weary and discouraged that he slipped into town under cover of darkness in order to avoid a public reception planned in his honor. The main thing he wanted now was rest, which he hoped would enable him to forget the final lap of his seventy-day round-trip journey through Central Kentucky.

No such rousing welcome had been planned for Bragg, whose problem on his return was the avoidance, not of praise, but of blame amounting to downright condemnation. Though he had never courted or apparently even desired popularity, much preferring to be respected for the sternness of his discipline rather than admired for the warmth of his nature — of which, in truth, he had little — this opprobrium, heaped on the shoulders of the man who had conceived and led the most successful offensive so far launched by a Confederate commander outside the strict national limits, seemed to him as unfair as it was unrealistic. Where Lee had failed, for example, he (Bragg) had succeeded, not only with a smaller army against longer odds, but with far fewer casualties and far greater material results; yet Lee was praised and he was blamed. In his final report of the campaign, submitted some months later, though he avoided comparisons, he attempted to refute his critics point by point. Whatever there was of failure, or shortcoming, he assigned to the backwardness of the expected Kentucky volunteers, who by their lack of native patriotism — so he called or thought of it — had forced him to travel the long road back to Tennessee with 20,000 unused muskets in his wagons. Nor was he reticent in summing up his gains:

> *Though compelled to yield to largely superior numbers and fortuitous circumstances a portion of the valuable territory from which we had driven the enemy, the fruits of the campaign were very large and have had a most important bearing upon our subsequent military operations here and elsewhere. With a force enabling us at no time to put more than 40,000 men of all arms and in all places in battle, we had redeemed North Alabama and Middle Tennessee and recovered possession of Cumberland Gap, the gateway to the heart of the Confederacy. We had killed, wounded, and captured no less than 25,000 of the enemy; taken*

over 30 pieces of artillery, 17,000 small-arms, some 2,000,000

cartridges for the same; destroyed some hundreds of wagons and

brought off several hundreds more with their teams and harness

complete; replaced our jaded horses by a fine mount; lived two

months upon supplies wrested from the enemy's possession;

secured material to clothe the army, and finally secured subsist-

ence from the redeemed country to support not only the army

but also a large force of the Confederacy to the present time.

Though some of this was actually understated, it made no real impression on his critics. They were not so much concerned with what he had done, which admittedly was considerable, as they were with what he had not done. In fact, their complaints in this respect were so immediately vociferous that on October 23, the day after he reached Knoxville, Bragg was summoned to Richmond by a wire from the Adjutant General, who informed him: "The President desires . . . that you will lose no time in coming here." Amid rumors that he was about to be relieved, he caught an eastbound train the following morning, thus avoiding a meeting with Kirby Smith, who arrived that night.

★ ★ ★ *W*hatever weight Davis and Cooper might attach to Bragg's claims in determining whether to sustain or fire him, Lincoln and Halleck apparently were inclined not only to accept them at face value, but also to deduct them from what little credit his opponent had left in their direction. Receiving Buell's dispatch of October 17, wherein he announced that he was abandoning the pursuit to return to Nashville, the general-in-chief replied next morning: "The great object to be attained is to drive the enemy from Kentucky and East Tennessee. If we cannot do it now we need never to hope for it." This was followed by another wire, in which Halleck brought Lincoln's logic to bear by indirect quotation, reinforcing the protest he had made the day before: "The capture of East Tennessee should be the main object of your campaign. You say it is the heart of the enemy's resources; make it the heart of yours. Your army can live there if the enemy's can. . . . I am directed by the President to say to you that your army must enter East Tennessee this fall, and that it ought to move there while the roads are passable. . . . He does not understand why we cannot march as the enemy marches, live as he lives, and fight as he fights, unless we admit the inferiority of our troops and of our generals."

★

Logic was a knife that could cut both ways, however, and prewar service in the Adjutant General's office had made Buell familiar with its use. He replied October 20 with a long, closely reasoned exegesis on the difficulties of what was being required of him. But that was not what Lincoln and Halleck wanted to hear. Besides, as an indication of his progress, the sequential headings on his telegrams — Mount Vernon, Crab Orchard, Danville — spoke a clearer language than their contents. Despite his former suggestion that "the present time is perhaps as convenient as any for making any change that may be thought proper," Buell's military life line was running out much faster than he thought. Previously, after being relieved, he had been restored to command partly as a result of political pressure in his favor; but such pressure as was being exerted now was in the opposite direction. His old enemy Governor Morton, for example, was wiring Lincoln: "The butchery of our troops at Perryville was terrible. . . . Nothing but success, speedy and decided, will save our cause from utter destruction. In the Northwest distrust and despair are seizing upon the hearts of the people." Armed with this, and presently reinforced by similar expressions of displeasure from Yates of Illinois and Tod of Ohio, Halleck told Buell on October 22: "It is the wish of the Government that your army proceed to and occupy East Tennessee with all possible dispatch. It leaves to you the selection of the roads upon which to move to that object. . . . Neither the Government nor the country can endure these repeated delays. Both require a prompt and immediate movement toward the accomplishment of the great object in view — the holding of East Tennessee."

Buell now had his orders, the first specific ones he had received. But before he could put them into execution (and on the same day Bragg left Knoxville, bound for Richmond) the following was delivered:

Washington, October 24

Maj. Gen. D. C. Buell, Commanding, &c.:

General: The President directs that on the presentation

of this order you will turn over your command to Maj. Gen.

W. S. Rosecrans, and repair to Indianapolis, Ind., reporting from

that place to the Adjutant General of the Army for further orders.

Very respectfully, your obedient servant,

H. W. Halleck

General-in-Chief.

★　★　★

★

*Lincoln and McClellan (center),
flanked by other Federal officers,
face each other near the Antietam
battlefield two weeks after the
nation's bloodiest day.*

SIX

Lincoln's Late-Fall Disappointments

1862 ★ ★ ★ ★ ★ **Buell was not the first nor was he the last** of the blue-clad puppets whose strings had been cut, or would be cut, in what turned out to be a season of dismissals. Others had been or were about to be packed away in their boxes, mute, their occupations gone like Othello's and themselves removed, like him, from "the big wars, That make ambition virtue." Halleck, from his position near the vital center, had forecast the political weather at the outset, back in August, when he told a friend: "I can hardly describe to you the feeling of disappointment here in the want of activity," and added: "The Government seems determined to apply the guillotine to all unsuccessful generals. It seems rather hard to do this where the general is not in fault, but perhaps with us now, as in the French Revolution, some harsh measures are required."

The ax was descending. Pope's head rolled before Buell's; McDowell, too — though admittedly he was more sinned against than sinning — was gone, complaining wistfully as he went: "I did not ask to be relieved. I only asked for a court." Even the navy, barnacle-encrusted during the nearly fifty peacetime years since the War of 1812, had stretched some necks beneath the blade. Down on the Gulf, glad to be breathing salt air after the Vicksburg-*Arkansas* fiasco, Farragut gave his late-summer and early-fall attention to the

★

Texas coast, where the blockaders worked without the advantage of a lodgment on the mainland. With this in mind, he sent out three expeditions in as many months. The first attacked Corpus Christi in mid-August but, having no occupation troops, withdrew after giving the place a pounding. Next month the second expedition went up Sabine Pass, wrecked the railroad bridge and the fort at Sabine City, captured a pair of rebel steamers, and retired again to the bay. The third was more ambitious, being aimed at Galveston. It was also more successful. Two regular gunboats and two converted ferries hit the port on October 5, drove the Confederates out with a few well-aimed salvos, then landed a token force of 260 men commanded by a colonel; after which, by a tacit understanding, the warships patrolling the bay refrained from further shelling on condition that the rebels would not move artillery into Galveston over the two-mile-long bridge connecting the island town with the mainland. Alabama was now the only southern state with an unoccupied coast, and Farragut had redeemed, at least in part, his midsummer performance up the Mississippi.

Gratifying as this redemption was to Secretary Welles — whom Lincoln dubbed "Father Neptune" and sometimes "Noah" — it also called attention to the contrast between the Tennessee sailor's make-up and that of his former upriver partner, the Boston Brahmin Charles H. Davis, who had run into little but trouble since he replaced Foote as flotilla commander on the upper Mississippi, back in May. He was, as one of his officers said, "a most charming and lovable man," author of two esoteric books, and a member of the commission which had planned the strikes at Hatteras and Port Royal, but it was becoming increasingly apparent that he lacked what Farragut had and what Foote had had before him: a hard-driving, bulldog, cut-and-slash aggressiveness, a preference for action at close quarters, and a burning sense of personal insult at the slightest advantage gained by an opponent at his expense. Since it was this quality, or combination of qualities, which would be needed for the work that lay ahead on the big river, Welles decided Captain Davis had to go. In mid-October he acted. Davis was eased upstairs to the Bureau of Navigation, where he would find work better suited to his intellectual capacities.

There was little that was surprising in this removal. What was surprising was the Secretary's choice of a successor: David Dixon Porter. Porter was only a junior commander, so that to give him the job Welles had to disappoint and outrage more than eighty senior officers. Besides, there were personal drawbacks. Like his brother Dirty Bill, Porter was not above claiming other men's glory as his own; he would stretch or varnish the truth to serve his purpose; he would undermine a superior; he would promise a good deal more than he could deliver — all of which he had done at New Orleans, and then had gone on to do them again at Vicksburg. Yet he had virtues, too, of the sort which Othello said proceeded from ambition in "the big wars." Like Lincoln in his pre-Manassas judg-

An abrasive self-promoter, Admiral David Dixon Porter had few friends, but no one doubted his reputation as a first-rate gunboat commander.

ment of John Pope, Welles apparently believed that "a liar might [yet] be brave and have skill as an officer." Weighing the virtues against the vices, the gray-bearded brown-wigged naval head confided in his diary: "Porter is but a Commander. He has, however, stirring and positive qualities, is fertile in resources, has great energy, excessive and sometimes not overscrupulous ambition; is impressed with and boastful of his own powers, given to exaggeration in relation to himself — a Porter infirmity — is not generous to older and superior living officers, whom he is too ready to traduce, but is kind and patronizing to favorites who are juniors; is given to cliquism, but is brave and daring like all his family. He has not the conscientious and high moral qualities of Foote to organize the flotilla, and is not considered by some of our best naval men a fortunate officer. His selection will be unsatisfactory to many, but his field of operations is peculiar, and a young and active officer is required for the duty to which he is assigned."

Having decided that the credits overbalanced the debits, in weight if not in number, Welles called Porter into his office and informed him that he was being sent as an acting rear admiral to take charge of the navy on the western waters. The order was dated October 9; Porter, who had come north on leave, hoping to cure a touch of fever he had contracted in the region to which his chief was now returning him, accepted both the assignment and the promotion

★

as no more than his due. Six days later he was in Cairo, where he assumed command of the 125 vessels comprising the Mississippi Squadron, together with 1300 officers, only twenty-five of whom had been in the old navy, and approximately 10,000 sailors. What he would do with these boats and officers and men — and whether Welles would be sustained by circumstance in his choice of a man whose character he doubted — remained to be seen.

At any rate, Buell and Davis had been brought down. And now as October wore toward a close, giving occasion in the East for a mocking revival of "All Quiet Along the Potomac," Lincoln was after larger game. In fact he was after the top-ranking man in the whole U.S. Army: George B. McClellan. The other two had been wing shots — targets of opportunity, so to speak — but this one he was stalking with care, intending to catch him on the sit.

According to some observers this should not be difficult, since that was the Young Napoleon's accustomed attitude. The managing editor of the New York *Tribune*, for example, had written privately in late September, a week

As October wore toward a close, giving occasion in the East for a mocking revival of "All Quiet Along the Potomac," Lincoln was after larger game.

after the Battle of Antietam, that one of his reporters had just returned from the army, "and his notion is that it is to be quiet along the Potomac for some time to come. George, whom Providence helps according to his nature, has got himself on one side of a ditch, which Providence had already made for him, with the enemy on the other, and has no idea of moving. Wooden-head at Washington will never think of sending a force through the mountains to attack Lee in the rear, so the two armies will watch each other for nobody knows how many weeks, and we shall have the poetry of war with pickets drinking from the same stream, holding friendly converse and sending newspapers across by various ingenious contrivances." In other words, this Indian summer, with its firm roads and its fair skies tinged with woodsmoke, was to be wasted, militarily, like the last one, in getting ready for a movement which bad weather would postpone. Whether the country would stand for another such winter of apparent inactivity Lincoln did not know. But he himself could not; nor did he intend to.

On the first day of October, without sending word that he was coming, he boarded a train and rode out to Western Maryland to see the general and his army. McClellan, however, got word that he was on the way and met

★

him at Harpers Ferry. Pleased to find that the President had brought no politicians with him, "merely some western officers," McClellan wrote his wife: "His ostensible purpose is to see the troops and the battlefield; I incline to think that the real purpose of his visit is to push me into a premature advance into Virginia. I may be mistaken, but think not."

He was not mistaken. That was precisely why Lincoln had come; "I went up to the field to try to get [McClellan] to move," he said later. But as usual when he was face to face with Little Mac, discussing military matters, he got nowhere. Apparently he did not really try very hard; the primary inertia was too great. When he urged an advance, McClellan went into an explanation of shortages and drawbacks, and Lincoln dropped the subject. According to the general, "He more than once assured me that he was fully satisfied with my whole course from the beginning; that the only fault he could possibly find was that I was perhaps too prone to be sure that everything was ready before acting, but that my actions were all right when I started." Later they sat on a hillside, Lincoln with his long legs drawn up so that his knees were almost under his chin, and McClellan afterwards wrote that Lincoln told him: "General, you have saved the country. You must remain in command and carry us through to the end." When McClellan said that this would be impossible — "The influences at Washington will be too strong for you, Mr President. I will not be allowed the required time for preparation" — Lincoln replied: "General, I pledge myself to stand between you and harm."

It was a three-day visit, and much of the time was spent reviewing the troops. The President "looked pale," according to one veteran who saw him, while another remarked that as he "rode around every battalion [he] seemed much worn and distressed and to be looking for those who were gone." Doubtless he was thinking of the fallen, but he was also thinking of the men he saw — and of what they represented. A Union surgeon noted that Lincoln was "well received" by the soldiers, "but by no means so enthusiastically as General McClellan." Lincoln did not mind this much. What he minded was the thought that this gave rise to. "The Army of the Potomac is my army as much as any army ever belonged to the man that created it," McClellan told a member of his staff about this time. "We have grown together and fought together. We are wedded and should not be separated." The army felt that way, too, and Lincoln knew it. He also knew that if the soldiers felt it strongly enough, mutiny would follow any order for the general's removal from command. This was much on his mind during the visit, and resulted in a curious scene. Just before dawn of the second morning, he woke O. M. Hatch, an Illinois friend. "Come, Hatch," he said, "I want you to take a walk with me." Together they climbed to a hilltop overlooking the camps, and as sunrise lighted the valley where the troops lay waiting for reveille, Lincoln made an abstracted gesture, indicating the tented plain below. "Hatch, Hatch," he said in a husky voice, barely above a whisper. "What is all this?" His companion was confused. "Why, Mr Lincoln, this is the Army of the Potomac," he replied. Lincoln shook his head. "No, Hatch, no. This is General McClellan's bodyguard."

He returned to Washington, October 4. Two days later Halleck astonished McClellan with a telegraphic dispatch: "The President directs that you cross the Potomac and give battle to the enemy or drive him south. Your army must move now while the roads are good. . . . I am directed to add that the Secretary of War and the General-in-Chief concur with the President in these instructions." McClellan replied that he was "pushing everything as rapidly as possible in order to get ready for the advance." Beyond this bare acknowledgment, however, the only sign he gave that he had received the directive was a step-up in the submission of requisitions for more supplies of every description. He wanted shoes, hospital tents, and horses: especially horses, the need for which was presently emphasized by Jeb Stuart, who once more covered himself with glory at the Young Napoleon's expense.

Under instructions from Lee to scout the Federal dispositions — and, if possible, destroy the railroad bridge over the Conococheague near Chambersburg, which would limit McClellan's rail supply facilities to the B & O — Stuart crossed the Potomac above Martinsburg at early dawn, October 10. He had with him 1800 horsemen and four guns. By noon he was across the Pennsylvania line, approaching Mercersburg. Soon after dark, the lights of Chambersburg were in view. Demanding and receiving the surrender of the place, he appointed Wade Hampton "Military Governor," quite as if he intended to stay there all fall, and bivouacked that night in the streets of the town. There were two disappointments. A bank official had escaped with all the cash in the vault, and the Conococheague bridge, being built of iron, proved indestructible. However, there were material compensations, including the capture and parole of 280 bluecoats, the opportunity to spend Confederate money in well-stocked Pennsylvania stores, and the impressment of more than a thousand excellent horses. Many of these last were draft animals of Norman and Belgian stock, and it was fortunate that they were seized in harness, since no southern quartermaster could furnish collars large enough for the big-necked creatures soon to be hauling rebel guns and wagons. Their former owners, never having seen an actual secessionist, were under the impression that Stuart's troopers were Federal soldiers, sent to harass farmers suspected of disloyalty, and many of them protested indignantly as the raiders led their heavy-footed animals away: "I'm just as good a Union man as any of you!"

Jeb's men had come nearly forty miles to reach their assigned objective, stirring up a hive of enemy cavalry in the process, and now the problem was how to get them back. Stuart met it as he had done before. When the column formed outside Chambersburg next morning, he led it, not southwest in the direction he had come from, but due east. Though he would have to ride more than twice as far to reach the Potomac by this route, it gave him the advantage of being unexpected along the way. The gray-jackets whooped at this evidence that they were about to repeat their Peninsula performance by staging another "Ride Around McClellan." Eastward they rode, beyond the Blue Ridge, on through Cashtown, where they stopped to feed the horses, then turned south, avoiding the college town of Gettysburg, eight miles off. Late that afternoon they recrossed the Pennsylvania line and entered Emmitsburg; beyond which, riding in darkness now and frequently changing to captured horses to spare their own, they forded the Monocacy. Some fought sleep by dismounting to walk a mile or so from time to time. Others slumped in their saddles and frankly slept, their snores droning loud above the hoofclops.

Word of the raid had spread to Washington by now. "Not a man should be permitted to return to Virginia," Halleck wired McClellan, who replied: "I have given every order necessary to insure the capture or destruction of those forces, and I hope we may be able to teach them a lesson they will not

Jeb Stuart's men help themselves to U.S. Army clothing at the Federal depot in Chambersburg, Pennsylvania, during the October "Ride Around McClellan."

soon forget." But that was not to be. Sunday morning, October 12, near the mouth of the Monocacy — where Lee had crossed with his whole army, marching north the month before — Stuart broke through a weak link in the cordon, splashed across the Potomac, and regained the safety of the Confederate lines. He had two men missing, victims most likely of commandeered Yankee whiskey, and a handful slightly wounded. That seemed to him a small price to pay for the nearly three hundred bluecoats paroled at Chambersburg and the thirty-odd public officials brought back as hostages to secure the release or considerate treatment of Southerners now in Union hands. More than a quarter of a million dollars in public and railroad property had been destroyed, and in exchange for about sixty lame or worn-out animals abandoned along the way, the gray troopers had brought 1200 horses back from Pennsylvania for service under the Stars and Bars. Most satisfactory of all — at least to Stuart, who thus once more had justified his plume — was the knowledge that all this had been accomplished in the immediate presence of more than 100,000 enemy soldiers whose commander, midway through the raid, had announced his intention to "teach [the rebels] a lesson" by effecting their capture or destruction.

Instead it was McClellan who had been taught a lesson, though whether he would profit from it was doubtful; apparently he had failed to absorb much from the same lesson when it was first administered, four months ago on the Peninsula. Now as then, he was the object of much derision, North and South — only this time Lincoln himself led the chorus. He was aboard a steamer, returning from a troop review at Alexandria, when someone asked him: "Mr President, what about McClellan?" Without looking up, Lincoln drew a circle on the deck with the ferrule of his umbrella. "When I was a boy we used to play a game," he said, " 'Three Times Round, and Out.' Stuart has been round him twice. If he goes around him once more, gentlemen, McClellan will be out."

A new and biting note of mockery was coming into the President's references to the commander of the Army of the Potomac. Formerly this had been restricted mainly to comments on Little Mac's political suggestions — as when the governor of Massachusetts asked what Lincoln was going to reply to some advice McClellan had offered on a civil matter; "Nothing," Lincoln said. "But it made me think of the man whose horse kicked up and stuck his foot through the stirrup. He said to the horse, 'If you are going to get on I'll get off.' " Thus he had dealt with McClellan the would-be statesman, reserving his respect for McClellan the soldier. Now this too was fading. On the day after Stuart got back from his raid, Lincoln sent the circumnavigated Young Napoleon a long letter full of advice, in effect a lecture on strategy and tactics. "You remember my speaking to you of what I called your over-cautiousness. Are you not over-cautious when you assume that you cannot do what the enemy is constantly doing? Should you not claim to be at least his equal in prowess, and act upon the claim? . . . Exclusive of the water-line, you are now nearer Richmond than the enemy is by the route you can and he must take. Why can you not reach there before him, unless you admit that he is more than your equal on the march? . . . I would press closely to him, fight him if a favorable opportunity should present, and at least try to beat him to Richmond on the inside track. I say 'try'; if we never try, we shall never succeed." That was the main thing, as Lincoln saw it: Beat him. A stalemate would not serve. Even a repulse was not enough. "We should not so operate as to merely drive him away. As we must beat him somewhere or fail finally, we can do it, if at all, easier near to us than far away. If we cannot beat the enemy where he now is, we never can, he being again within the intrenchments of Richmond. . . . It is all easy if our troops march as well as the enemy, and it is unmanly to say they cannot do it." He added: "This letter is in no sense an order."

Thus Lincoln. But McClellan apparently had as little respect for Lincoln the would-be strategist as Lincoln had for McClellan the would-be statesman. October's perfect weather went sliding by, and the army hugged its camps

> *That was the main thing, as Lincoln saw it:*
> *Beat him. A stalemate would not serve.*
> *Even a repulse was not enough.*

while its commander, despite his own chief quartermaster's protest that "no army was ever more perfectly supplied than this one has been as a general rule," continued to call for more and more supplies. He also wanted more soldiers, believing himself outnumbered, though his strength report of October 20 listed 133,433 men "present for duty," with an "aggregate present" of 159,860. Next day Halleck wired him: "Telegraph when you will move, and on what lines you propose to march." McClellan replied that he was nearly ready, but when he followed this with an urgent request for more horses, claiming that the ones he had were broken down by arduous service and weakened by foot-and-mouth disease, Lincoln lost his temper. "I have just read your dispatch about sore-tongued and fatigued horses," he wired on October 25. "Will you pardon me for asking what the horses of your army have done since the battle of Antietam that fatigues anything?"

McClellan was upset. "It was one of those little flings that I can't get used to when they are not merited," he wrote his wife, and he protested at some length to Lincoln the following day, defending his troopers and announcing that the long-awaited movement of his army across the Potomac had begun. Mollified, the President replied that he had "intended no injustice to any, and if I have done any I deeply regret it. To be told, after more than five weeks' total inaction of the army . . . that the cavalry horses were too much fatigued to move, presents a cheerless, almost hopeless, prospect for the future, and it may have forced something of impatience in my dispatch." McClellan had an apology, such as it was, yet his gloom was unrelieved. Through it he saw plainly what was coming. When one of his corps commanders indicated a spot on the map where he thought the next great battle would be fought, he nodded agreement but added sadly: "I may not have command of the army much longer. Lincoln is down on me."

Lincoln was indeed down on him. Though he wired that he was "glad to believe you are crossing," privately he was saying that he was tired of trying to "bore with an auger too dull to take hold." However, he had a final secret test in mind. Lee's army, drawn up around Winchester, was farther from Richmond than McClellan's, which was crossing the Potomac below Harpers Ferry; "His route is the arc of a circle, while yours is the chord," Lincoln had said in the tactics lecture, two weeks before. If, in spite of this disadvantage, the Confederate commander managed to interpose his troops between the advancing Federals and his capital, McClellan would be out. So Lincoln decided, and kept his decision to himself, watching and waiting. He waited long. It took the blue host nine days to cross the river and begin its southward creep, east of the Blue Ridge, toward a concentration around Warrenton. By that time, Lee — unmolested — had shifted half his army to Culpeper, squarely across the Federal line of march. McClellan had failed the test, and Lincoln's mind was made up. He would remove him.

Fearing that this was about to happen, old Francis Blair pled against it with all the persuasion learned in a lifetime spent advising Presidents. McClellan was the Union's one best hope for preservation, he declared. Lincoln disagreed. "I said I would remove him if he let Lee's army get away from him, and I must do so. He has got the slows, Mr Blair."

★ ★ ★ *He* would remove him: but not just yet. November 4 was the first Tuesday in the month, which meant that it was election day in most of the northern states, and therefore not a propitious time for disturbing voters who were disturbed enough already. Even Chase, who vied with Stanton in the intensity of his desire to see McClellan ousted, admitted privately that it was inexpedient to fire the general on the eve of the congressional elections, lest the Administration's motives be misconstrued as a sop to the radicals. There was a widespread conviction among conservatives that the Preliminary Emancipation Proclamation had been sop enough in that direction. Political unrest found its basis there, together with objection to arbitrary arrests and the general lack of satisfaction with the prosecution of the war itself, which seemed to have stalled on every front. Nor was this dissatisfaction limited to moderates and conservatives. Iowa Senator J. W. Grimes, a loyal Republican whose constituents had voted heavily for Lincoln in 1860, was saying flatly: "We are going to destruction as fast as imbecility, corruption and the wheels of time can carry us." Lyman Trumbull of Lincoln's home state was complaining bitterly of a "lack of affirmative, positive action and business talent in the cabinet," while to Governor Andrew of Massachusetts it seemed that "the President has never yet seemed quite sure that we [are] in a war at all."

Such remarks were straws in the wind, down which Democrats sniffed victory in November. And in many instances they got it. New York, Pennsylvania, Ohio, Indiana — all of which had gone solidly Republican in the election held two years ago — sent Democratic delegations to the House of Representatives. So did Illinois, where Lincoln's good friend Leonard Swett went down in defeat to John T. Stuart, the President's former law partner, who thus made one among the nine Democrats elected as opposed to five Republicans. New Jersey, which had split its vote before, now went solidly Democratic; Wisconsin, on the other hand, now split her six-man delegation down the middle. Although the number of Democratic congressmen increased from 44 to 75 as a result of this election, the Republicans would remain the majority party because they managed to carry three widely scattered regions: New England, the Border States, and the Far West. Such comfort as Lincoln found in this was considerably soured, however, by the fact that most observers saw in the individual defeats a rebuke of the party leader and a rejection of his policies on the conduct of the war. The friendly *New York Times* ran the election story under the heading, "Vote of Want of Confidence," and in Lincoln's own home state the Salem *Advocate* declared: "We saw the President of the United States stretching forth his hand and seizing the reins of government with almost absolute power, and yet the people submitted. On the 4th day of November, 1862, the people arose in their might, they uttered their voice, like the sound of many waters, and tyranny, corruption and maladministration trembled."

Lincoln took it philosophically, though he found it hard to do so, remarking that he felt like the boy who stubbed his toe on the way to see his girl; he was too big to cry, he said, and it hurt too much to laugh. One thing it did, at any rate, however it came out. It cleared the way for action on McClellan. November 5, before the election tabulations were complete, Lincoln had the orders for his removal drawn up. The following evening they were given to Brigadier General C. P. Buckingham, the so-called "confidential assistant adjutant-general to the Secretary of War," who left with them next morning, November 7, aboard a special train bound for McClellan's headquarters at Rectortown, near Manassas Gap. The first snowfall of winter was whitening the

Rhode Island politician and carbine inventor Ambrose Burnside had little confidence in his own ability to command an army.

North Virginia landscape and the car in which he rode was drafty; but Buckingham did not wonder that an officer with so much rank as his was being exposed to such discomfort and employed as a sort of overdressed messenger boy, Stanton having explained that McClellan might refuse to relinquish command of his army if the order was presented to him by a man with anything less than stars on his shoulders. Even with them, the Secretary had added darkly, there was a strong possibility of some such mutinous action on the part of the commander of the Army of the Potomac. He advised the brigadier to make his arrival unannounced, thus gaining the military advantage of a surprise attack.

It was still snowing at 11 o'clock that night. McClellan sat alone in his tent, ending the day as usual with a letter to his wife, who was busy getting settled in their new home at Trenton, New Jersey. Nothing in his manner showed that the proposed surprise had failed; but it had. He knew that Buckingham had arrived early that evening, and he knew what his arrival probably meant. Whatever there was of real surprise lay in the fact that, instead of coming directly from the depot to army headquarters here at Rectortown, the War Department emissary had ridden down to Salem, five miles south, where Burnside's corps was posted. Presently, however, this too was explained. A knock came at the tent pole, and when McClellan looked up from his letter, calling for whoever it was to enter, the canvas flap lifted and there stood Buckingham and Burnside, snow collected on the crowns and brims of their hats and sifted into the folds of their greatcoats. Behind his facial ruff of dark brown whiskers —

★

also lightly powdered with snow, so that it resembled a badly printed trademark — "Dear Burn" looked both embarrassed and distressed.

McClellan knew what that meant, too, but for the present he gave no sign of this. He invited the visitors in, quite as if for an informal midnight chat, and for a time he and Buckingham exchanged pleasantries, Burnside sitting glumly by, looking rather as if he had been struck a rather hard rap on the head. Finally, though, the staff brigadier remarked that he had come to deliver some papers; and with that he passed them over. There were two of them, both dated November 5. Lincoln having authorized Halleck, "in [his] discretion, to issue an order [removing McClellan] forthwith, or so soon as he may deem proper," the general-in-chief had deemed it proper to act without delay:

> *Major General McClellan, Commanding, &c.:*
>
> *General: On receipt of the order of the President,*
> *sent herewith, you will immediately turn over your*
> *command to Major General Burnside, and repair to*
> *Trenton, N.J., reporting, on your arrival at that place,*
> *by telegraph, for further orders.*
>
> *Very respectfully, your obedient servant.*

The second was from the Adjutant General's office, and was a direct quotation of the first sentence of Lincoln's message to Halleck:

> *By direction of the President of the United States, it*
> *is ordered that Major General McClellan be relieved from*
> *the command of the Army of the Potomac, and that*
> *Major General Burnside take the command of that army.*
>
> *By order of the Secretary of War.*

Neither of the orders being really any stronger than the other, it appeared that the Young Napoleon's superiors considered two blows likelier to floor him than just one. However that might have been, he kept his balance under the double impact. He read both sheets, then said with a smile and in the same pleasant tone as before: "Well, Burnside, I turn the command over to

★

Doffing his hat, McClellan bids farewell to the Army of the Potomac near Warrenton, Virginia, on November 10, 1862.

you." Close to tears, the Indiana-born Rhode Islander implored McClellan to stay with him for a day or two while he began to get accustomed to handling the reins. He had not wanted this job; had, in fact, refused it twice already, pleading incompetence, and once again this evening when Bucking-ham first came to Salem — that was why they had arrived so late; he had spent two hours argu-ing against his appointment — but Buckingham had reminded him that this was no request, it was a double-barreled order; he had no choice. Besides, the staff brigadier had added, if Burnside declined the command it would go to Hooker. That decided the matter; he had accepted, and all he asked now was that Little Mac stay with him for a couple of days to help him get settled in the driver's seat.

McClellan agreed, and the two generals went back out into the snowy night.

Alone again, the deposed commander took up his pen and returned to his letter: "Another interruption — this time more important. It was in the shape of Burnside, accompanied by Gen. Buckingham. . . . Alas for my poor country! I know in my inmost heart she never had a truer servant." He did not say, as he had said before, that this was a temporary step-down, that he would be recalled when things went as wrong for Burnside as they had gone for Pope. He was through and he knew it. But he added: "Do not be at all worried — I am not. I have done the best I could for my country; to the last I have done my duty as I understand it. That I must have made many mistakes I cannot deny. I do not see any great blunders; but no one can judge

★

of himself. Our consolation must be that we have tried to do what was right."

All that really remained to be done was say goodbye to the army whose affection for him was, in the end, his most enduring monument. Next day, when the order for his removal was published, the reaction combined disbelief and horror, both of which gave way to rage, which in turn was tempered by sadness. The various corps, drawn up for a farewell exchange of salutes, broke ranks as they had done before at his approach. Now as before, they crowded around him, touched his boots, and stroked the flanks of his horse, only this time the tears were produced by sorrow, not by jubilation. Nor had all the anger been drained off. "Send him back! Send him back!" they cried in his wake, as if their shouts could be heard in the capital, fifty miles away. The Irish brigade cast its colors in the dust for him to ride over; "but, of course," one observer wrote, "he made them take them up again." The same man heard a general say he "wished to God that McClellan would put himself at the head of the army and throw the infernal scoundrels at Washington into the Potomac." Another yelled: "Lead us to Washington, General — we'll follow you!" Burnside shared the prevailing gloom, still so badly choked up that when one division commander, having voiced his regrets to McClellan, turned to him and offered congratulations, the new army head could hardly speak. "Couch, don't say a word about it," he implored.

McClellan accepted this adulation with as much satisfaction as ever, possibly more, but he remained strangely calm in the midst of it and did nothing to encourage the various expressions of resentment. "The officers and men feel terribly about the change," he wrote his wife on the second night after receiving the order for his removal. "I learn today that the men are very sullen and have lost their good spirits entirely." This was putting it mildly indeed; but the truth was, he had lost much of his former flamboyance. Even his written farewell to his soldiers was comparatively restrained. "In you I have never found doubt or coldness," he told them, and he added: "We shall ever be comrades in supporting the Constitution of our country and the nationality of its people."

That was all; or almost all. November 11 he took his final leave of them, riding down to Warrenton Junction, where a train was waiting to carry him away. After receiving the salute of a 2000-man detachment stationed here, he boarded the train and took his seat. But before the engineer could obey the highball, the troops broke ranks, surrounded the car, then uncoupled it and ran it back, yelling threats against the Administration and insisting that McClellan should not leave. "One word, one look of encouragement, the lifting of a finger," one witness later declared, "would have been a signal for a revolt against lawful authority, the consequences of which no man can measure." Instead, McClellan stepped onto the front platform and delivered a short address to the men, who had fallen silent as soon as he appeared. "Stand by General Burnside as you have stood by me, and all will be well," he said. Calmed, the soldiers recoupled the car and the train pulled out, followed by "one long and mournful huzza [as the men] bade farewell to their late commander." His route led through the capital, but he had already told his wife: "I shall not stop in Washington longer than for the next train, and will not go to see anybody."

In their tears, in their passionate demonstrations of affection for this man who moved them in a way no other general ever had or ever would, it was as if the soldiers had sensed a larger meaning in the impending separation; it was as if they knew they were saying goodbye to something more than just one stocky brown-haired man astride a tall black horse. It was, indeed, as if they were saying goodbye to their youth — which, in a sense, they were. Or it might also have been prescience, intimations of mortality, intimations of suffering down the years. There had been Pope, and now it appeared that there would be others more or less like him. Knowing what that meant, they might well have been weeping for their own lot, as well as for McClellan's. "My army," he had called them from the start, and it was true. He had made them into what they were, and whatever they accomplished he would accomplish too, in part, even though he would no longer be at their head.

That was no doubt his greatest satisfaction; but there were others, no less welcome for being delayed. Five years after the guns had cooled and were parked in town squares and on courthouse lawns, with sparrows building nests in their muzzles, he received what was perhaps his finest professional compliment, and received it from the man who had occupied the best of all possible positions from which to formulate a judgment. Asked then who was the ablest Federal general he had opposed throughout the war, Robert E. Lee replied without hesitation: "McClellan, by all odds."

★ ★ ★ **M**cClellan was gone, and others were gone with him: Fitz-John Porter, for example, who was relieved from command by authority of the same message Lincoln had sent Halleck on November 5, relieving Little Mac. His corps went to Hooker, whose own had been severely cut up at Antietam, and Porter himself was brought back to Washington to face charges for having failed to obey Pope's order for an attack on the Confederate right "at or near Manassas, in the State of Virginia, on or about the 29th day of August, 1862." The court having convicted him, Lincoln ordered that he be "cashiered and dismissed from the service . . . and forever disqualified from holding any office of trust or profit under the Government of the United States." Winged thus by a stray pellet from the blast that felled his chief, Porter had to wait long for vindication. It came at last, officially, nearly a quarter of a century later, when Congress in 1886 commissioned him a regular-army colonel, to rank from 1861, and permitted him to retire immediately thereafter, without back pay but with honor.

One other major figure was to go, though not entirely: Benjamin Butler was too useful a man, and too powerful a politician, to be assigned to limbo alongside Buell and McClellan. Like them he was a Democrat, but he was blatantly so — with the result that what had been for them a disadvantage was for him a downright blessing. So long as he occupied a high position in the army, the Administration could not be accused of conducting a strictly Republican war, whereas his dismissal would have exactly the reverse effect. Butler of course was aware of this advantage, and operated accordingly. What was more, he was efficient, particularly as an administrator. Yet for all his ingenuity in dealing with the problems attending the occupation of New Orleans (he had not only succeeded in making the Creoles "fear the stripes" in his flag, he had also brought them some of the sanitary benefits of Lowell, Massachusetts, including an intensive flushing-out of their sewers and an equally intensive regulation of their morals) the squint-eyed general had not fulfilled his early promise as a terror to the rebels in the field. Of late, in fact, he had entirely neglected that side of military life, even having gone so far as to pull his troops out of Baton Rouge in order to avoid a return engagement with the Confederates who had attacked the place in early August. Obviously he would not do for the bloody work Lincoln now saw would have to be done if the war was ever to end. However, the disposition of Butler was no large problem. His talents were so manifold that he would be about as useful in one place as another. He could be shifted.

Fortunately for Lincoln's purpose he had a replacement there at hand, in the form of the commander of the Washington defenses. Banks, like Butler, was a Massachusetts politician, so that to exchange them, one for another, would not upset the voters of their region. Besides, Banks was resourceful, energetic, and pugnacious: a combination of qualities all too rare of late, in more places than New Orleans. In short, he was just the kind of man Lincoln thought he wanted for the job he had in mind. It was true that wherever he had fought he had been whipped, sometimes rather spectacularly, but this had not been the result of any unwillingness to fight; quite the reverse — and generally it had been against Stonewall Jackson, whom he would be unlikely to encounter down in Louisiana or up the Mississippi. That was where Lincoln intended to send him. On November 8, the day after Buckingham left for Rectortown with the orders placing Burnside in command of the Army of the Potomac, Lincoln had the Adjutant General issue an order assigning Banks "to the command of the Department of the Gulf, including the State of Texas," and the following day he had Halleck write the new commander a letter of instructions, explaining the purpose — or, more strictly speaking, purposes — for which he was being transferred so far south.

General Nathaniel Banks was derisively nicknamed "Commissary" after his defeat in the Shenandoah.

Vicksburg and Mobile were to be his primary objectives, and he was to have the coöperation of the navy in effecting their reduction. "The President regards the opening of the Mississippi River as the first and most important of all our military and naval operations," he was told, "and it is hoped that you will not lose a moment in accomplishing it." Following this, Halleck continued — quite as if the thing had been done already with a flourish of the pen — Banks was to move eastward from Vicksburg to Jackson, "and thus cut off all connection by rail between Northern Mississippi . . . and Atlanta . . . the chief military depot of the rebel armies in the West." This done, he would return approximately to his starting point in order to "ascend with a naval and military force the Red River as far as it is navigable, and thus open an outlet for the sugar and cotton of Northern Louisiana." Not even then did Halleck allow him time for a breather. "It is also suggested that, having Red River in our possession, it would form the best base for operations in Texas." There at last he closed with the assurance, "These instructions are not intended to tie your hands or to hamper your operations in the slightest degree . . . and I need not assure you, general, that the Government has unlimited confidence not only in your judgment and discretion, but also in your energy and military promptness."

Although this was clearly one of the largest tasks ever assigned a commander in all the history of warfare — and unquestionably the most difficult ever assigned a nonprofessional who, after eighteen months in the field and a major share in three campaigns, lacked so much as a single tactical victory to his credit — Banks shared Halleck's "unlimited confidence" that the thing could be done and that he was the man to do it. Summoned to Washington and informed that he would be given 20,000 reinforcements to accompany him on the coastal voyage to New Orleans — one expeditionary force would sail from New York, the other from Hampton Roads — the New Englander was delighted. "Everything is favorable for my purpose," he had replied to an earlier warning order. "I shall obtain troops at once, and be ready for movement as early as you wish. . . . Requisitions will be made and forwarded by mail. No material delay will occur, unless for want of transports." Now, having conferred in person with Lincoln and Halleck as to the details of the multi-faceted project, he was more enthusiastic than ever. There was "much to do," he said as he departed for New York, but he would "lose no time."

Lincoln was delighted, too: not only by the prospect of seeing so much accomplished, but also by the unfamiliar experience of having sat face to face with a commander who recognized the worth of time and the military fruits that haste could gather. Moreover, it augured well for larger matters. For all the vastness of the project thus assigned to Banks, the main value of his operations would be diversionary, serving 1) to drain off rebel front-line troops by threatening their rear, and 2) to distract the enemy high command from concentrating against the Federal main effort, about to be exerted against their front. After a hundred thousand casualties and a year and a half of successes, near-successes, and sickening failures — the last, as Lincoln saw them, being mainly due to the vacillation and nonaggressiveness of generals like Buell and McClellan, who, desiring combat less than they feared defeat, believed in preparation more than they believed in movement — a victory pattern had emerged. Three southern cities were the three main northern objectives. Richmond, Chattanooga, and Vicksburg were the brain, heart, and bowels of the rebellion. A successful blow struck any one of the three might well prove fatal, in time, to the corpus as a whole; but *three* successful blows, struck simultaneously, would produce immediate results. Whatever movement followed then, on the part of the creature named Rebellion, would be no more than death throes and the setting in of rigor mortis.

Immediate results being what he was after, Lincoln had assigned these three main objectives to the commanders of the three main armies of the Union: Burnside, Rosecrans, and Grant. He himself had chosen the first and second, and he had sustained the third against strident demands for his dismissal, saying of him: "I can't spare this man. He fights." He believed he could say it of the other two as well. Whatever shortcomings they might develop under pressure (Grant's, for instance, was said to be whiskey; hearing which, the President was supposed to have asked what brand he drank, intending to send a barrel each to all his other generals) it seemed unlikely that a distaste for combat was going to be the flaw in any case. All three had fought, and fought hard: Burnside at Roanoke Island and Antietam, Rosecrans in West Virginia and at Corinth, Grant at Belmont, Donelson, and Shiloh — which was practically to call the roll of all the victories the army could lay claim to, east of the Mississippi, even by stretching the point in an instance or two or three. So had Banks fought hard, and though admittedly it had been with less success, Lincoln believed that the war had reached a stage where hard fighting, sustained by the superior resources of the nation, would create its own success. At any rate, that was what he was asking for now: hard fighting. And with this in mind, as Commander in Chief, he had placed his major armies under leaders he considered most likely to give it to him without delay.

★ ★ ★   *S*o he thought, this melancholy man with his incurable optimism: only to find that what his high hopes mainly afforded him — once more, alas — was another occasion for exploring the gap that yawned between conception and execution. One by one, two by two, and finally all four together, his hand-picked generals failed his expectations as to haste. And, paradoxically, he discovered that the reason for delay, in all four cases, was just those superior resources which he had thought assured them victory.

★

Banks was first, the most enthusiastic of the lot. He had scarcely been gone from the capital a week before the President saw a monster requisition the Massachusetts general submitted, calling for mountains of supplies and thousands of horses to haul them through the jungles of the Lower South. Horses were a sore subject with Lincoln just now, anyhow, and when he was assured by the chief quartermaster that the requisition could not "be filled and got off within an hour short of two months," he wrote Banks a letter in which anger vied with sorrow for predominance. "I have just been overwhelmed and confounded," he declared, and continued: "My dear general, this expanding and piling up of impedimenta has been so far almost our ruin, and will be our final ruin if it is not abandoned. . . . When you parted with me you had no such ideas in your mind. I know you had not, or you could not have expected to be off so soon as you said. You must get back to something like the plan you had then or your expedition is a failure before you start. You must be off before Congress meets. You would be better off anywhere, and especially where you are going, for not having a thousand wagons doing nothing but hauling forage to feed the animals that draw them, and taking at least 2000 men to care for the wagons and animals, who otherwise might be 2000 good soldiers." In closing he added a further admonition: "Now, dear general, do not think this is an ill-natured letter; it is the very reverse. The simple publication of this requisition would ruin you."

As usual in cases where the offense presaged delay, Banks had what he considered a reasonable explanation. Two days later, November 24, he replied that the request for supplies "was drawn up by an officer who did not fully comprehend my instructions, and inadvertently approved by me without sufficient examination." In other words, he had signed without looking. "My purpose has not been changed since I left Washington," he assured Lincoln, "and I have waited [for] nothing not absolutely necessary." Apparently, though, a great many items fell in that category; for the waiting continued. Banks kept saying he would be off any day now, but the disillusioned President had doubts. And his doubts were valid. Banks' purpose might not have changed, but his schedule had. November went out; December came in; Banks remained at his New York starting point. Finally, on December 4, he sailed for Fort Monroe. How long he would stay there before continuing on to New Orleans, Lincoln did not know.

Anyhow, he had a good deal more on his mind by then. Troubles of a similar nature, involving delay, but derived from a different and even more unexpected source, were looming in the West: specifically in Grant's department, and even more specifically in U. S. Grant himself. After the ill-wind fiasco at Iuka and the bloody repulse of the rebels at Corinth, which he had missed, Grant had been sounding oddly unlike himself. When Halleck, after the latter fight, asked why he did not press the defeated and retreating foe — "Why order a return of our troops? Why not . . . pursue the enemy into Mississippi, supporting your army on the country?" — Grant replied that an army could not "subsist itself on the country except in forage. . . . Disaster would follow in the end." This did not sound like the Grant of old, who never spoke of disaster except with the intention of inflicting it, and presently he was sounding even less so, calling urgently for reinforcements in expectation of having to fight another battle. This fall, in fact, his aggressive instincts mostly seemed reserved for the Jews in his department. "Refuse all permits to come south of Jackson for the present," he wired Hurlbut at that place, adding: "The Israelites especially should be kept out." He instructed his railroad superintendent to "give orders to all conductors on the road that no Jews are to be permitted to travel on the railroad southward from any point. They may go north and be encouraged in it; but they are such an intolerable nuisance that the department must be purged of them."

Lincoln would not have admired this talk of purges, not only because it ran counter to his personal belief in the equality of men before the law (whether the law was military or civil) but also because it could be applied to a father or mother on the way to visit a soldier son; for there were, of course, Jewish soldiers in all the nation's armies — even Grant's. In time this would be called to his attention, but for the present Lincoln was disturbed enough at the general's tone in regard to the pursuit of a beaten foe. One explanation was given by Rosecrans in a private letter to Halleck, written on the day before he was ordered north to replace Buell. He complained of "the spirit of mischief among the mousing politicians on Grant's staff," spoke of Grant becoming "sour and reticent," and asked to be "relieved from duty here." When a fighter Lincoln respected as much as he did Rosecrans asked for a transfer, apparently all was not well in the area he wished himself away from. Also — as always — there was talk that Grant had reverted to his old fondness for the bottle. Doubtless, too, Lincoln heard gossip similar to what a Chicago reporter heard from his fellow passengers as he rode south about this time on a train bound for Memphis. Officers and men returning from leaves and furloughs declared that Grant "never did amount to anything, and never would. He had been kicked out of the United States Army once, and would be again. He was nothing but a drunken, wooden-headed tanner, that would not trouble the country very long. &c. &c."

Whatever his past successes, Vicksburg was too important a prize for its capture to hinge entirely on the problematic advance of a man who was the subject of so many ugly rumors and whose character, even aside from the truth or falseness of such talk, seemed to have undergone a discouraging reversal. At any rate, Lincoln in this case had provided not one but two extra strings for the bow that was to be bent in that direction. While Banks was moving upriver against the place, supported by warships from Farragut's fleet, and Grant was marching overland down the Mississippi Central from Grand Junction, a third force was to descend the river from southern Illinois, its mission being to

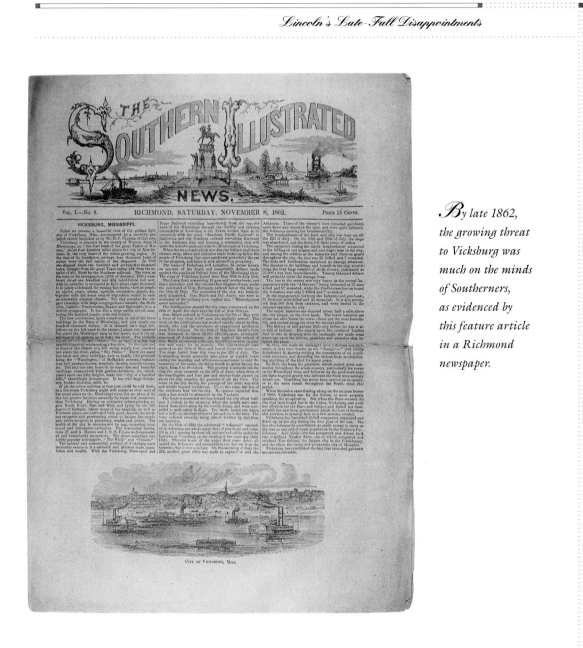

By late 1862, the growing threat to Vicksburg was much on the minds of Southerners, as evidenced by this feature article in a Richmond newspaper.

coöperate with Porter's ironclad flotilla for an attack on the stronghold which Jefferson Davis had called "the Gibraltar of the West." This third force was irregular and highly secret in nature, its purpose known only to three men: Lincoln, Stanton, and its commander, John McClernand. They had created it — out of the whole cloth, so to speak. McClernand had come north on leave in late September, saying privately that he was "tired of furnishing brains" for Grant's army, and had appealed to his friend the President to "let one volunteer officer try his abilities." In accordance with the plan he submitted, Stanton gave him on October 21 a confidential order authorizing him "to proceed to the States of Indiana, Illinois, and Iowa, and to organize the troops remaining in those States and to be raised by volunteering or draft . . . to the end that, when a sufficient force not required by the operations of General Grant's command shall be raised, an expedition may be organized under General McClernand's command against Vicksburg . . . to clear the Mississippi River and open navigation to New Orleans." A presidential indorsement further authorized him to show this confidential document "to Governors, and even others, when in his discretion he believes so doing to be indispensable to the progress of the expedition."

Armed with this order, which he saw as placing his star in the ascendant — his ambition had not been lessened by the singeing he took at Donelson while seeking the bubble reputation at the cannon's mouth — McClernand left for his home state in late October, there to begin assembling the force which he believed would put him not only in Vicksburg but also in the White House. Even the first of these steps would take time, however; and time, he knew, was the foe of secrecy. Sure enough, by early November Grant began hearing what he called "mysterious rumors of McClernand's command." Glad as he had been to get rid of his fellow Illinoisan, he did not want him back in his department at the head of a rival army. When Halleck — whom the three lawyers had also not let in on their secret — informed him that Memphis would "be made the depot of a joint military and naval expedition on Vicksburg," Grant took alarm and wired back: "Am I to understand that I lie still here while an expedition is fitted out from Memphis, or do you want me to push as far south as possible? Am I to have Sherman move subject to my orders, or is he and his forces reserved for some special service?" Halleck replied blandly: "You have command of all troops sent to your department, and have permission to fight the enemy where you please."

That was enough for Grant. Receiving Halleck's go-ahead message near Grand Junction on November 11, he had cavalry in Holly Springs two days later. He followed at once with the infantry, established a supply base there, and continued his advance down the Mississippi Central. By December 1 his cavalry was across the Hatchie, the rebels fading back. Still Grant followed. Within another week he had occupied Oxford, fifty miles beyond his starting point, setting up a command post in the courthouse and repairing the railroad in his rear. . . . Whatever else McClernand's behind-the-scenes maneuver might accomplish in the end, it had effected at least one thing before it even got beyond the plans-and-training stage: Grant's mind had emerged from the tunnel it had entered after Shiloh. He was himself again, or anyhow he appeared to be, and this in itself was encouraging to Lincoln. However, he could also see that in North Mississippi, as elsewhere along the thousand-mile front, the fine autumn weather had mostly gone to waste, so far as offensive operations were concerned. Grant was still 150 air-line miles from Vicksburg, and neither Banks nor McClernand had even begun to move.

★

Here in the East, delay was especially discouraging for being close at hand; Lincoln's torture, as a result, was not unlike that of Tantalus, who saw the surface of the pool recede each time he bent to drink. In this case, too, he was soon obliged to suspect that he had made an error in personal judgment, no matter how well founded that judgment had seemed at the time he acted on it. In addition to native combativeness, demonstrated on independent service, Burnside had other qualities which had caused Lincoln to overrule his twice-repeated protest that he was not competent to command the Army of the Potomac, despite the fact that his rank entitled him to the post. Less than three years older than McClellan, he had been his friend before and during the war and had taken no part in the bickering that surrounded him. It was Lincoln's hope that this would ease the blow and soften the reaction when "McClellan's bodyguard" got the news that its hero had been replaced. Also, Burnside had no political opinions: a lack that might have been expected to spare him the mistrust and enmity of the Jacobins who had hounded his predecessor. Both calculations, one regarding the army, the other Congress, appeared to have been valid at the outset. For a time, they even worked; or else they seemed to. But the President was not long in finding out that both had been something less than inclusive. According to one general in a group who came to congratulate Burnside on his promotion, he thanked them "and then, with that transparent sincerity which made everyone believe what he said, he added that he knew he was not fit for so big a command, but he would do his best." The witness remarked: "One could not help feeling a certain tenderness for the man. But when a moment later the generals talked among themselves, it was no wonder that several shook their heads and asked how we could have confidence in the fitness of our leader if he had no confidence in himself?" Such in part was the reaction in the army he was about to lead into battle. As for the radicals in Congress, it soon became apparent that an absence of politics was by no means a recommendation in their eyes. They had no objection to politics, per se; they merely insisted that the politics be Republican. All they really knew of Burnside was that he was the acknowledged friend of the man whose ruin they were proud to have helped accomplish, and they were prepared to do as much for him in turn, if on closer acquaintance it appeared that he deserved it.

Such objections were mainly personal, however, and Lincoln did not share them, or if he did he thought them incidental. His main concern was with Burnside as a strategist, a seeker after battle: which was where his doubts came in. Aware that the President wanted immediate action, and had in fact removed his predecessor for not giving it to him, the new commander immediately prepared a plan which he submitted for approval. Not liking the army's present location — which seemed to him uncomfortably similar to the one John Pope had occupied before he came to grief — Burnside had the notion of converting the advance just east of the Blue Ridge into a feint, under cover of which he would "accumulate a four or five days' supply for the men and animals; then make a rapid move of the whole force to Fredericksburg, with a view to a movement upon Richmond from that point." This was the so-called "covering approach" which Lincoln had always favored, since it protected Washington. But in this case he thought the plan defective, in that it made the southern capital the primary Federal objective, not Lee's army, which in fact it seemed that Burnside was attempting to avoid. Halleck felt that way about it, too, and on November 12 went down to Warrenton for a talk with the lush-whiskered general, who argued forcefully in favor of the change of base. Still doubtful, Halleck returned to Washington and reported the discussion to the President. Lincoln too was unconvinced, but he was so pleased at the prospect of early action — here in the East, if nowhere else — that he agreed to let Burnside go ahead — or, more strictly speaking, sideways, then ahead — provided he moved fast. Halleck passed the word to Warrenton on the 14th: "The President has just assented to your plan. He thinks that it will succeed, if you move very rapidly; otherwise not."

Burnside did move rapidly, "very rapidly." Despite the tremendous supply problems which went with having an "aggregate present" of approximately 250,000 officers and men for whose welfare he was responsible — 150,441 in the field force proper, 98,738 in the capital defenses — the fact was, he had turned out to be an excellent administrator. On the day he received Lincoln's qualified assent to an eastward shift, he regrouped his seven corps into Right, Left, and Center "Grand Divisions" of two corps each, respectively under Sum-

ner, Franklin, and Hooker, leaving the seventh in "independent reserve" under Sigel. With his army thus reorganized for deft handling, he took up the march for Falmouth the following day, November 15. Sumner went first, followed on subsequent days by Franklin, Hooker, and the cavalry. Moving down the north bank of the Rappahannock, which thus covered the exposed flank of the column, the Right Grand Division arrived on the 17th and the others came along behind on schedule. Burnside himself reached Falmouth on the 19th, just in advance of the rear-guard elements. Proudly he wired Washington: "Sumner's two corps now occupy all the commanding positions opposite Fredericksburg. . . . The enemy do not seem to be in force." So far, indeed, except for an occasional gray cavalry vedette across the way, the only sign of resistance had come from a single rebel battery on the heights beyond the historic south-bank town, and it had been smothered promptly by counterbattery fire. Lincoln had asked for speed, and Burnside had given it to him. He seemed about to give him all else he had asked for, too — hard fighting — for he added: "As soon as the pontoon trains arrive, the bridge will be built and the command moved over."

But there was the rub. Burnside had left the sending of the pontoons to Halleck, who in turn had left it to a subordinate, and somewhere along

The delayed arrival of pontoon trains like the one shown here prevented Burnside from making an unopposed crossing of the Rappahannock River.

the chain of command the word "rush" had been dropped from the requisition. The army waited a week, during which a three-day rain swelled the fords and turned the roads into troughs of mud. Still the pontoons did not come. On the eighth day they got there; but so by then had something else; something not nearly so welcome. "Had the pontoon bridge arrived even on the 19th or 20th, the army could have crossed with trifling opposition," Burnside notified Halleck on the 22d. "But now the opposite side of the river is occupied by a large rebel force under General Longstreet, with batteries ready to be placed in position to operate against the working parties building the bridge and the troops in crossing." Vexed that his forty-mile change of base, executed with such efficiency and speed that it had given him the jump on his wily opponent, had gained him nothing by way of surprise in the end, he said flatly: "I deem it my duty to lay these facts before you, and to say that I cannot make the promise of probable success with the faith that I did when I supposed that all the parts of the plan would be carried out. . . . The President said that the movement, in order to be successful, must be made quickly, and I thought the same."

Lincoln was distressed: not only because of the delay, which he had predicted would be fatal to the success of the campaign, but also because the new commander, in the face of all those guns across the river, seemed to believe it was part of his duty to expose his army to annihilation by way of payment for other men's mistakes. November 25, the day the first relay of pontoons reached Falmouth, the President wired: "If I should be in a boat off Aquia Creek at dark tomorrow (Wednesday) evening, could you, without inconvenience, meet me and pass an hour or two with me?" He made the trip, saw Burnside and the situation — which he characterized by understatement as "somewhat risky" — then returned to Washington, worked out a supplementary plan of his own, and sent for the general to come up and discuss it with him and Halleck. As he saw it, the enemy should be confused by diversionary attacks, one upstream from Fredericksburg, the other on the lower Pamunkey, each to be delivered by a force of about 25,000 men and the latter to be supported by the fleet. Both generals rejected the plan, however, on grounds that it would require too much time for preparation. So Lincoln, with his argument stressing haste thus turned against him, had to content himself with telling Burnside to go back to his army and use his own judgment as to when and where he would launch an assault across the Rappahannock.

Burnside returned to Falmouth on the next to last day of November. His notion was to strike where Lee would least expect it, and the more he thought about the problem, the more it seemed to him that this would be at Fredericksburg itself, where Lee was strongest. Accordingly, he began to mass his 113,000 effectives — Sigel having been posted near Manassas — along and behind the north-bank heights, overlooking the streets of the Rappahannock town whose citizens had already been given notice to evacuate their homes.

November was gone by then, however. In the East as in the West, to Lincoln's sorrow, there had been no fall offensive, only a seemingly endless preparation for one which had not come off.

Between these two East-West extremes, the trouble in Middle Tennessee, while similar to the trouble in Virginia and North Mississippi, was in its way even more exasperating. Burnside and Grant at least regretted the delay and expressed a willingness to end it, but Rosecrans not only would not say that he regretted it, he declared flatly that he would not obey a direct order to end it until he personally was convinced that his hard-marched army was ready for action, down to the final shoenail in the final pair of shoes. This came as a shock to Lincoln, who had expected Old Rosy's positivism to take a different form. He would have been less surprised, no doubt, if he had known Grant's reaction when that general learned in late October that his then subordinate was leaving. "I was delighted," he later wrote, adding: "I found that I could not make him do as I wished, and had determined to relieve him from duty that very day."

In the East as in the West, to Lincoln's sorrow, there had been no fall offensive, only a seemingly endless preparation for one which had not come off.

Whatever reasons lay behind Rosecrans' reluctance to move forward, they could not have proceeded from any vagueness in his instructions, which were covered in a letter Halleck sent him along with his appointment as Buell's successor: "The great objects to be kept in view in your operations in the field are: First, to drive the enemy from Kentucky and Middle Tennessee; second, to take and hold East Tennessee, cutting the line of railroad at Chattanooga, Cleveland, or Athens, so as to destroy the connection of the valley of Virginia with Georgia and the other Southern States. It is hoped that by prompt and rapid movements a considerable part of this may be accomplished before the roads become impassable from the winter rains." After emphasizing "the importance of moving light and rapidly, and also the necessity of procuring as many of your supplies as possible in the country passed over," the general-in-chief concluded on an even sterner note: "I need not urge upon you the necessity of giving active employment to your forces. Neither the country nor the Government will much longer put up with the inactivity of some of our armies and generals."

There he had it, schedule and all; even the name of the army was changed, so that what had been called the Army of the Ohio was now the Army of the Cumberland, signifying the progress made, as well as the progress looked forward to. He knew well enough that Buell had been relieved because the authorities in Washington lacked confidence in his inclination or ability to get these missions accomplished in a hurry. That, too — in addition to the reluctance shown in declining the same appointment a month before — was why Thomas had been passed over in order to give the job to Rosecrans, whom they apparently considered the man to get it done. As a sign of this confidence, Halleck at once agreed to let him do what he had been unwilling to grant Buell. That is, he allowed him to return to Nashville with the army, agreeing at last with Buell's old contention that this was the best starting point for an advance on Chattanooga. Having won this concession, Rosecrans moved into the fortified Tennessee capital, and while butternut cavalry under Morgan and Forrest tore up tracks in his rear and slashed at his front, he set about reorganizing his command, more or less in the manner of Burnside, into Right, Left, and Center "Wings" of four divisions each. Gilbert having faded back into the obscurity he came out of, these went respectively to McCook, Crittenden, and Thomas. The mid-November effective strength of the army was 74,555 men — as large or larger, it was thought, than the enemy force at Murfreesboro, thirty-odd miles southeast — but Rosecrans still had not advanced beyond the outskirts of Nashville. He was hoping, he said, for a sudden rise of the Tennessee River to cut off the rebels' retreat; in which case, as he put it, "I shall throw myself on their right flank and endeavor to make an end of them." For the present, however, he confided, "I am trying to lull them into security, that I do not intend soon to move, until I can get the [rail]road fully opened and throw in a couple of millions of rations here."

The Confederates might be lulled by his apparent inactivity, but his own superiors were not. Alarmed by this casual reference to "a couple of millions of rations" — followed as it was by urgent requisitions for "revolving rifles," back pay, "an iron pontoon train long enough to cross the Tennessee," and much else — Halleck told him sternly on November 27: "I must warn you against this piling up of impediments. Take a lesson from the enemy. Move light." The Tennessee commander protested that he was asking for nothing that was not "indispensable to an effectual and steady advance, which is the only one that will avail us anything worth the cost." By now it was December, and Rosecrans had begun to sound more like Buell than Buell himself had done. Halleck lost his temper, wiring curtly: "The President is very impatient. . . . Twice have I been asked to designate someone else to command your army. If you remain one more week in Nashville, I cannot prevent your removal." Rosecrans, unintimidated, bristled back at him: "Your dispatch received. I reply in few but earnest words. I have lost no time. Everything I have done was necessary, absolutely so; and has been done as rapidly as possible. . . . If the Government which ordered me here confides in my judgment, it may rely on my continuing to do what I have been trying to do — that is, my whole duty. If my superiors have lost confidence in me, they had better at once put someone in my place and let the future test the propriety of the change. I have but one word to add, which is, that I need no other stimulus to make me do my duty than the knowledge of what it is. To threats of removal or the like I must be permitted to say that I am insensible."

Now Lincoln knew the worst. With autumn gone and winter at hand, not a single one of the three major blows he had hoped for and designed had been struck. Right, left, and center, for all he knew — and he had observed signs of this with his own eyes, down on the Rappahannock — all that had been accomplished in each of these three critical theaters was a fair-weather setting of the stage for a foul-weather disaster. Halleck was saying of him during this first week in December: "You can hardly conceive his great anxiety," and Lincoln himself had told a friend the week before: "I certainly have been dissatisfied with the slowness of Buell and McClellan; but before I relieved them I had great fears I should not find successors to them who would do better; and I am sorry to add that I have seen little since to relieve those fears."

★ ★ ★ hese words were written in a letter to Carl Schurz, a young German emigrant whom the Republican central committee had sent to Illinois four years ago to speak in Lincoln's behalf during the senatorial race against Douglas. Grateful for this and later, more successful work, Lincoln appointed him Minister to Spain in 1861, and when Schurz resigned to come home and fight, the President made him a brigadier under Frémont in the Alleghenies. After the fall election returns were in, he wrote Lincoln his belief that they were "a most serious reproof to the Administration" for placing the nation's armies in "the hands of its enemies," meaning Democrats. "What Republican has ever had a fair chance in this war?" Schurz asked, apparently leaving his own case out of account, and urged: "Let us be commanded by generals whose heart is in the war." Lincoln thought this over and replied: "I have just received and read your letter of [November] 20th. The purport of it is that we lost the late elections and the Administration is failing because the war is unsuccessful, and that I must not flatter myself that I am not justly to blame for it. I certainly know that if the war fails, the Administration fails, and that I will be blamed for it, whether I deserve it or not. And I ought to be blamed if I could do better. You think I could do better; therefore you blame me already. I think I could not do better; therefore I blame you for blaming me."

Having thus disposed of the matter of blame, he passed on to the matter of hearts. "I understand you now to be willing to accept the help of men who are not Republicans, provided they have 'heart in it.' Agreed. I want no others. But who is to be the judge of hearts, or of 'heart in it'? If I must discard my own judgment and take yours, I must also take that of others; and by the time I should reject all I should be advised to reject, I should have none left, Republicans or others — not even yourself. For be assured, my dear sir, there are men who have 'heart in it' that think you are performing your part as poorly as you think I am performing mine. . . . I wish to disparage no one, certainly not those who sympathize with me; but I must say I need success more than I need sympathy, and that I have not seen the so much greater evidence of getting success from my sympathizers than from those who are denounced as the contrary."

He closed with a suggestion that the citizen soldier come to see him soon at the White House: which Schurz did, arriving early one morning, and was taken at once to an upstairs room where he found the President sitting before an open fire, his feet in large Morocco slippers. Told to pull up a chair, he did so: whereupon Lincoln brought his hand down with a slap on Schurz's knee. "Now tell me, young man, whether you really think that I am as poor a fellow as you have made me out in your letter." He was smiling, but Schurz could not keep from stammering as he tried to apologize. This made the tall man laugh aloud, and again he slapped his visitor's knee. "Didn't I give it to you hard in my letter? Didn't I? But it didn't hurt, did it? I did not mean to, and therefore I wanted you to come so quickly." Still laughing, he added: "Well, I guess we understand one another now, and it's all right." They talked for the better part of an hour, and as Schurz rose to leave he asked whether he should keep on writing letters to the President. "Why, certainly," Lincoln told him. "Write me whenever the spirit moves you."

It was Schurz's belief that the visit had done Lincoln good, and unquestionably it had. Busy as he was with the details of office, not all of which were directly connected with the war, he had all too few occasions for relaxation, let alone laughter, the elixir he had always used against his natural melancholia. Out in Minnesota, for example, John Pope had been more successful against the marauding Sioux than he had against Lee and Jackson. He had defeated Chief Little Crow in battle and brought the surviving braves before a military court which sentenced 303 of them to be hanged. Reviewing the list, Lincoln reduced to thirty-eight the number slated for immediate execution and ordered the rest held, "taking care that they neither escape nor are subjected to any unlawful violence." This was of course only one distraction among many, the most troublesome being the host of importunate callers, all of whom wanted some special favor from him. Sometimes he lost patience, as when he told a soldier who came seeking his intervention in a routine army matter: "Now, my man, go away.

★

Lincoln's beloved, and often pampered, son Tad poses in a custom-made officer's uniform complete with gauntlets and sword.

I cannot attend to all these details. I could as easily bail out the Potomac with a spoon!" But mostly he was patient and receptive. He put them at ease, heard their complaints, and did what he could to help them. When a friend remarked, "You will wear yourself out," he shook his head and replied with a sad smile: "They don't want much; they get but little, and I must see them."

One place of refuge he had, the war telegraph office, and one companion whose demands on his time apparently brought him nothing but pleasure, Tad. Often he would combine the two, taking his son there with him during the off-hours, when the place was quiet, with only a single operator on duty. He would sit at a desk, reading the accumulated flimsies, while the nine-year-old went to sleep on his lap or rummaged around in search of mischief, which he seldom failed to find. John Hay once remarked that Tad "had a very bad opinion of books, and no opinion of discipline." The former was mainly his father's fault. "Let him run," Lincoln said. "There's time enough yet for him to learn his letters and get poky." So was the latter; for since the death of Willie,

*Having crossed over to the Federal side of the
Rappahannock, a Confederate picket barters
tobacco for a northern newspaper.*

eight months before, this youngest child had been overindulged by way of double compensation. "I want to give him all the toys I did not have," Lincoln
explained, "and all the toys I would have given the boy who went away." Nor
would he allow his son to be corrected. Once when they were at the telegraph
office Tad wandered into the adjoining room, where he found the combination
of black ink and white marble-topped tables quite irresistible. Presently the
operator, whose name was Madison Buell, saw what was being done. Indignant
at the ruin, he seized the dabbler by the collar and marched him out to his
father, pointing through the open door at the irreparable outrage. Lincoln
reacted promptly. Rising, he took the boy in his arms, unmindful of the hands
still dripping ink. "Come, Tad," he said; "Buell is abusing you," and left.

In these and other ways he sought relaxation during this season which had opened with reverses and closed before the big machine could overcome the primary inertia which had gripped it when it stalled. Such large-scale battles as had been fought — Antietam, Corinth, Perryville — had been set down as Union victories; but they had been near things at best — particularly the first and the last, which the rebels also claimed — and what was more, all three had been intrinsically defensive; which would not do. It would do for the insurgents, whose task was merely to defend their region against what they called aggression, but not for the loyalists, whose goal could be nothing short of conquest. Besides, the defensive encouraged the fulfillment of Lincoln's two worst fears: utter war-weariness at home, and recognition for the Confederacy abroad. Other developments might prolong the war, but these two could lose it, and he had taken their avoidance as his personal responsibility. During the period just past, he had sought to prevent the first by appealing directly to the people for confidence in his Administration, and to forestall the second by issuing the Preliminary Emancipation Proclamation. How well he had done in both cases he did not know; it was perhaps too soon to tell, though here too the signs were not encouraging. Some said the fall elections were a rejection of the former, while the latter had been greeted in some quarters — including England, so far as could be judged from the public prints — with derision.

He would wait and see, improvising to meet what might arise. Meanwhile, the armies were getting into position at last for another major effort — and, incidentally, fulfilling the *Tribune* reporter's prediction about "the poetry of war." Down on the Rappahannock, for example, another of Greeley's men overheard the following exchange between two pickets on opposite banks:

"Hallo, Secesh!"

"Hallo, Yank."

"What was the matter with your battery Tuesday night?"

"You made it too hot. Your shots drove the cannoneers away, and they haven't stopped running yet. We infantry men had to come out and withdraw the guns."

"You infantry men will run, too, one of these fine mornings."

The Confederate picket let this pass, as if to say it might be so, and responded instead with a question:

"When are you coming over, bluecoat?"

"When we get ready, butternut."

"What do you want?"

"Want Fredericksburg."

"Don't you wish you may get it!"

★   ★   ★

★

Shelby Foote

Ohio troops (foreground and at right) defend a ford on the Columbia River near Gallatin, Tennessee, from marauding Confederate cavalry on the far bank.

Davis: Lookback and Outlook

1862 ★ ★ ★ ★ ★ As if in accordance with the respective limitations of their available resources — which of course applied to men as well as to the food they ate, the powder they burned, and the shoes and clothes and horses they wore out — while Lincoln was getting rid of experienced commanders, Davis was making use of those he had. Yet this difference in outlook and action was not merely the result of any established ratio between profligacy and frugality, affordable on the one hand and strictly necessary on the other; it was, rather, an outgrowth of the inherent difference in their natures. Lincoln, as he said, was more in need of success than he was in need of sympathy. And while this was also true of Davis, he placed such value on the latter quality — apparently for its own sake — that its demands for reciprocal loyalty, whatever shortcomings there might be in regard to the former, were for him too strong to be denied.

Braxton Bragg and R. E. Lee were cases in point. Ever since the western general began his retreat from Harrodsburg, Davis had been receiving complaints of dissension in the ranks of the Army of Kentucky, along with insistent demands that its commander be removed: in spite of which (if not, indeed, because of them; for such agitations often seemed to strengthen instead of weaken Davis's will) the summons Bragg found waiting for him in Knoxville had not

★

been sent with any notion of effecting his dismissal, but rather with the intention of giving him the chance to present in person his side of the reported controversy. When he got to Richmond, October 25, the President received him with a smile and a congratulatory handshake. On the face of it, both were certainly deserved: the first because it was not Davis's way to dissolve a friendship or condemn any man on the basis of hearsay evidence, and the second because, of the three offensives designed to push Confederate arms beyond the acknowledged borders of secession, only Bragg's had been even moderately successful. In fact, "moderately" was putting it all too mildly. Whatever else had been left undone, a campaign which relieved the pressure on Chattanooga and recovered for the Confederacy all of northwest Alabama, as well as eastern and south-central Tennessee, including Cumberland Gap — not to mention the fact that its two columns had inflicted just under 14,000 battle casualties while suffering just over 4000, and had returned with an enormous train of badly needed supplies

---

"If you choose to rip up the Kentucky campaign you can tear Bragg into tatters."

— William J. Hardee

---

and captured matériel, including more than thirty Union guns — could scarcely be called anything less than substantial in its results. What was more, Bragg had conceived and, in conjunction with Kirby Smith, executed the whole thing, not only without prodding from above, but also without the government's advance permission or even knowledge. Initiative such as that was all too rare. Davis heard him out, and though he did not enjoy hearing his old friend and classmate Bishop Polk accused of bumbling and disloyalty, sustained him. Bragg was told to rejoin his army, which meanwhile was moving rapidly by rail, via Stevenson, Alabama, from Knoxville to Tullahoma and Murfreesboro, where it would threaten Nashville and block a Federal advance from that direction.

Polk was summoned to the capital as soon as Bragg had left it. Invited to present his side of the controversy, the bishop came armed with documents — messages from Bragg to him, messages from him to Bragg, and affidavits provided by fellow subordinates, similarly disaffected — which he believed would protect his reputation and destroy his adversary's, or at any rate neutralize the poison lately poured into the presidential ear. "If you choose to rip up the Kentucky campaign you can tear Bragg into tatters," Hardee told him. However, Davis urged him to put them away, appealing to his patriotism as well as his churchman's capacity for forgiveness, and the bishop agreed

★

to go back and do his Christian best along those lines. By way of compensation, the President handed him his promotion to lieutenant general, a new rank lately authorized by Congress at the same time it legalized the previously informal division of the armies into "wings" and corps. That was gratifying. Equally so was the news that his friend Hardee's name appeared immediately below his own on the seven-man list of generals so honored.

Above them both — next to the very top, in fact — was Kirby Smith, who thus was rewarded for his independent accomplishments in Kentucky, even though he had written to the War Department soon after his return, complaining acidly of Bragg's direction of the campaign during its later stages and requesting transfer to Mobile or elsewhere, anywhere, if staying where he was would require further coöperation with that general. Davis himself replied to this on October 29. He agreed that the campaign had been "a bitter disappointment" in some respects, but he also felt that events should not be judged by "knowledge acquired after they transpired." Besides, having talked at length with Bragg that week, he could assure Smith that "he spoke of you in the most complimentary terms, and does not seem to imagine your dissatisfaction." Davis admitted some other commanders might "excite more enthusiasm" than the dyspeptic North Carolinian, but he doubted that they would be "equally useful" to the country. In motion now for Middle Tennessee, Bragg would need reinforcements in order to parry the Federal counterthrust from Nashville. Where were they to be procured if not from Smith? He asked that, and then concluded: "When you wrote your wounds were fresh, your lame and exhausted troops were before you. I hope time may have mollified your pain and that future operations may restore the confidence essential to cheerfulness and security in campaign."

That was enough for Smith, whose admiration for Davis was such that, if the President requested it, he would not only coöperate with Bragg, he would even serve under him if it was absolutely necessary. Grateful, Davis sent for him to come to Richmond in early November. Smith went and, like Polk, gave the President his personal assurance that his rancor had been laid by — as indeed it had. A week later he sent Bragg his strongest division, Stevenson's, and neither Smith nor any member of his staff permitted himself a public word of criticism of the leader of the Kentucky campaign for the balance of the war. Returning to Knoxville by way of Lynchburg (where he had convalesced from his Manassas wound and married the young lady who had nursed him) he had an unexpected encounter during a change of trains. "I saw Gen. Bragg," he wrote his wife; "everyone prognosticated a stormy meeting. I told him what I had written to Mr. Davis, but he spoke kindly to me & in the highest terms of praise and admiration of 'my personal character and soldierly qualities.' I was astonished but believe he is honest & means well."

Breckinridge was already with Bragg: in fact, had preceded the army to its present location. Following the repulse at Baton Rouge, after wiring Hardee to "reserve the division for me," he had reached Knoxville in early October with about 2500 men. Reinforced by an equal number of exchanged prisoners, he had been about to start northward in order to share in the "liberation" of his native Bluegrass, when he received word that Bragg was on the way back and wanted him to proceed instead to Murfreesboro, where he was to dispose his troops "for the defense of Middle Tennessee or an attack on Nashville." He got there October 28, joining Forrest, who had been deviling the Federals by way of breaking in his newly recruited "critter companies." Bragg's 30,000 veterans arrived under Polk and Hardee ten days later, and when Stevenson's 9000-man division marched in from Knoxville shortly afterward, the army totaled 44,000 infantry and artillery effectives, plus about 4000 organic cavalry under Wheeler. This was by no means as large a force as Rosecrans was assembling within the Nashville intrenchments, but Bragg did not despair of whipping him when he emerged. Returning from Richmond with assurances of the President's confidence, he set about the familiar task of drilling his troops and stiffening the discipline which Buell had admired. Meanwhile, he turned Forrest and Morgan loose on Rosecrans, front and rear. "Harass him in every conceivable way in your power," he told them. And they did, thus fulfilling the anticipation announced in general orders, November 20: "Much is expected by the army and its commander from the operations of these active and ever-successful leaders."

Nor were the infantry neglected in their commander's announcement of his hopes. Having posted Stevenson's division in front of Manchester, Hardee's corps at Shelbyville, and Polk's at Murfreesboro — the latter now including Breckinridge, so that Polk had three and Hardee two divisions — Bragg announced in the same general order that the army had a new name: "The foregoing dispositions are in anticipation of the great struggle which must soon settle the question of supremacy in Middle Tennessee. The enemy in heavy force is before us, with a determination, no doubt, to redeem the fruitful country we have wrested from him. With the remembrance of Richmond, Munfordville, and Perryville so fresh in our minds, let us make a name for the now Army of Tennessee as enviable as those enjoyed by the armies of Kentucky and the Mississippi."

★ ★ ★ *P*resumably this was the best that could be done in that direction: Davis had sustained the army commander and persuaded his irate subordinates to lay aside their personal and official differences in order to concentrate on the defense of the vital center in Tennessee. South and west of there, however, the problem was not one of persuading delicate gears to mesh, but rather one of filling the near vacuum created by the bloody repulse Van Dorn and Price had suffered in front of Corinth. Vicksburg was obviously about to become the target for a renewed

*Confederate raiders savaged the Federal hinterland in
northern Tennessee, burning Columbia River steamboats
(above) and attacking Union-controlled rail lines.*

endeavor by Federal combinations. What these would be, Davis did not know, but whatever they were, they posed a problem that would have to be met before they got there. He met it obliquely, so to speak, by turning initially to a second problem, seven hundred miles away, whose solution automatically provided him with a solution to the first.

This was the problem of Charleston, where the trouble was also an outgrowth of dissension. John Pemberton, in command there, had been a class-mate of Bragg's and had several of that general's less fortunate characteristics, including an abruptness of manner which, taken in conjunction with his north-ern birth, had earned him a personal unpopularity rivaling the North Carolin-ian's. Indeed, not being restricted to the army, it surpassed it. He was "wanting in polish," according to one Confederate observer, "and was too positive and domineering . . . to suit the sensitive and polite people among whom he had been thrown." As a result, he had not been long in incurring the displeasure of Governor Pickens and the enmity of the Rhetts, along with that of other Charlestonians of influence, who by now were clamoring for his removal. They wanted their first hero back: meaning Beauregard. It was a more or less familiar cry to Davis, for others were also calling for the Creole, still restoring his "shat-tered health" at Bladon Springs. In mid-September two Louisiana congressmen brought to the President's office a petition signed by themselves and fifty-seven fellow members, requesting the general's return to command of the army that had been taken from him. Davis read the document aloud, including the signa-tures, then sent for the official correspondence relating to Beauregard's removal for being absent without leave. This too he read aloud, as proof of justice in his action on the case, and closed the interview by saying: "If the whole world were to ask me to restore General Beauregard to the command which I have already given to General Bragg, I would refuse it."

In any case, he had decided by then to use him in the opposite direc-tion: meaning Charleston. Orders had been drawn up in late August, appointing Beauregard to command the Department of South Carolina and Georgia, with headquarters in Charleston. Whether he would accept the back-area appoint-ment, which amounted in effect to a demotion, was not known. Yet there should have been little doubt; for the choice, after all, lay between limited action and *in*action. *"Nil desperandum* is my motto," he had declared, chafing in idle-ness earlier that month, "and I feel confident that ere long the glorious sun of Southern liberty will appear more radiant than ever from the clouds which obscure its brilliant disk." He wanted a share in scouring those clouds away. Receiving the orders in early September, he told a friend: "If the country is will-ing I should be put on the shelf thro' interested motives, I will submit until our future reverses will compel the Govt to put me on duty. I scorn its motives and present action." He wired acceptance, took the cars at Mobile on September 11, and received a tumultuous welcome on the 15th when he returned to the city whose harbor had been the scene of his first glory.

This not only freed the embittered Charlestonians of Pemberton; it also freed Pemberton for the larger duty Davis had in mind, along with his promotion as seventh man on the seven-man list of new lieutenant generals. Slender and sharp-faced, the forty-eight-year-old Pennsylvanian had been pro-Southern all his adult life, choosing southern cadets as his West Point friends and later marrying a girl from Old Point Comfort. He was, indeed, an out-and-out States Righter, and it was generally known in army circles that in making his choice of sides in the present conflict, despite the fact that two of his brothers had joined a Philadelphia cavalry troop, he had declined a Federal colonelcy in order to accept a commission as a Confederate lieutenant colonel and assignment to Norfolk, where he had been charged with organizing Virginia's cavalry and artillery. Efficiency at that assignment had won him a brigadier's stars and transfer to Charleston, where his ability as an administrator — whatever his shortcomings

"I feel confident that ere long the glorious sun of Southern liberty will appear more radiant than ever from the clouds which obscure its brilliant disk."

— P. G. T. Beauregard

when it came to social converse — had won him another promotion and eventually still another, along with another transfer, in connection with the larger duty Davis had in mind. This was for Pemberton to take charge of a department created October 1, consisting of the whole state of Mississippi and that part of Louisiana east of the Mississippi River. Instructed to "consider the successful defense of those States" — one already invaded from the north, the other already invaded from the south — "as the first and chief object of your command," he was told to proceed at once to his new post: which he did. Arriving October 14, he established department headquarters at Jackson, Mississippi.

There were, as usual, objections. Mainly these came from men over whose heads he had been advanced in his rush up the ladder of rank, including Van Dorn and Lovell, here in his own department, as well as others back in the theater he had come from; "officers who," as one of them protested, "had already distinguished themselves and given unquestioned evidence of capacity, efficiency, and other soldierly qualities." By this last, the disgruntled observer meant combat — for Pemberton had seen none since the Mexican War. Also, it was felt that he lacked the flexibility of mind necessary to independent command of a region under pressure from various directions. But the fact was, Davis had already taken this into consideration. Pemberton's main job would be to keep a bulldog grip on Vicksburg and Port Hudson, denying free use of the Mississippi to the Federals and keeping the stretch of river between those two bastions open as a Confederate supply line connecting its opposite banks. Inflexibility in the performance of such a job — even tactical and strategic near-sightedness, of which the new commander was also accused by those who had known him in the East — might turn out to be a positive virtue when he was confronted, as surely he would be, by combinations which well might cause a more "flexible" man to fly to pieces. So Davis reasoned, at any rate, when he assigned the Northerner to defend his home state. And at least one Vicksburg editor agreed, declaring that Pemberton's arrival at last demonstrated that the far-off Richmond government had not "failed to appreciate the vast importance of preserving this important region" and that Mississippians were no longer "to be put off and imposed upon with one-horse generals."

Whatever their resentment of his rapid rise, his northern birth, his lack of exposure to gunfire, and his uncongenial manner, Pemberton's by-passed fellow officers — even Van Dorn, whose ruffled feathers Davis smoothed by explaining that the appointment had been made, not to overslough him, but to unburden him of paperwork and other back-area concerns, in order to free him for the offensive action which he so much preferred — would doubtless have been less envious if they had been able to compare the magnitude of the new commander's "first and chief object" with the means which he had inherited for effecting it. He had fewer than 50,000 troops of all arms in his entire department: 24,000 under Van Dorn and Price — disaffected Transmississippians for the most part, anxious to get back across the river for the close-up protection of their homes — and another 24,000 mainly comprising the permanent garrisons of Vicksburg and Port Hudson. Even without knowledge of the three-pronged Federal build-up now in progress north and south of these two critical points (a combined force of more than 100,000 men, supported by the guns of two fleets) it was obvious that the difficulties of the assignment would be exceeded only by the clamor which would follow if he failed, whatever the odds.

★ ★ ★ *H*ere too, however, Davis had done what he could and as he thought best. Having sustained Bragg, installed Pemberton, and incidentally disposed of Beauregard, he found it in a way a relief to give his attention to the army closest to the capital: for its troubles, although manifold, were at least of a different nature. Though Lee's invasion had been less profitable than Bragg's, and his repulse far bloodier, no one could accuse him of unwillingness to exploit any

★

236

opening the enemy afforded, regardless of the numerical odds or the tactical risks of annihilation. As a result, such disaffection as arose was not directed against him, either by his army or by the public it protected, but against Congress, which bridled at passing certain measures Lee suggested for the recruitment of new men, the establishment of proper supply facilities for the benefit of the men he had — including the more than 10,000 who now were marching barefoot in the snow — and the authority to tighten discipline.

The President supported Lee in the controversy and wrote him of the scorn he felt for their opponents, who were reacting simultaneously to rumors that the enemy was about to advance on Richmond from Suffolk: "The feverish anxiety to invade the North has been relieved by the counter-irritant of apprehension for the safety of the capital in the absence of the army, so long criticised for a 'want of dash,' and the class who so vociferously urged a forward movement, in which they were not personally involved, would now be most pleased to welcome the return of that army. I hope their fears are as poor counselors as was their presumption." He assured the Virginian, "I am alike happy in the confidence felt in your ability, and your superiority to outside clamor, when the uninformed assume to direct the movements of armies in the field." Lee replied characteristically: "I wish I felt that I deserved the confidence you express in me. I am only conscious of an earnest desire to advance the interests of the country and of my inability to accomplish my wishes."

Davis left the field work to Lee, while he himself took up the fight with Congress throughout its stormy second session, which extended from mid-August to mid-October. Two of the general's recommendations resulted in much violent debate: 1) that a permanent court martial be appointed, with authority to inflict the death penalty in an attempt to reduce straggling and desertion, and 2) that the Conscription Act be extended to include all able-bodied men between the ages of eighteen and forty-five. The first of these suggestions was not only not acceptable to the law-makers, it led to vigorous inquiries as to whether such powers had not been overexercised already. But it was the second which provoked the greatest furor, especially after Davis gave it presidential support. Yancey was particularly vitriolic, shouting that if he had to have a dictator, he wanted it to be Lincoln, "not a Confederate." Joe Brown of Georgia thought so too, declaring that the people had "much more to apprehend from military despotism than from subjection by the enemy." A Texas senator added point to the assertion, as here applied, by recalling that it had been conscription which "enabled [Napoleon] to put a diadem on his head." Davis met these charges with a bitterness matching that of the men who made them; and in the end he won the fight. Conscription was extended, but not without the estrangement of former loyal friends whose loss he could ill afford. As always, he was willing to pay the price, though it was becoming increasingly steep in obedience to the law of diminishing utility.

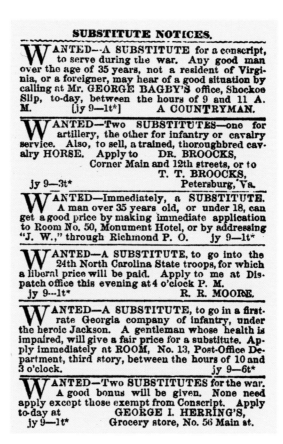

Advertisements in the Richmond Dispatch seek men willing to serve as substitutes for fainthearted draftees, a practice that was subject to widespread abuse.

At any rate the measure helped secure for Lee the men he badly needed, and while Davis engaged these wranglers in the army's rear, the bluecoats to its front were obligingly idle, affording time for rest, recruitment, and reorganization of its shattered ranks. The need for these was obvious at a glance. Recrossing the Potomac, only fourteen of the forty brigades had been led by brigadiers, and many of them had dwindled until they were smaller than a standard regiment. Yet the return of stragglers and convalescents, along with the influx of conscripts, more than repaired the shortage in the course of the five-week respite the Federals allowed. By October 10, Lee's strength had risen to 64,273 of all arms, and within another ten days — on which date McClellan reported 133,433 present for duty in the Army of the Potomac — he had 68,033, or better than half as many as his opponent. High spirits, too, were restored. Pride in their great defensive fight at Sharpsburg, when the odds had been even longer, and presently their jubilation over Stuart's second "Ride Around McClellan," solidified into a conviction that the Army of Northern Virginia was more than a match for whatever came against it, even if the Yankees continued to fight as well as they had fought in Maryland. Shortages of equipment there still were, especially of shoes and clothes, but these were accepted as rather the norm and relatively unimportant. A British army observer, visiting Lee at the time, expressed surprise at the condition of the trousers of the men in Hood's division, the rents and tatters being especially apparent after the first files had passed in review. "Never mind the raggedness, Colonel," Lee said quietly. "The enemy never sees the backs of my Texans."

He spoke, the colonel observed, "as a man proud of his country and confident of ultimate success." However, this was for the southern commander a time of personal sorrow. Soon after October 20 he heard from his wife of the death on that date of the second of his three daughters. She was twenty-three years old and had been named for his mother, born Ann Carter. He turned to some official correspondence, seeking thus to hide his grief, but presently an aide came into the tent and found him weeping. "I cannot express the anguish I feel at the death of my sweet Annie," he wrote home.

Work was still the best remedy, he believed, and fortunately there was plenty to occupy him. The previously informal corps arrangement was made official in early November with the promotion of Longstreet and Jackson, respectively first and fifth on the list of lieutenant generals. By that time, more-over, the Federals had crossed the river which gave their army its name, and Lee had divided his own in order to cover their alternate routes of approach, shifting Old Pete down to Culpeper while Stonewall remained in the lower Valley, eager to pounce through one of the Blue Ridge gaps and onto the enemy flank. But this was not Pope; this was McClellan. He maneuvered skillfully, keeping the gaps well plugged as he advanced against the divided Confederates. Then suddenly, inexplicably, he stopped. For two days Lee was left wondering: until November 10, that is, when he learned that Little Mac had been relieved. The southern reaction was not unmixed. Some believed that the Federals would be demoralized by McClellan's removal, while others found assurance in the conviction that his successor would be more likely to commit some blunder which would expose the blue host to destruction. Lee, however, expressed regret at the departure of a familiar and respected adversary. "We always under-stood each other so well," he said wryly. "I fear they may continue to make these changes till they find someone whom I don't understand."

When Burnside shifted east in mid-November, Lee's first plan was to occupy the line of the North Anna, twenty-five miles south of the Rappa-hannock. From there he would draw the bluecoats into the intervening wintry swamps and woodlands, then move forward and outflank them in order to slash at them from astride their line of retreat. If successful, this would have been to stage a Sedan eight years ahead of the historical schedule; Jackson, for one, was very much in favor of it. If on the other hand the Confederates con-tested the Rappahannock crossing, where the position afforded little depth for

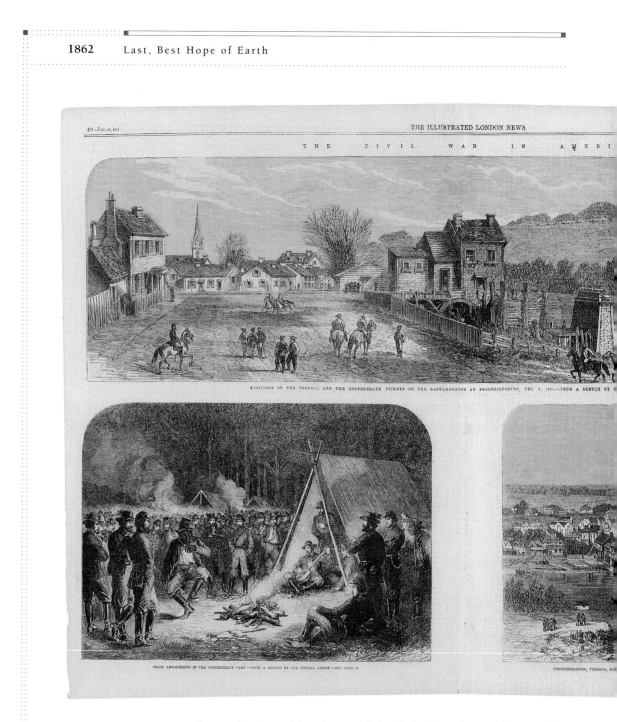

THE ILLUSTRATED LONDON NEWS

POSITIONS OF THE FEDERAL AND THE CONFEDERATE PICKETS ON THE RAPPAHANNOCK AT FREDERICKSBURG, DEC. 4, 1862.—FROM A SKETCH BY

NIGHT AMUSEMENTS IN THE CONFEDERATE CAMP.—FROM A SKETCH BY OUR SPECIAL ARTIST.—SEE PAGE 41.

FREDERICKSBURG, VIRGINIA, SO

maneuver and was dominated by the north-bank heights, it was Stonewall's opinion that they would "whip the enemy, but gain no fruits of victory." However, Lee did not want to give up the previously unmolested territory and expose the vital railroad to destruction; so while Burnside balked at Falmouth, awaiting the delayed pontoons, the southern commander moved Longstreet onto the heights in rear of Fredericksburg. This suited Old Pete fine; for the position offered all the defensive advantages he most admired, if only "the damned Yankees" could be persuaded to "come to us."

★

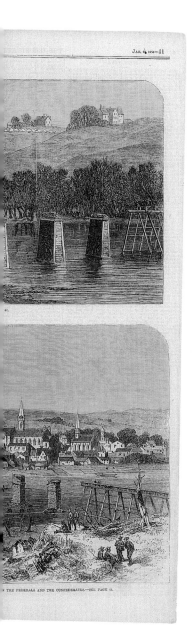

A January 1863 edition of The Illustrated London News featured two views of Fredericksburg's riverfront (top and right) and a Confederate camp scene.

Apparently they were coming, here or somewhere near here, but they were taking their time about it. ("When are you coming over, blue-coat?" "When we get ready, butternut.") For ten days Lee left the vigil to Longstreet, withholding Jackson for a flank attack if Burnside crossed upstream. Then, as the indications grew that a crossing would be attempted here, he sent for Stonewall, whose troops began to file into position alongside Longstreet's on the first day of December. By that time the army had grown to 70,000 infantry and artillery, plus 7000 cavalry, and its spirit was higher than ever, despite the fact that one man in every six was barefoot. They now bore with patience, one officer remarked, "what they once would have regarded as beyond human endurance." Even a four-inch snowfall on the night of December 5, followed by bitter cold weather, failed to lower their morale. Rather, they organized brigade-sized snowball battles, during which their colonels put them through the evolutions of the line, and thus kept in practice while waiting for the Yankees to cross the river flowing slate gray between its cake-icing banks.

Lee shared their hardships and their confidence. Sometimes, though, alone in his tent, he was oppressed by sorrow for the daughter who had died six weeks ago. "In the quiet hours of the night, when there is nothing to lighten the full weight of my grief," he wrote home, "I feel as if I should be overwhelmed. I have always counted, if God should spare me a few days after this Civil War has ended, that I should have her with me, but year after year my hopes go out, and I must be resigned." Mainly his consolation was his army. Though he told his wife, "I tremble for my country when I hear of confidence expressed in me. I know too well my weakness, and that our only hope is in God," his admiration for the men he led was almost without bounds. "I am glad you derive satisfaction from the operations of the army," he replied to a congratulatory letter from his brother. "I acknowledge nothing can surpass the valor and endurance of our troops, yet while so much remains to be done, I feel as if nothing had been accomplished. But we must endure to the end, and if our people are true to themselves and our soldiers continue to discard all thoughts of self and to press nobly forward in defense alone of their country and their rights, I have no fear of the result. We may be annihilated, but we cannot be conquered. No sooner is one [Federal] army scattered than another rises up. This snatches from us the fruits of victory and covers the battlefield with our dead. Yet what have we to live for if not victorious?"

It was this spirit which made Lee's army "terrible in battle," and it was in this spirit that he and his men awaited Burnside's crossing of the Rappahannock.

★ ★ ★   Off in the Transmississippi, the sixth of the new lieutenant generals, Theophilus Holmes, had established headquarters at Little Rock and from there was surveying a situation which was perhaps as confusing for him as the one near Malvern Hill, where he had cupped a deaf ear in the midst of a heavy bombardment and declared that he thought he "heard firing." If he was similarly bewildered it was no wonder, considering the contrast between the geographical vastness of his command and the slimness of his resources. In addition to Texas and Missouri, the two largest states of the old Union, he was theoretically responsible for holding or reclaiming Arkansas, Indian Territory, West Louisiana, and New Mexico, in all of which combined he had fewer than 50,000 men, including guerillas. These last were sometimes as much trouble to him as they were to the enemy, especially as an administrative concern, and even the so-called "regulars" were generally well beyond his reach, being loosely connected with headquarters, if at all, by lines of supply and communication which could only be characterized as primitive, telegraph wire being quite as rare as railroad iron. By late October, after three months of pondering the odds, he had begun to consider not only the probability of total defeat, but also the line of conduct he and his men would follow in the wake of that disaster. In this he showed that, whatever his physical shortcomings and infirmities, his spirit was undamaged. "We hate you with a cordial hatred," he told an Indiana colonel who came to Little Rock bearing messages under a flag of truce. "You may conquer us and parcel out our lands among your soldiers, but you must remember that one incident of history: to wit, that of all the Russians who settled in Poland not one died a natural death."

Moreover, his three department commanders — John Magruder, Richard Taylor, and Thomas Hindman, respectively in charge of Texas, West

Louisiana, and Arkansas — shared his resolution, but not his gloom. All three were working, even now, on plans for the recovery of all that had been lost. Prince John for example, as flamboyant in the Lone Star State as ever he had been in the Old Dominion, was improvising behind the scenes a two-boat cotton-clad navy with which he intended to steam down Buffalo Bayou and re-take Galveston, the only Federal-held point in his department. Taylor's ambition was longer-ranged — as well it had to be; New Orleans was occupied by something more than ten times as many soldiers and sailors as he had in his whole command — but he had hopes for the eventual recapture of the South's first city, along with the lower reaches of the Father of Waters itself. Meanwhile, having recovered from the mysterious paralysis which had gripped his legs on the eve of the Seven Days, thus preventing any addition to the reputation he had won under Jackson in the Valley, he was working hard with what little he had in the way of men and guns, seeking first to establish dispersed strong-points with which to forestall a further penetration by the gunboats and the probing Union columns, after which he intended to swing over to the offensive and reclaim what had been lost to amphibious combinations heretofore considered too powerful to resist with any substantial hope of success.

Of the three, so far, it was Hindman who had accomplished most, however, and against the longest odds. Operating in a region which had been stripped of troops when Van Dorn crossed the Mississippi back in April, he yet had managed to raise and equip an army of 16,000 men, and with them he had already begun to launch an offensive against Schofield, who had about the same number for the protection of the Missouri border. By late August, Hindman was across it; or anyhow a third of his soldiers were, and he was preparing to join them with the rest. Skirting Helena, where 15,000 Federals were intrenched — they now were under Brigadier General Frederick Steele, Curtis having moved on to St Louis and command of the department, belatedly rewarded for his Pea Ridge victory — the Confederate advance occupied Newtonia, beyond Neosho and southwest of Springfield. All through September they stayed there, 2500 Missouri cavalry under Colonel J. O. Shelby and about 3000 Indians and guerillas, called in to assist in holding the place until Hindman arrived with the other two thirds of his hastily improvised army. Shelby was a graduate of the prewar Kansas border conflict, a stocky, heavily bearded man approaching his thirty-second birthday. Called "Jo" for his initials, just as Stuart was called "Jeb," and wearing like him an ostrich plume attached to the upturned brim of a soft felt hat, he was a veteran of nearby Wilson's Creek and of Elkhorn Tavern, forty miles to the south. With him out front, and the stone walls of the town to fight behind, the garrison was more than a match for a 4000-man column Schofield sent to retake Newtonia on the last day of September. The Confederates broke the point of the counterthrust and drove the bluecoats north. However, learning three days

ℋentucky-born cavalryman J. O. Shelby and his "Iron Brigade" were the scourge of Federal forces in Missouri.

later (October 3: Van Dorn and Price were moving against Corinth) that the Federals had been reinforced to thrice their former strength, they fell back next day in the direction of the Boston Mountains, Shelby skillfully covering the retreat with a succession of slashing attacks and quick withdrawals.

Hindman was not discouraged by this turn of events. In fact, he saw in it certain advantages. Schofield should be easier to whip if he advanced into Arkansas, lengthening his lines of supply — and lengthening, too, the distance he would have to backtrack through the wintry woods in order to regain the comparative security of Missouri. Under such disadvantages, a simple repulse might be transformed into a disaster. At any rate, Hindman intended to do all he could to bring about that result. But as he prepared to move forward in early November, consolidating the segments of his army, he received news that was discouraging indeed. It came from Holmes, who had just received in Little Rock a dispatch from Richmond, dated October 27 and signed by the Secretary of War: "Coöperation between General Pemberton and yourself is indispensable to the preservation of our connection with your department. We regard this as an object of first importance, and when necessary you can cross the Mississippi with such part of your forces as you may select, and by virtue of your rank direct the combined operations on the eastern bank."

This meant, in effect, that Hindman's offensive would have to be abandoned. And when it was followed in mid-November by a specific request from the Adjutant General ("Vicksburg is threatened and requires to be reinforced. Can you send troops from your command — say 10,000 — to operate either opposite to Vicksburg or to cross the river?") Holmes perceived that it meant the abandonment, not only of his hopes for regaining Missouri, but also of his hopes for hanging onto Arkansas. "I could not get to Vicksburg in less than two weeks," he protested. "There is nothing to subsist on between here and there, and [Steele's] army at Helena would come to Little Rock before I reached Vicksburg."

However, he need not have worried. He was not going anywhere. Nor was Hindman's offensive to be interrupted: at any rate not by anyone in

Richmond, and least of all by Thomas Jefferson's grandson George Randolph. Presently it became fairly clear that the original dispatch sent by that official, though couched in the form of a military directive, was in effect an act of political suicide, whereby the Confederacy lost the third of its several Secretaries of War.

★ ★ ★   *J*oe Johnston was one of the first to get inside news of the impending disruption in the President's official family, and what was more he got it at first hand. His Seven Pines wound had proved troublous, resulting in what the doctors called "an obstinate adhesion of the lungs to the side, and a constant tendency to pleurisy," for which the prescribed treatments were "bleedings, blisterings, and depletions of the system." All three were stringently applied: in spite of which, having sufficiently recovered by early November to begin taking horseback exercise — "My other occupation," he told a friend, "is blistering myself, to which habit hasn't yet reconciled me" — the general called at the War Department on the 12th of that month to report himself fit for duty. Closeted with the Secretary, he learned that the government intended to send him West, where his assignment would be to coördinate the efforts of Bragg and Pemberton for the defense of Tennessee and Mississippi. Perceiving that each was not only too weak to reinforce the other, but also most likely too weak to handle what was coming at him — particularly the latter, since the Federals were certain to make Vicksburg their prime objective in the offensive they were clearly about to launch — Johnston at once suggested that the best solution would be to bring additional troops from the Transmississippi to assist in the east-bank defense of the big river.

Randolph replied that he had reached the same decision, more than two weeks ago, and read to his fellow Virginian the dispatch he had sent Holmes. When he had finished, he smiled rather strangely and took up another document, which he also read aloud. It was dated today and signed by Jefferson Davis: "I regret to notice that in your letter to General Holmes of October 27, a copy of which is before me, you suggest the propriety of his crossing the Mississippi and assuming command on the east side of the river. His presence on the west side is not less necessary now than heretofore, and will probably soon be more so. The coöperation designed by me was in co-intelligent action on both sides of the river of such detachment of troops as circumstances might require and warrant. The withdrawal of the commander from the Trans-Mississippi Department for temporary duty elsewhere would have a disastrous effect, and was not contemplated by me."

Johnston recognized the tone, having received such directives himself. He knew, too, what response this son of Thomas Jefferson's oldest daughter was likely to make to such a letter. The question was, what had made him so deliberately provoke it? Yet Johnston knew the answer here as well. Eight months of service as "the clerk of Mr Davis," sometimes learning of vital military decisions only after they had been made and acted on, had brought home to Randolph the truth of one observer's remark "that the real war lord of the South resided in the executive mansion." The message to Holmes, sent without previous consultation with the Commander in Chief, was in the nature of a gesture of self-assertion, desperate but necessary to the preservation of his self-respect. And now he accepted the consequences. Two days later, having added an indorsement to the offending document sent by Davis — "Inclose a copy of this letter to General Holmes, and inform the President that it has been done, and that [Holmes] has been directed to consider it as part of his instructions" — he submitted his formal resignation.

This had been neither intended nor expected by Davis, who up to now had been highly pleased with Randolph as a member of his cabinet. Except for two particulars, he had not even disapproved of the Secretary's decision to bring troops across the river to assist in the defense of Vicksburg. In fact, he himself ordered this done that same week, when he had the Adjutant General send Holmes the request for 10,000 men to be used for this very purpose. What he objected to, most strenuously, were the two particulars: 1) that Holmes himself was advised to cross, which would leave his department headless, and 2) that the thing had been done behind his back, without his knowledge. It was this last which disturbed him most. As Commander in Chief he saw himself as chief engineer of the whole vast machine; if adjustments were made without his knowledge, a wreck was almost certain. In this case, however, receiving the tart letter of resignation, he sought to prevent a break by suggesting a personal interview at which he and the Virginian could discuss their differences. Randolph declined, and Davis would bend no further. "As you thus without notice and in terms excluding inquiry retired," he replied, "nothing remains but to give you this formal notice of the acceptance of your resignation."

G. W. Smith, recovered from the collapse he had suffered when Johnston's fall left him in charge of the confused and confusing field of Seven Pines, had been serving as commander of the Richmond defenses ever since Lee and his army departed to deal with Pope, back in August. Now Davis found a further use for the former New York Street Commissioner by assigning him to serve as head of the War Department during the three-day interim, which he himself spent in search of a permanent — if the word could be used properly in reference to a position which, so far, had been so impermanent — replacement for Randolph, who retired at once to private life and subsequently "refugeed" in Europe with his family.

Once more the Old Dominion had been left without a representative among the President's chief advisers, and once more Davis solved the problem, this time by appointing James A. Seddon to be Secretary of War. A

Richmond lawyer who had served two terms as U.S. Congressman from the district, a former occupant of the present Confederate White House, and a descendant of James River grandees, Seddon ranked about as high in the complicated Virginia caste system as even Randolph did, with the result that his selection was a source of considerable satisfaction to those who had become accustomed to looking down their noses at what they called "the middle-class atmosphere" of official Richmond. Moreover, he had a reputation as a scholar and a philosopher, though what service this would be to him in his new position was unknown; he had had no previous military experience whatever. Nor was his appearance reassuring. "Gaunt and emaciated," one observer called him, "with long straggling hair, mingled gray and black." He was forty-seven, but looked much older, perhaps because of chronic neuralgia, which racked him nearly as badly as it racked Davis. He looked, in fact, according to the same diarist, "like a dead man galvanized into muscular animation. His eyes are sunken and his features have the hue of a man who has been in his grave a full month."

At any rate, whatever his lack of the kind of training which would have cautioned him to guard his flanks and rear, it soon became apparent that he did not intend to expose himself to attack from above, as his predecessor had done. Johnston went to him on November 22, the new Secretary's first full day in office, and renewed his suggestion that troops be ordered east from the Transmississippi. Seddon listened sympathetically. But when Johnston received his orders two days later, assigning him to the region lying between the Blue Ridge Mountains and the Mississippi River, he was surprised to find that they contained no reference to troops not already within those limits. "The suggestion was not adopted or noticed," he afterwards recorded dryly.

★ ★ ★ *D*avis had a higher opinion of Johnston's abilities at this stage than the Virginian probably suspected. "I wish he were able to take the field," the President had told Mrs Davis during the general's convalescence. "Despite the critics, who know military affairs by instinct, he is a good soldier, never brags of what he did do, and could at this time render most valuable service." In no way, indeed, could the Commander in Chief have demonstrated this confidence more fully than by assigning him, as soon as he was fairly up and about, to what was called "plenary command" of the heartland of the Confederacy, an area embracing all of Tennessee, Mississippi, and Alabama, together with parts of North Carolina, Florida, and Georgia, including the main regional supply base at Atlanta. Moreover, he placed on him no restrictions within that geographical expanse, either as to his movements or the location of his headquarters, which he was instructed to establish "at Chattanooga, or such other place as in his judgment will best secure facilities for ready communication with the troops within the limits of his

Recovered from the wound he received at Seven Pines, Joe Johnston was anxious for a new command. His enthusiasm waned, however, when he learned of his new assignment in the West.

command, and will repair in person to any part of said command wherever his presence may, for the time, be necessary or desirable."

These instructions embodied a new concept of the function of departmental command, which in turn had been prompted by the example of R. E. Lee in his conduct of the defense of his native state. Lee's achievements here in Virginia, before as well as after he had been given field command, were in a large part the result of a successful coördination of the efforts of separate forces, either through simultaneous actions at divergent points — as when Jackson took the offensive in the Valley, threatening Washington to play on Lincoln's fears, while Johnston delayed McClellan's advance up the Peninsula — or through rapid concentration against a common point, as when all available forces were brought together for the attack which opened the Seven Days and accomplished the deliverance of Richmond. Subsequent repetition of this strategy, with a similar coördination of effort, had brought about the "suppression" of Pope and opened the way for invasion of the North, removing the war to that

★

extent beyond the Confederate border. Now it was Davis's hope that such methods, which had won for southern arms the admiration of the world and for Lee a place among history's great captains, would result in similar achievements in the West and give to the commander there a seat alongside Lee in Valhalla.

Choice of Johnston for the post was prompted by more than the fact that he was entitled to it by rank. Not only did Davis consider him a "good soldier" who could "render most valuable service," but the Virginian had also been asked for already by two of the three generals who would be his chief subordinates. During their recent visits to the capital, Bragg and Kirby Smith had both expressed an eagerness to have him over them, and doubtless Pemberton would be equally delighted to have the benefit of his advice, along with whatever reinforcements would become available in times of crisis as a result of the shuttle service the new theater commander was expected to establish between his several departments. How well he would do — whether he was potentially another Lee, and whether Bragg and Pemberton would serve him as well as Longstreet and Jackson had served the eastern commander — remained to be seen. So far, however, the resemblance had been anything but striking. His first reaction, expressed in a letter sent to the Adjutant General on the day he received the appointment, was a protest that his forces were "greatly inferior in number to those of the enemy opposed to them, while in the Trans-Mississippi Department our army is very much larger than that of the United States." He also complained of the presence of the Tennessee River, "a formidable obstacle" which divided his two main armies, and found it highly irregular that his department commanders — by an arrangement which Davis had designed "to avoid delay" — would be in direct correspondence with the War Department. This combination of drawbacks and irregularities, discerned by him before he even left Richmond, had already led him to suspect what he later stated flatly: "that my command was a nominal one merely, and useless."

Depressed by these several misgivings, he began at once to make arrangements for his journey west, and five days later he was off, accompanied by his wife and a new staff. In the interim, however, he found time to attend a farewell breakfast given in his honor and also in the hope that it would effect a reconciliation between two of his political friends, Senators Foote and Yancey, who had quarreled despite the common bond of their detestation of Davis. Under the healing influence of their admiration for Johnston, along with that of a bountiful meal accompanied by champagne, the two statesmen forgot their differences. Presently Yancey called for fresh glasses and proposed a toast. "Gentlemen, let us drink to the only man who can save the Confederacy. General Joseph E. Johnston!" All applauded, drank their wine, and took their seats: whereupon the guest of honor rose, glass in hand, and responded. "Mr Yancey," he said firmly, "the man you describe is now in the field — in the person of General Robert E. Lee. I will drink to his health." Not to be outdone, the silver-tongued Yancey rose and countered: "I can only reply to you, sir, as the Speaker of the House of Burgesses did to General Washington: 'Your modesty is only equaled by your valor.' " Again the celebrants applauded and drank the balding general's health. But he remained taciturn and preoccupied, as if his mind was already engaged by the frets he knew awaited him in the West.

In the course of the five-day trip to Chattanooga, delayed by no less than three railroad accidents, Johnston was much wearied, despite the ministrations of his wife and the cheers from station platforms along the way. Early on the morning of December 4 he got there. After resting briefly, he issued an order formally accepting his new responsibilities, although his gloom was unrelieved. "Nobody ever assumed a command under more unfavorable circumstances," he wrote to a friend in Richmond that same day.

———————— ∽∽∾ ————————

★ ★ ★   *J*ohnston's gloom, though it was not shared by the people in general, East or West — nor, for that matter, by those who cheered him from station platforms as he traveled from one to the other — was nonetheless reflected in the value of their dollar. After holding at 1.5 through August, it fell in October to 2, in November to 2.9, and by December it had dropped to 3. Statistics were dreary at best, however, except perhaps for those who dealt in money as a commodity. It was in terms of what the stuff would buy, shoved coin by coin across a counter or laid down bill by badly printed bill, that the meaning of such quotations really struck home. Now with winter hard upon the upper South, coal was $9 a handcart load and wood $16 a cord. Bacon was 75¢ a pound, sugar five cents higher. Butter was $1.25 and coffee twice that. To the despair of Richmond housewives, laundry soap was 75¢ a cake, flour $16 a barrel, and potatoes $6 a bushel.

For those of an analytical turn of mind, accustomed to looking behind effects for causes, it was more or less clear that the cause behind this particular close-to-home effect was the failure of the Confederacy's one concerted effort at invasion, East and West. Yet even here their reaction contained a good deal more of pride than of regret. "It was to be expected," Davis had told them, back at the outset, ". . . that [this war] would expose our people to sacrifices and cost them much, both of money and blood. . . . It was, perhaps, in the ordination of Providence that we were to be taught the value of our liberties by the price we pay for them." In the light of this, Bragg's thousand-mile hegira through Kentucky and Lee's bloody defense of the Sharpsburg ridge became for their countrymen, not occasions for despair, but instances for the promotion of the growth of national pride and the evocation of applause from those who

★

watched from afar. "Whatever may be the fate of the new nationality," the London *Times* was saying, "in its subsequent claims to the respect of mankind it will assuredly begin its career with a reputation for genius and valour which the most famous nations might envy."

Such public praise was welcome, as were certain private remarks from that same quarter. Thomas Carlyle, for example — though he pleased neither side with a reference to the American war as the burning out of a dirty chimney, a conflagration which could be regarded only with satisfaction by neighbors too long plagued by soot — amused and gladdened Southerners by subsequently professing his impatience with people who were "cutting each other's throats, because one half of them prefer hiring their servants for life, and the other by the hour." Most gratifying of all, however, were the observations colorfully expressed in the course of a banquet speech made at Newcastle, October 7, by Chancellor of the Exchequer William E. Gladstone. Professing the kindliest feeling toward the people of the North — "They are our kin. They were . . . our customers, and we hope they will be our customers again" — he denied that the British government had "any interest in the disruption of the Union." But he also declared, with particular emphasis: "There is no doubt that Jefferson Davis and other leaders of the South have made an army. They are making, it appears, a navy. And they have made what is more than either; they have made a nation." This was greeted with applause and cheers. "Hear, hear!" the diners cried. When they subsided, Gladstone added: "We may anticipate with certainty the success of the Southern States so far as regards their separation from the North."

Coming as it did from the third-ranking member of the Cabinet, the statement was assumed to reflect the views of the Government: which it did, except that Palmerston and Russell considered it precipitate and unpropitious: which it was, the Prime Minister having recently advised the Foreign Secretary that he thought it best to "wait awhile and see what may follow" Lee's retreat from Maryland. What had followed was the Preliminary Emancipation Proclamation, and though this document was greeted with sneers on the one hand and confusion on the other, it too provided an occasion for more waiting. Gladstone's outburst caused an immediate drop in the price of cotton, which apparently would soon be plentiful as a result of the lifting of the blockade, as well as an increase of activity by Members of Parliament sympathetic to the North. On October 22, two weeks after the Newcastle speech, Palmerston wrote Russell: "We must continue to be mere lookers-on till the war shall have taken a more decided turn."

On that same day, the French Emperor granted Slidell an audience at St Cloud during which he let the Confederate minister understand that he considered the time ripe for joint mediation by France, England, and Russia. "My own preference is for a proposition of an armistice of six months," he said. "This would put a stop to the effusion of blood, and hostilities would probably never be resumed. We can urge it on the high grounds of humanity and the interest of the whole civilized world. If it be refused by the North, it will afford good reason for recognition, and perhaps for more active intervention." Eight days later, as good as his word — and with his eye still fixed on the promised hundred thousand bales of cotton — he addressed, through his Minister of Foreign Affairs, a dispatch to his ambassadors at St Petersburg and London, proposing that the three governments "exert their influence at Washington, as well as with the Confederates, to obtain an armistice." Russia's answer was emphatic: "In our opinion, what ought specially to be avoided [is] the appearance of any

pressure whatsoever of a nature to wound public opinion in the United States and to excite susceptibilities very easily aroused at the bare idea of foreign intervention." England's was scarcely less so, Russell declining for the reason "that there is no ground at the present moment to hope that the Federal government would accept the proposal suggested, and a refusal from Washington at the present time would prevent any speedy renewal of the offer."

Napoleon, then, was as far as ever from those hundred thousand bales, and so was the Confederacy from recognition by the powers of Europe. England was to blame; for France could act without Russia, but not without England; England swung the balance. And yet, admittedly, Southerners already had much to be thankful for, if not from the British government, then at least from British individuals: particularly the owners of and workers in shipyards up the Mersey. Gladstone's remark that the Confederates "are making, it appears, a navy" was based on solid ground — ground which, indeed, was of his own countrymen's making. In late July, a powerful new screw steamer known mysteriously as the *290* had steamed down from Liverpool, supposedly on a trial run, but headed instead for the open sea and a rendezvous off the Azores, where she took on provisions, coal, and guns, struck her English colors in favor of the Stars and Bars, swore in a crew, and exchanged her numerical designation for a name: the *Alabama*. She was the second to follow this course. Four months before, another such vessel, called the *Oreto*,

The largest of the three unfinished hulls visible in this scene of Liverpool's bustling shipyard is believed to be that of the future commerce raider Alabama.

had accomplished this same metamorphosis from merchantman to raider, and already she was at work as the Confederate cruiser *Florida,* her mission being the high-seas destruction of Federal commerce. Commanded by Captain J. N. Maffit, she was to take thirty-four prizes before her career ended two years later; but it was the *Alabama* which did most in this direction, provoking a rise of more than 900 percent in U.S. marine insurance and the transfer of over seven hundred Union merchant ships to British registry. Also, she gave the South another hero in the person of her skipper, Captain Raphael Semmes, a fifty-three-year-old Maryland-born Alabamian, known to his crew — mostly foreigners off the docks of Liverpool, whom he referred to as "a precious set of rascals" — as "Old Beeswax" because of the care he gave his long black needle-sharp mustachios.

He had had considerable experience at this kind of work as captain of the *Sumter,* the first of the rebel raiders. A commander in the old navy, ensconced in comfort as head of the Lighthouse Board in Washington, he had gone south in February of the year before and offered his services to the new government in Montgomery. Secretary Mallory sent him back north on a purchasing expedition, and when he returned informed him that the Confederacy had acquired a small propeller steamer of 500 tons. She was tied up to a New Orleans wharf, he added, awaiting a chance to slip past the Federal blockaders in order to undertake disruption of the sea lanes. "Mr Secretary, give me that ship," Semmes said. "I think I can make her answer the purpose." Mallory gave him what he asked for, along with general instructions: "On reaching the high seas you are to do the enemy's commerce the greatest injury in the shortest time. Choose your own cruising grounds. Burn, sink, and destroy, and be guided always by the laws of the nations and of humanity." That was in mid-April; Semmes made his escape from the mouth of the Mississippi on the last day of June, and took his first prize four days later. In the course of the next seven months he took seventeen more barks, brigantines, and schooners, which he captured, burned, or ransomed in the Gulf and the Atlantic. Bottled up in Gibraltar from January to April, he sold the *Sumter,* discharged her crew, and took passage for Southampton. Late in May he left for Nassau, intending to board a blockade runner there and get back home. If the navy had another ship for him, he would take it; if not, he planned to transfer to the army. What awaited him at Nassau, however, were instructions for him to return to England and assume secret command of the *290-Alabama.*

He took over, officially, off the island of Terceira on August 24, when the cruiser was formally commissioned. Having named the *Florida* for his native state, Mallory had named this second English-built warship for the state in which the Confederacy itself was born. Bark-rigged, with handsome, rakish lines, she was 235 feet in length, 32 feet in the beam, and displaced a thousand tons. Her armament was eight guns, three 32-pounders on each broadside and two pivot guns on the center line, one a 7-inch rifle and the other an 8-inch smoothbore. Two 300-horsepower engines gave her a speed of ten knots on steam alone, but with the help of her sails and a friendly wind she could make nearly fifteen, which approached top speed for sea-going ships of the time. When traveling under sail alone — as she often would, to conserve fuel; the 275 tons of coal in her bunkers were barely enough for eighteen days of steaming at moderate speed — her two-bladed screw could be triced up into a propeller well, clear of the water, and thus afford no drag. To her crew of 24 gray-clad officers and 120 men, she was a beautiful thing on her commissioning day. Her brass was bright; her decks were clean and fragrant; her taunt-hauled rigging gleamed with newness. To Semmes himself she seemed "a bride with the orange wreath about her brows, ready to be led to the altar."

Led instead on her shakedown cruise, she took her first prize twelve days later, the whaling schooner *Ocmulgee* of Edgartown, Massachusetts, caught with her sails furled, a dead whale moored alongside, and her crew busy strip-

---

She took her first prize twelve days later, the whaling schooner Ocmulgee of Edgartown, Massachusetts, caught with her sails furled, a dead whale moored alongside, and her crew busy stripping blubber.

---

ping blubber. Brimming with sperm oil, she was valued at $50,000 and made a spectacular conflagration. Semmes took her crew aboard the *Alabama*, released them next day within sight of land, their whaleboats loaded to the gunnels with all they had managed to salvage before their ship was burned, and continued his search for other prizes. Before September was over he had taken ten. In October he took eleven. By early December he had raised the total to twenty-six, removing from each its chronometer, which he added to the others in his collection, including the eighteen transferred from the *Sumter*, and wound them regularly by way of counting tally.

By now his fame, or infamy, was established. To Northerners, despite the invariable courtesy and consideration he showed his temporary captives, he was a bloodthirsty pirate, an "Algerine corsair." To his crew, often vexed that he allowed no individual pillage, he seemed no such thing. In time, despite the strangeness of his manner, including the fact that he seldom spoke to anyone, and the tightness of his discipline — "Democracies may do very well for the land," he once explained, "but monarchies, and pretty absolute monarchies at that, are

Maligned as a pirate in this northern cartoon, Captain Raphael Semmes of the Alabama consistently treated the crews of the ships he took with dignity.

the only successful governments for the sea" — the officers and men of the *Alabama* paid him not only his due of absolute obedience, but also the homage of genuine affection. It was not a question of patriotism. Few of the officers and none of the men were even Americans, let alone Southerners; they were mostly English, Welsh, and Irish, with a scattering of French, Italian, Spanish, and Russian sailors among them. Their allegiance was to him and the *Alabama*. They liked to watch his gray eyes glint blue when he sighted a prize off on the bulge of the horizon, and they approved of his Catholic devoutness, knowing that he began and ended each day on his knees before the little shrine in his cabin.

Blurred by distance, to his countrymen he was something less — and also something more. He was, in fact, a member of that growing band of heroes who, as the *Alabama* began her career with the burning of the *Ocmulgee,* seemed about to make good the impossible claims and threats with which the fire-eaters had prefaced the reality of war. Lee was crossing the Potomac, Bragg was on the march for Kentucky, and Kirby Smith was in Lexington; Semmes was therefore proof that the South could take the offensive at sea as well as on land. Moreover, though those others had been turned back, he kept on, taking prizes which he burned or sank or, if it was impractical to remove their crews and passengers to safety, released on "ransom bond." This last, sometimes resorted to when the cruiser was crowded to capacity with captives, was an agreement between

Semmes and the master of the vessel, whereby the latter pledged the owner to pay a stipulated amount "unto the President of the Confederate States of America . . . within thirty days after the conclusion of the present war." It was, in effect, a bet that the South would win, and as such it did much to increase the pride of Southerners in their lawyer-raider, who thus expressed before the eyes of the world their confidence in the outcome of their struggle for independence.

Another cause for pride in southern arms derived from an older source: in fact, from the oldest source of all. Though Lee and Bragg and Kirby Smith had returned from their expeditions, disappointing the hopes that had gone with them, Beauregard — the original hero, back on the scene of his original triumph — had not been long in justifying the cheers with which Charlestonians had greeted his return. October 22, five weeks after his arrival, a Federal attempt to cut the Charleston & Savannah Railroad at Pocotaligo, midway between those two coastal cities, was foiled when 4500 bluecoats under Ormsby Mitchel — within eight days of sudden death from yellow fever — were thrown back to their landing boats by half as many rebels. Casualties were 340 and 163, respectively. "Railroad uninjured," Beauregard wired Richmond. "Abolitionists left dead and wounded on the field. Our cavalry in hot pursuit." Old Bory was himself again.

★ ★ ★ *S*light though they were — by comparison, that is, with the resounding double failure, East and West, of the Confederacy's first concerted attempt at all-out invasion — these late fall and early winter successes, afloat and ashore, did much to sustain or restore the confidence of the southern people. Besides, they could tell themselves, the strategic offensive was for extra: a device to be employed from time to time, not so much with the intention of keeping the graybacks north of the Potomac or the Cumberland, but rather of establishing an interlude for harvesting the crops in forward areas and thereby gaining a breathing spell in which the natives could enjoy at least a temporary freedom from the oppressive presence of the bluecoats. It was the strategic defensive that counted; it was this they had been pledged to by their President when he told the world, "All we ask is to be let alone." And in this — considering the odds — they had been singularly successful: especially in the East, where three full-scale attempts at invasion had been smashed and a fourth halted dead in its tracks when its commander was retired for the second time. In the West, too, there was occasion for rejoicing and self-congratulation. After a long season of reverses, a series of collapses under inexorable pressure, the front of the principal sector had been advanced a hundred and fifty miles, from North Mississippi to Middle Tennessee; on the Mississippi itself, the upper and lower Union fleets, conjoined triumphantly above Vicksburg, had been sundered and sent their separate ways by a single homemade ironclad; while across the river, in Arkansas, an army created seemingly out of thin air was on the march for Missouri.

All this was much, enough indeed to satisfy the hungriest of seekers after glory, and the thought of such accomplishments went far toward offsetting the pain of earlier reverses. However, to ease the ache was not to cure the ailment; the effect of the worst of the early reverses still remained. Norfolk was lost, and with it the one hope for the home construction of a Confederate deep-sea navy. So — continuing clockwise, down and around the coast — were the North Carolina sounds, Port Royal and Fort Pulaski, Brunswick and Fernandina, Jacksonville and St Augustine, Apalachicola and Pensacola, Biloxi and Pass Christian, Ship Island and Galveston. All these were tangent hits, mainly painful to southern pride (and to southern pocketbooks, augmenting as they did the effectiveness of the Federal blockade) but there were others that hurt worse, being vital. Nashville was gone, and so were New Orleans and Memphis. At the time of their loss, people had told themselves that these cities would be recovered, along with the outlying points around the littoral, once the pressure in front had been relieved. Apparently, though, that had been mere whistling in the dark. Four times now the pressure had eased up: after First Manassas, Wilson's Creek, the evacuation of Corinth, and Second Manassas: yet in all four instances the southern commanders who tried to take advantage of the respite gained were either repulsed when they moved forward or else they fell back eventually of their own accord. In fact, of the four advances which had followed these events — Johnston's into northern Virginia, Price's into northern Missouri, Bragg's into Kentucky, and Lee's into Maryland — all but Bragg's had wound up south of the point from which they had been launched. It was small wonder then, at this stage, that Southerners discounted the advantages of the offensive, considering how little had been gained from three of these four attempts and how much had been lost by two others, Shiloh and Baton Rouge, even though both were generally referred to as tactical victories and were prime sources of the glory, which, so far, had been the South's chief gain from twenty months of war.

Yet glory was a flimsy diet at best, containing far more of what Southerners called "suption" than of substance. No one realized this better than Davis, who had had an overplus of glory down the years and who, familiar with it as he was, knew how little real sustenance it afforded. Moreover, as a professional soldier, in touch with every department of the army he commanded, he not only recognized the odds his country faced in its struggle for independence; he saw that they were lengthening with every passing month as the North's tremendous potential was converted into actuality. In that sense, not only was time against him; even success was against him, for each northern reverse brought on a quickening of the tempo of conversion. And yet, paradoxically, it was time for which he was fighting. Time alone could bring into being, in the North, the discouragement — the sheer boredom, even — which was the South's chief hope for victory if foreign intervention failed to materialize, as now seemed likely.

Meanwhile, there were the odds to face, and Davis faced them. He did not know what future combinations were being designed for the Confederacy's destruction, but he knew they would be heavy when they came. Here in the East, Lee could be trusted to cope with whatever forces the Union high command might conceive to be his match. Likewise in the Transmississippi, though the outlook was far from bright, Hindman's improvisations, Magruder's theatrical ingenuity, and Taylor's hard-working common sense gave promise of achieving at least a balance. It was in the West — that region between the Blue Ridge and the Mississippi, where Federal troops had scored their most substantial gains — that the Commander in Chief perceived the gravest danger. Whether Johnston would prove himself another Lee, coördinating the efforts of his separate armies in order to frustrate those of his opponents, remained to be seen. So far, though, the signs had not been promising. A gloom had descended on the gamecock general, who seemed more intent on acquiring troops from outside

As the war dragged on, President Jefferson Davis personally assumed more and more of the burden of securing southern independence in the face of ever-increasing odds.

his department than on setting up a system for the mutual support of those within it. Also, there were continuing rumors of dissension in Bragg's army. All this seemed to indicate a need for intervention, or at any rate a personal inspection, by the man who had designed the new command arrangement in the first place. Davis had not been more than a day's trip from Richmond since his arrival in late May of the year before, but now in early December he packed his bags for the long ride to Chattanooga and Vicksburg. Thus he would not only see at first hand the nature of the problems in the region which was his home; he would also provide an answer to those critics who complained that the authorities in the capital had no concern for what went on outside the eastern theater.

★ ★ ★ **O**ne drawback this had, and for Davis it was of the kind that could never be taken lightly. The trip would mean another separation from the family he had missed so much while they were in North Carolina for the summer. "I go into the nursery as a bird may go to the robbed nest," he had written his wife in June, and he added: "My ease, my health, my property, my life I can give to the cause of my country. The heroism which could lay my wife and children on any sacrificial altar is not mine." For all the busyness and anxiety of those days and nights when McClellan's campfires rimmed the east, the White House had seemed to him an empty thing without the laughter of his sons and the companionship of the woman who was his only confidante. "I have no attraction to draw me from my office now," he wrote, "and home is no longer a locality."

In September they returned, to his great joy. Mrs Davis found him thinner, the failing eye gone blinder and the lines grooved deeper in his face. "I have no political wish beyond the success of our cause," he had written her, "no personal desire but to be relieved from further connection with office. Opposition in any form can only disturb me inasmuch as it may endanger the public welfare." But the critics were in full bay again as the fall wore on, including his own Vice President, and it was clear to his wife that he was indeed disturbed. At the outset, back in Montgomery, he had spoken of "a people united in heart, where one purpose of high resolve animates and actuates the whole." Lately this evaluation had been considerably modified. "Revolutions develop the high qualities of the good and the great," he wrote, "but they cannot change the nature of the vicious and the selfish." He had this to live with now, this change of outlook, this reassessment of his fellow man: with the result that he was more troubled by neuralgia than ever, and more in need of his wife's ministrations. Present dangers, front and rear, had given even pretended dangers an increased reality and had added to his sympathy for all sufferers everywhere, including those in the world of light fiction. One day, for example, when he was confined to bed with a cloth over his eyes and forehead, she tried to relieve the monotony by reading to him from a current melodramatic novel. He was so quiet she thought he was asleep, but she did not stop for fear of waking him. As she approached the climax of the story, wherein the bad man had the heroine in his power and was advancing on her for some evil purpose, Mrs Davis heard a voice exclaim: "The infernal villain!" and looking around saw her husband sitting bolt upright in bed, with both fists clenched.

Whether this was the result of too much imagination, or too little, was a question which would linger down the years. But some there were, already, who believed that nothing except short-sightedness could hide the eventual outcome of the long-odds struggle from anyone willing to examine the facts disclosed in the course of this opening half of the second year of conflict. Senator Herschel V. Johnson of Georgia, Stephen Douglas's running-mate in the 1860 election and now a prominent member of the Confederate Congress, replied to a question from a friend in late October: "You ask me if I have confidence in the success of the Southern Confederacy? I pray for success but I do not expect success. . . . The enemy in due time will penetrate the heart of the Confederacy . . . & the hearts of our people will quake & their spirits will yield to the force of overpowering numbers." He saw the outcome clearly, and he found it unavoidable. "The enemy is superior to us in everything but courage, & therefore it is quite certain, if the war is to go on until exhaustion overtake the one side or the other side, that we shall be the first to be exhausted."

Whether or not this would be the case — whether the South, fighting for such anachronisms as slavery and self-government, could sustain the conflict past the breaking point of northern determination — Davis did not know. Much of what his dead friend Albert Sidney Johnston had called "the fair, broad, abounding land" had already fallen to the invaders. How much more would fall, or whether the rising blue tide could be stemmed, was dependent on the gray-clad men in the southern ranks and the spirit with which they followed their star-crossed battle flags. Just now that spirit was at its height. "We may be annihilated," the first soldier of them all had said, "but we cannot be conquered." Davis thought so too, though he offered no easy solutions in support of his belief. Now in December, as he prepared to leave on his journey to the troubled western theater, he could only repeat what he had told his wife in May: "I cultivate hope and patience, and trust to the blunders of our enemy and the gallantry of our troops for ultimate success."

★ ★ ★

*T*he Treasury building (right)
and the White House (center)
face out over an open tract that
will become Washington's
Mall after the war.

EIGHT

Lincoln: December Message

1862 ★ ★ ★ ★ ★ ★

"Our cause, we love to think, is specially God's," the Connecticut theologian Horace Bushnell told his Hartford congregation. "Every drum-beat is a hymn; the cannon thunder God; the electric silence, darting victory along the wires, is the inaudible greeting of God's favoring word." His belief that the evil was all on the other side was based on a conviction that war had come because willful men beyond the Potomac had laid rude hands on the tabernacle of the law. "Law . . . is grounded in right, [and] right is a moral idea, at whose summit stands God, as the everlasting vindicator." Thus the logic came full circle: "We associate God and religion with all we are fighting for, and we are not satisfied with any mere human atheistic way of speaking as to means, or measures, or battles, or victories, or the great deeds to win them."

The assertion that this was a holy war — in fact, a crusade — was by no means restricted to those who made it from a pulpit. "Vindicating the majesty of an insulted Government, by extirpating all *rebels,* and fumigating their nests with the brimstone of unmitigated Hell, I conceive to be the holy purpose of our further efforts," a Massachusetts colonel wrote home to his governor from Beaufort, South Carolina, and being within fifty air-line miles of the very birthplace of rebellion, he added: "I hope I shall . . . do something . . . in 'The Great Fumiga-

★

tion,' before the sulphur gives out." Just what it was that he proposed to do, with regard to those he called "our Southern brethren," he had announced while waiting at Annapolis for the ship that brought him down the coast. "Do we fight them to avenge . . . insult? No! The thing we seek is *permanent* dominion. And what instance is there of permanent dominion without changing, revolutionizing, absorbing, the institutions, life, and manners of the conquered peoples? . . . They think we mean to take their *Slaves*. Bah! We must take their *ports,* their *mines,* their *water power,* the very *soil* they plough, and develop them by the hands of our *artisan* armies. . . . We are to be a regenerating, colonizing power, or we are to be whipped. Schoolmasters, with howitzers, must instruct our Southern brethren that they are a set of d----d fools in everything that relates to . . . modern civilization. . . . *This army* must *not come back.* Settlement, migration must put the seal on battle, or we gain nothing."

Tecumseh Sherman, biding his time in Memphis — where sharp-eyed men with itchy palms had followed in the wake of advancing armies, much as refuse along the right-of-way was sucked into the rearward vacuum of a speeding locomotive — threw the blame in another direction. "The cause of the war is not alone in the nigger," he told his wife, "but in the mercenary spirit of our countrymen. . . . Cincinnati furnishes more contraband goods than Charleston, and has done more to prolong the war than the State of South Carolina. Not a merchant there but would sell salt, bacon, powder and lead, if they can make money by it." So the volatile red-haired general wrote, finding his former nerve-jangled opinion reinforced by the difficulties since encountered all along the fighting front. "If the North design to conquer the South, we must begin at Kentucky and reconquer the country from there as we did from the Indians. It was this conviction then as plainly as now that made men think I was insane. A good many flatterers now want to make me a prophet."

Prophet or not, he could speak like one in an early October letter to his senator brother: "I rather think you now agree with me that this is no common war. . . . You must now see that I was right in not seeking prominence at the outstart. I knew and know yet that the northern people have to unlearn all their experience of the past thirty years and be born again before they will see the truth." None of it had been easy thus far, nor was it going to be any easier in the future. The prow of the ship might pierce the wave, yet once it was clear of the vessel's stern the wave was whole again: "Though our armies pass across and through the land, the war closes in behind and leaves the same enemy behind. . . . I don't see the end," he concluded, "or the beginning of the end, but suppose we must prevail and persist or perish." He saw only one solution, an outgrowth of the statement to his wife that the Federal armies would have to "reconquer the country . . . as we did from the Indians." What was required from here on was harshness. "We cannot change the hearts of the people of the South," he told his friend and superior Grant: "but we can make war so terrible that they will realize the fact that however brave and gallant and devoted to their country, still they are mortal and should exhaust all peaceful remedies before they fly to war."

★ ★ ★   **F**or Lincoln, too, it was a question of **"prevail and persist or perish."** For him, moreover, there was the added problem of coördinating the efforts — and, if possible, reconciling the views — of these three random extremists, together with those of more than twenty million other individuals along and behind the firing line. The best way to accomplish this, he knew, was to unite them under a leader whose competence they believed in and whose views they would adopt as their own, even when those views came into conflict with their preconceptions. In facing this task, he started not from scratch, but from somewhere well behind it. "The President is an honest, plain, shrewd magistrate," *Harper's Weekly* had told its readers a year ago this December. "He is not a brilliant orator; he is not a great leader. He views his office as strictly an executive one, and wishes to cast responsibility, as much as possible, upon Congress." This tallied with the view of Attorney General Edward Bates, who wrote in his diary after attending a cabinet meeting held at about the same time, "The President is an excellent man, and in the main wise, but he lacks will and purpose, and I greatly fear he has not the power to command."

Since then, a good many high-placed men — including Bates, who had seen Cameron banished and the bricks applied to Stanton — had had occasion to learn better: though not all. The poet Whittier, for example, saw victory only through a haze of *ifs*. "The worst of the *ifs* is the one concerning Lincoln," he privately declared. "I am much afraid that a domestic cat will not answer when one wants a Bengal tiger." His fellow poet William Cullen Bryant agreed. "The people after their gigantic preparation and sacrifice have looked for an adequate return, and looked in vain," he editorialized in the New York *Evening Post*. "They have seen armies unused in the field perish in pestilential swamps. They have seen their money wasted in long winter encampments, or frittered away on fruitless expeditions along the coast. They have seen a huge debt roll up, yet no prospect of greater military results." Wendell Phillips, bitter as ever, continued to aim an indignant finger at the White House. "The North has poured out its blood and money like water; it has leveled every fence of constitutional privilege," he declaimed, "and Abraham Lincoln sits today a more unlimited despot than the world knows this side of China. What does he render for this unbounded confidence? Show us something," he cried in the direction he was pointing, "or I tell you that within two years the indignant reaction of the people will hurl the Cabinet in contempt from their seats."

Confronted with such judgments handed down by public men, who thus came between him and his purpose of unification, Lincoln kept his temper

★

and his poise. If he failed in his attempts to win these critics over by means of personal discussion, face to face in his office — "What is he wrathy about? Why does he not come down here and have a talk with me?" — he went beyond them to the people. Sometimes he did so in cold print, as in the case of his answer to Greeley's "Prayer of Twenty Millions," but generally he proceeded in a manner that was strangely intimate in its effect, acting on a larger stage the role he had played in Illinois. In Washington, as in Springfield, he received all comers, and for the most part he received them with a sympathy which, by their own admission, equaled or exceeded their deserving. He shook their hands at frequent public receptions held in the White House, which was his home and yet belonged to them; he attended the theater, a form of relaxation which kept

This allegorical painting shows New York's antiwar Tammany Hall faction chaining Lincoln to the Constitution while he battles the Confederate dragon.

him still within their view; he drove or rode, almost daily, through the spoke-like streets of the hive-dense city, returning the looks and salutes of men and women and children along the way. Thousands touched him, heard him, saw him at close range, and scarcely one in all those thousands ever forgot the sight of that tall figure, made still taller by the stovepipe hat, and the homely drape of the shawl across the shoulders. Never forgotten, because it was unforget-table, the impression remained, incredible and enduring, imperishable in its singularity — and, finally, dear.

Millions who did not see him saw his picture, and this too was a part of the effect. Widely broadcast as it was — the result of recent developments in photography and the process of reproduction — his had become, within two crowded years, the most familiar face in American history. At first sight this might appear to be a liability. The Paris correspondent of the *New York Times,* for example, sent home a paragraph titled "Lincoln's Phiz in Europe," in which he suggested the wisdom of declaring an embargo on portraits of the President, at least so far as France was concerned: "The person represented in these pictures looks so much like a man condemned to the gallows, that large numbers of them have been imposed on the people here by the shopkeepers as Dumollard, the famous murderer of servant girls, lately guillotined near Lyons. Such a face is enough to ruin the best of causes. . . . People read the name inscribed under it with astonishment, or rather bewilderment, for the thing appears more like a hoax than a reality." Yet here, too, something worked in his favor. It was as if, having so far overshot the mark of ugliness, the face was not to be judged by or-dinary standards. You saw it not so much for what it was, as for what it held. Suffering was in it; so were understanding, kindliness, and determination. "None of us to our dying day can forget that countenance," an infantryman wrote on the occasion of a presidential visit to the army. "Concentrated in that one great, strong, yet tender face, the agony of the life and death struggle of the hour was revealed as we had never seen it before. With a new understanding, we knew why we were soldiers."

Herein lay the explanation for much that otherwise could not be un-derstood — by Jefferson Davis, for one, who had expressed "contemptuous as-tonishment" at seeing his late compatriots submit to what he called "the mere edict of a despot." They did not see their submission in that light. "I know very well that many others might . . . do better than I can," Lincoln had told the cabi-net in September, "and if I were satisfied that the public confidence was more ful-ly possessed by any one of them than by me, and knew of any constitutional way he could be put in my place, he should have it. I would gladly yield it to him. But . . . I do not know that, all things considered, any other person has more [of the confidence of the people]; and, however this may be, there is no way in which I can have any other man put where I am. I am here. I must do the best I can, and bear the responsibility of taking the course which I feel I ought to take." Though these words were spoken in private, their import carried over: with the result that such power as he seized — and it was much, far more in fact than any President had ever had before, in peace or war — was surrendered by the people in confidence that the power was not being seized for its own sake, or even for Lincoln's sake, but rather for the sake of preserving the Union. They gave him the power, along with the responsibility, glad to have a strong hand on the reins.

This fear of weakness had been the source of their gravest doubt through the opening year of conflict, as well as the subject of the editors' most frequent complaint — Lincoln was lacking in "will and purpose." Now they knew that their fears had been misplaced. A Kentucky visitor, turning to leave the White House, asked the President what cheering news he could take home to friends. By way of reply, Lincoln told him a story about a chess expert who had never met his match until he tried his hand against a machine called the Automaton Chess Player, and was beaten three times running. Astonished, the defeated expert got up from his chair and walked slowly around and around the machine, examining it minutely as he went. At last he stopped and leveled an accusing finger in its direction. "There's a man in there!" he cried. Lincoln paused, then made his point: "Tell my friends there is a man in here."

★ ★ ★ **S**omething else he was, as well — a literary craftsman — though so far this had gone unrecognized, unnoticed, and for the most part would remain so until critics across the Atlantic, unembarrassed by proximity, called attention to the fact. Indeed, complaints had been registered that he wrote "like a half-educated lawyer" with little or no appreciation for the cadenced beauties latent in the English language, awaiting the summons of the artist who knew how to call them up. That there was such a thing as the American language, available for literary purposes, had scarcely begun to be suspected by the more genteel, except as it had been employed by writers of low dialog bits, which mainly served to emphasize its limitations. Lincoln's jogtrot prose, compacted of words and phrases still with the bark on, had no music their ears were attuned to; it crept by them. However, an ambiguity had been sensed. Remarking "the two-fold working of the two-fold nature of the man," one caller at least had observed the contrast between "Lincoln the Westerner, slightly humorous but thoroughly practical and sagacious," and "Lincoln the President and statesman . . . seen in those abstract and serious eyes, which seemed withdrawn to an inner sanctuary of thought, sitting in judgment on the scene and feeling its far reach into the future."

Here was a clew; but it went uninvestigated. Apparently it was miracle enough that a prairie lawyer had become President, without pressing matters further to see that he had also become a stylist. In fact, so natural and unlabored had his utterance seemed, that when people were told they had an artist in the White House, their reaction was akin to that of the man in Moliére who discovered that all his life he had been speaking prose. "I am here. I must do the best I can," Lincoln had said, and that best included this. Natural perhaps it was; unlabored it was not. Long nights he toiled in his workshop, the "inner sanctuary" from which he reached out to the future, and here indeed was the best clew of all. For he worked with the dedication of the true artist, who, whatever his sense of superiority in other relationships, preserves his humility in this one. He knew, as a later observer remarked, "the dangers that lurk in iotas." There were days when callers, whatever their importance, were turned away with the explanation that the President was at work: which meant writing.

A series of such days came in November, and the occasion was the preparation of a message to Congress, which would convene December 1. Lincoln saw already what would later become obvious, but was by no means obvious yet: that the war had ended one phase and was about to enter another. This message was intended to signal that event, bidding farewell to the old phase and setting a course for the new. Basically it was dedicatory, for there was need for dedication. The fury of Perryville, the blood that had stained the Antietam and sluiced the ridge in front of Sharpsburg, had reëmphasized the fact disclosed on a smaller scale at First Bull Run and Wilson's Creek, then augmented at Shiloh and the Seven Days, that both armies were capable of inflicting and withstanding terrible wounds. Though it was incredible that the ratio of increase would be maintained, there would be other Shilohs, other Sharpsburgs, other terrors. Men in their thousands now alive would presently be dead; homes so far untouched by sorrow would know tears; new widows and new orphans, some as yet unmarried or unborn, would be made — all, as Lincoln saw it, that the nation might continue and that men now in bondage might have freedom. In issuing the Preliminary Emancipation Proclamation he had made certain that there would be no peace except by conquest. He had weighed the odds and made his choice, foreseeing the South's reaction. "A restitution of the Union has been rendered forever impossible," Davis said. Lincoln had known he would say it; the fact was, he had been saying it all along. What he meant, and what Lincoln knew he meant, was that the issue was one which could only be settled by arms, and that the war was therefore a war for survival — survival of the South, as Davis saw it: survival of the Union, as Lincoln saw it — with the added paradox that, while neither of the two leaders believed victory for his side meant extinction for the other, each insisted that the reverse was true.

On the face of it, Davis had rather the better of his opponent in this contention, since the immediate and admitted result of a southern defeat would be that the South would go out of existence as a nation, however well it might survive in the sense that Lincoln intended to convey. The threat of national extinction was a sharper goad than any the northern leader could apply in attempting the unification he saw was necessary; therefore he determined to try for something other than sharpness. It was here that his particular talent, though so far it had gone unrecognized in general, could most effectively be brought to bear. As he had done against Douglas in the old days, so now in his long-range contest with Davis he shifted the argument onto a higher plane. Douglas had wanted to talk about "popular sovereignty," the right of the people of a region to decide for themselves the laws and customs under which they would live, but Lincoln had made slavery the issue, to the Little Giant's unavoidable discomfort. Similarly, in the present debate, while Davis spoke of self-government, Lincoln — without ever dropping the pretense that Davis was invisible, was in fact not there at all — appealed to "the mystic chords of memory" and "the chorus of the Union," then presently moved on to slavery

> *"While it has not pleased the Almighty to bless us with a return of peace, we can but press on, guided by the best light he gives us, trusting that in his own good time and wise way all will be well."*
>
> — Abraham Lincoln

and freedom, which Davis could no more avoid than Douglas had been able to do. Lincoln tarred them both with the same brush, doing it so effectively in the present case that the tar would never wear off, and managed also to redefine the Davis concept of self-government as destructive of world democracy, which was shown to depend on survival of the Union with the South as part of the whole. In thus discounting the claims of his opponent, he rallied not only his own people behind him, but also those of other lands where freedom was cherished as a possession or a goal, and thus assured nonintervention. Davis in time, like other men before and since, found what it meant to become involved with an adversary whose various talents included those of a craftsman in the use of words.

A case in point was this December message. It was a long one, nearly fifty thousand words, and it covered a host of subjects, all of them connected directly or indirectly with the war. "Fellow-Citizens of the Senate and House of Representatives," it opened. "Since your last annual assembling another year of health and bountiful harvest has passed, and while it has not pleased the Almighty to bless us with a return of peace, we can but press on, guided by the best light he gives us, trusting that in his own good time and wise way all will yet be well. . . . The civil war, which has so radically changed, for the moment, the occupations and habits of the American people, has necessarily disturbed the social condition and affected very deeply the prosperity of the nations with which we have carried on a commerce that has been steadily increasing throughout a period of half a century. It has at the same time excited political ambitions and apprehensions which have produced a profound agitation throughout the civilized world. . . . We have attempted no propagandism and acknowledged no revolution; but we have left to every nation the exclusive conduct and management of its own affairs. Our struggle has been, of course, contemplated by foreign nations with reference less to its own merits than to its supposed and often exaggerated effects and consequences resulting to those nations themselves. Nevertheless, complaint on the part of this government, even if it were just, would certainly be unwise."

After this rather mild and dry beginning, he passed at once — or the clerk did, for Lincoln did not deliver the message in person — to matters drier still. A new commercial treaty had been arranged with the Sultan of Turkey, while similar arrangements with Liberia and Haiti were pending. Financially, he was pleased to report, the country was quite sound. Treasury receipts for the July-through-June fiscal year were $583,885,247.06, and disbursements totaling $570,841,700.25 had left a balance of $13,043,546.81 to be carried over. Restlessness among the frontier tribes perhaps indicated that the Indian system needed to be remodeled. The Pacific Railway was being pushed toward completion. A Department of Agriculture had been established. . . . The clerk droned on, advising the squirming congressmen that these details "will claim your most diligent consideration," though this could hardly have been easy, comprising as they did nearly half of the long document. By now, the assembled politicians were nearly as restless as the red men on the frontier. Presently, however, approaching its mid-point, the message changed its tone.

"A nation may be said to consist of its territory, its people, and its laws. The territory is the only part which is of certain durability. 'One generation passeth away, and another generation cometh: but the earth abideth forever.' It is of the first importance to duly consider and estimate this ever-enduring part. That portion of the earth's surface which is owned and inhabited by the people of the United States is well adapted to be the home of one national family, and it is not well adapted for two or more. . . . There is no line, straight or crooked, suitable for a national boundary upon which to divide. Trace through, from east to west, upon the line between the free and slave country, and we shall find a little more than one-third of its length are rivers, easy to be crossed, and populated, or soon to be populated, thickly upon both sides; while nearly all its remaining length are merely surveyors' lines, over which people may walk back and forth without any consciousness of their presence."

Such an argument might have been advanced in support of the unification of Europe or the annexation of Canada, but presently the listeners saw what Lincoln was getting at. He was talking to the inhabitants of the region to which he himself was native, "the great interior region, bounded east by the Alleghenies, north by the British dominions, west by the Rocky Mountains, and south by the line along which the culture of corn and cotton meets. . . . Ascertain from the statistics the small proportion of the region which has as yet been brought into cultivation, and also the large and rapidly increasing amount of its products, and we shall be overwhelmed with the magnitude of the prospect presented. And yet this region has no seacoast, touches no ocean anywhere. As part of the nation, its people now find, and may forever find, their way to Europe by New York, to South America and Africa by New Orleans, and to Asia by San Francisco. . . . These outlets, east, west, and south, are indispensable to the well-being of the people inhabiting, and to inhabit, this vast interior region. Which of the three may be the best is no proper question. All are better than either, and all of right belong to that people and to their successors forever. True to themselves, they will not ask where a line of separation shall be, but will vow rather that there shall be no such line." After a pause, he added: "Our national strife springs not from our permanent part, not from the land we inhabit, not from our national homestead. . . . Our strife pertains to ourselves — to the passing generations of men; and it can without convulsion be hushed forever with the passing of one generation."

This brought him at last to what he considered the nub of the issue. "Without slavery the rebellion could never have existed; without slavery it could not continue." So far, he had not mentioned the Preliminary Emancipation Proclamation except to note that it had been issued; nor did he return to it now. What he returned to, instead, was his old plan for compensated emancipation, the one way he saw for bringing the war to an end "without convulsion." His plan, as expanded here, would leave to each state the choice of when to act on the matter, "now, or at the end of the century, or at any intermediary time." The federal government was to have no voice in the action, but it would bear the total expense by issuing long-term bonds as payment to loyal masters. To those critics who would complain that the expense was too heavy, Lincoln replied beforehand that it was cheaper to pay in bonds than in blood, as the country was doing now. Besides, even in dollars and cents the cost would be less. "Certainly it is not so easy to pay something as it is to pay nothing; but it is easier to pay a large sum than it is to pay a larger one. And it is easier to pay any sum when we are able, than it is to pay it before we are able. The war requires large sums, and requires them at once. The aggregate sum necessary for compensated emancipation of course would be large. But it would require no ready cash, nor the bonds even, any faster than the emancipation progresses. This might not, and probably would not, come before the end of the thirty-seven years."

★

*On Lincoln's express orders, work on
the Capitol continued despite the expense
and wartime shortages.*

At this point, apparently — at any rate, somewhere along the line —
the President had done some ciphering. By 1900, he predicted, "we shall probably have 100,000,000 of people to share the burden, instead of 31,000,000 as
now." This was no wild guess on Lincoln's part; or as he put it, "I do not state
this inconsiderately. At the same ratio of increase which we have maintained, on

an average, from our first national census of 1790 until that of 1860, we should in 1900 have a population of 103,208,415. And why may we not continue that ratio far beyond that period? Our abundant room — our broad national homestead — is our ample resource." The past seventy years had shown an average decennial increase of 34.6 percent. Applying this to the coming seventy years, he calculated the 1930 population at 251,680,914. "And we will reach this, too," he added, "if we do not ourselves relinquish the chance by the folly and evils of disunion, or by long and exhausting war springing from the only great element of national discord among us."

Descending from these rather giddy mathematical heights, Lincoln continued his plea for gradual emancipation, not only for the sake of the people here represented, but also for the sake of the Negroes, whom it would spare "the vagrant destitution which must largely attend immediate emancipation in localities where their numbers are very great." Whatever objections might be raised, he wanted one thing kept in mind: "If there ever could be a proper time for mere catch arguments, that time surely is not now. In times like the present, men should utter nothing for which they would not willingly be responsible through time and in eternity." And having thus admonished the assembly, after forcing it to accompany him on an excursion into the field of applied mathematics, he thought perhaps some note of apology — if not of retraction — was in order. "I do not forget the gravity which should characterize a paper addressed to the Congress of the nation by the Chief Magistrate of the nation. Nor do I forget that some of you are my seniors, nor that many of you have more experience than I in the conduct of public affairs. Yet I trust that in view of the great responsibility resting upon me, you will perceive no want of respect to yourselves in any undue earnestness I may seem to display." Apparently, however, this was intended not only to make amends for what had gone before, but also to brace them for what was to come. Nor was it long in coming. Hard on the heels of this apology for "undue earnestness," he threw a cluster of knotty, rhetorical questions full in their faces:

"Is it doubted, then, that the plan I propose, if adopted, would shorten the war, and thus lessen its expenditure of money and of blood? Is it doubted that it would restore the national authority and national prosperity, and perpetuate both indefinitely? Is it doubted that we here — Congress and Executive — can secure its adoption? Will not the good people respond to a united and earnest appeal from us? Can we, can they, by any other means so certainly or so speedily assure these vital objects? We can succeed only by concert. It is not 'Can any of us imagine better?' but 'Can we all do better?' Object whatsoever is possible, still the question recurs, 'Can we do better?' "

As the long message approached its end, Lincoln asked that question: "Can we do better?" Oratory was not enough. "The North responds . . .

sufficiently in breath," he had said of the reaction to the September proclamation; "but breath alone kills no rebels." He knew as well as Sherman the need for the nation to be "born again," and he would also have agreed with the New England major who this month wrote home that he sometimes felt like changing the old soldier's prayer into "O God, if there be a God, save my country, if my country is worth saving." A majority of 100,000 voters in Lincoln's own state, fearing the backwash of liberated slaves that would result from Grant's advance, had approved in November the adoption of a new article into the Illinois constitution prohibiting the immigration of Negroes into the state. He knew, too, the reaction of most of the lawmakers to the proposal he was now advancing — including that of Senator Orville Browning, his fellow Illinoisan and confidant, who would write in his diary of his friend's plea when he went home tonight: "It surprised me by its singular reticence in regard to the war, and some other subjects which I expected discussed, and by the hallucination the President seems to be laboring under that Congress can suppress the rebellion by adopting his plan of compensated emancipation." Yet according to Lincoln it was not he, but they, who were hallucinated and enthralled, and he told them so as the long message wore on toward a close: "The dogmas of the quiet past are inadequate to the stormy present. The occasion is piled high with difficulty, and we must rise with the occasion. As our case is new, so we must think anew and act anew. We must disenthrall ourselves, and then we shall save our country."

Then came the end, the turn of a page that opened a new chapter. And now, through the droning voice of the clerk, the Lincoln music sounded in what would someday be known as its full glory: "Fellow-citizens, we cannot escape history. We of this Congress and this Administration will be remembered in spite of ourselves. No personal significance or insignificance can spare one or another of us. The fiery trial through which we pass will light us down, in honor or dishonor, to the latest generation. We say we are for the Union. The world will not forget that we say this. We know how to save the Union. The world knows we do know how to save it. We — even we here — hold the power and bear the responsibility. In giving freedom to the slave, we assure freedom to the free — honorable alike in what we give and what we preserve. We shall nobly save or meanly lose the last, best hope of earth. Other means may succeed; this could not fail. The way is plain, peaceful, generous, just — a way which, if followed, the world will forever applaud, and God must forever bless."

★   ★   ★

★

Epilogue

★ ★ ★ *F*ollowing the Confederacy's second victory over Union forces on the plains of Manassas, Lee and Davis decided to invade northern soil. By abandoning their previous defensive strategy they hoped at least to give some relief to those areas of the Confederacy that had been savaged in recent months and, if their invasions were successful, to convince France and England that the Confederacy was indeed a viable entity.

Bragg from Chattanooga and Kirby Smith from Knoxville marched north. Kirby Smith moved toward Cincinnati but was stopped at Franklin, Kentucky, and withdrew to join Bragg, who threatened Louisville. Both were driven south following the Battle of Perryville.

Meanwhile, Lee had marched north into Maryland for possible strikes on the Union capital, Baltimore, or perhaps Philadelphia. He sent Jackson to capture Harpers Ferry, while he and Longstreet moved farther north. McClellan, again in charge of the Union forces, moved with unaccustomed speed, but a Confederate rear-guard action at South Mountain slowed the Federal pursuit, allowing Lee to concentrate his army on high ground west of Antietam Creek near Sharpsburg. There, on September 17, the two armies fought an all-day duel that resulted in more American casualties than any other single day in American history. That night and during the next day, each side, exhausted and disorganized, waited for a renewal of the contest that never came. The evening of the 18th, Lee withdrew across the Potomac into Virginia, leaving the field to McClellan, who did not pursue.

The North claimed victory, if only because it had been left in possession of the field, and Lincoln seized the occasion to release a Proclamation of Emancipation. It was largely a symbolic gesture—freeing the slaves only in those areas outside Federal control. While its effects were not immediately apparent, this gesture began to change the way Northerners, at least, would perceive the war. It would become a moral war for universal freedom.

Following these events, the lines of battle returned very near to where they had been prior to the unsuccessful invasions. Both presidents sought new strategies and altered chains of command hoping that fresh commanders might gain their side an advantage.

Ambrose Burnside, named by Lincoln to replace McClellan, would attempt another drive south, this time at Fredericksburg, only to have his attack shattered by massed Confederate artillery and infantry fire from atop Marye's Heights.

Meanwhile, Jefferson Davis would visit the West, hoping to raise the morale of soldiers and civilians alike. As he traveled some twenty-five hundred miles in twenty-five days, Confederate forces engaged in at least seven actions and won nearly all of them.

By the time Davis started his journey in early December 1862 Union General Sherman had already been thwarted in his attempt to get behind Vicksburg at Chickasaw Bluffs. While he traveled, the Federals failed at Fredericksburg. Grant's supply depot at Holly Springs was hit hard. There was fighting at Prairie Grove, and Galveston returned to Confederate hands. Bragg moved into central Tennessee but was stopped by Federals under Rosecrans in hellish terrain near Murfreesboro along Stones River—another Antietamesque, Pyrrhic, Yankee victory.

More victories would follow in the weeks after a weary but elated Davis returned to Richmond in early January. Burnside planned another strike at Fredericksburg. By moving a few, miles upstream, he hoped to cross the river with less opposition, but his attempt, later known as the Mud March, would be stopped, not by the Confederates but by bad weather. Four solid days of heavy rains turned the roads into troughs of slime that mired everything that attempted to travel them. Grant's Federals in the West would try a number of experiments—expanded canals, breached levees, and land movements among them—in unsuccessful attempts to by-pass Vicksburg. All would fail more because of the fickleness of the Mississippi and the roughness of the terrain than Confederate force of arms.

But there were problems, too. While French bankers were willing to float some loans through a risky bond issue—a venture that proved an economic disaster for the Confederacy—neither the French nor the English were any closer to recognizing the new-born nation. And there was unrest at home. Although the military seemed to be holding its own, the naval blockade, disrupted transportation and distribution systems, falling currency values and inflation, and just the simple wear and tear of being at war were taking a toll on the southern population. Beginning during Holy Week, first in Richmond, in Atlanta, and in Mobile, and then in other cities across the Confederacy, protests of rising prices would turn into full-fledged riots, with the burning and looting of stores, raiding of supply depots, and general chaos. War weariness had set in, and there seemed to be little relief in sight—the Yankees, "those people," as Lee called them—showed no signs of giving up the struggle.

★   ★   ★

★

$\mathcal{M}$ any books by many men, predominantly military experts or professional historians, went into the making of this work by a man who is neither, and of these the most useful, as well as the largest, were the 128-volume *War of the Rebellion: a Compilation of the Official Records of the Union and Confederate Armies* and the 30-volume *Official Records of the Union and Confederate Navies in the War of the Rebellion,* issued by the government in 1880-1901 and 1897-1927 respectively. There you hear the live men speak — there and in their diaries and letters, their newspapers and periodicals — although not always as they spoke in later life, when they got around to writing their memoirs, regimental histories, and a host of articles such as the ones collected in four large volumes and published in 1887 under the title *Battles and Leaders of the Civil War.* Early or late, taken in conjunction with the diplomatic correspondence and the congressional transcripts, these complete the first-hand testimony by soldiers and civilians, some of high rank, some of low rank, some of no rank at all. The evidence is in. All else is speculation or sifting, an attempt to reconcile differences and bring order out of multiplicity by sorting the fruits that have poured from this horn of plenty.

Biographies of the participants and studies of the war itself, in part or as a whole, make up the secondary sources. These are not only interesting and rewarding in their own right, filling in and deepening the over-all impression, but they also serve as a guide through the labyrinth. I found them invaluable on both counts: so much so, indeed, that while this narrative is based throughout on the original material referred to above, my obligations are equally heavy on this side of the line where it leaves off. I want to state here at the outset my chief debts, particularly to those works still available in bookstores. These include the following biographies, of and by the following men: of Lee by Douglas Southall Freeman, Scribner's, 1934-35: of McClellan by Warren W. Hassler, LSU Press, 1957: of Beauregard by T. Harry Williams, LSU Press, 1954: of Sherman by Lloyd Lewis, Harcourt, Brace, 1932: of Joe Johnston by G. E. Govan and J. W. Livingood, Bobbs-Merrill, 1956: of Sheridan by Richard O'Connor, Bobbs-Merrill, 1953: of Jackson by Burke Davis, Rinehart, 1954: of Kirby Smith by Joseph H. Parks, LSU Press, 1954: of Davis by William E. Dodd, Jacobs, 1907, and Hudson Strode, Harcourt, Brace, 1955: of Lincoln by Carl Sandburg, Harcourt, Brace, 1939; J. G. Randall, Dodd, Meade, 1945-55; and Benjamin P. Thomas, Knopf, 1952.

Among the more general works, my chief debts are to the following: *Lincoln Finds a General* by Kenneth P. Williams, Macmillan, 1949-56: *Lee's Lieutenants* by Douglas Southall Freeman, Scribner's, 1942-44: *The Army of Tennessee* by Stanley F. Horn, Bobbs-Merrill, 1941: *Civil War on the Western Border* by Jay Monaghan, Little, Brown, 1955: *Mr. Lincoln's Army* and *This Hallowed Ground* by Bruce Catton, Doubleday, 1951 and 1956: *Guns on the Western Waters* by H. Allen Gosnell, LSU Press, 1949: *Lincoln and His Generals* by T. Harry Williams, Knopf, 1952: *Statesmen of the Lost Cause* and *Lincoln's War Cabinet* by Burton J. Hendrick, Little, Brown, 1939 and 1946: *The North Reports the Civil War* by J. Cutler Andrews, University of Pittsburgh Press, 1955: *The Railroads of the Confederacy* by Robert C. Black, UNC Press, 1952: *The Life of Johnny Reb* and *The Life of Billy Yank* by Bell Irvin Wiley, Bobbs-Merrill, 1943 and 1952: *Reveille in Washington* by Margaret Leech, Harper, 1941: *The Beleaguered City* by Alfred Hoyt Bill, Knopf, 1946: *Experiment in Rebellion* by Clifford Dowdey, Doubleday, 1946: *The Civil War and Reconstruction* by J. G. Randall, Heath, 1937: *The Story of the Confederacy* by Robert S. Henry, Bobbs-Merrill, 1931: *The American Civil War* by Carl Russell Fish, Longmans, Green, 1937: *The Confederate States of America* by E. Merton Coulter, LSU Press, 1950. There were others but these were the main ones, and to each I owe much.

Other obligations, of a more personal nature, I also incurred during the five years that went into the writing of this first installment: to the John Simon Guggenheim Memorial Foundation, for an extended fellowship which made possible the buying of books and bread: to the superintendents, historians, and guides of the National Park Service, for unfailing industry and courtesy in helping me to get the look and feel of the various battlefields: to Robert N. Linscott and Robert D. Loomis of Random House, for combining enthusiasm and patience: to Mrs. O. B. Crittenden of the William Alexander Percy Memorial Library, Greenville, Mississippi, for the continuing loan of that institution's set of the *Official Records*. To all these I am grateful, as well as to friends in Memphis who had the out-of-hours grace to refrain from mentioning the Civil War.

★ ★ ★ A word I suppose is in order as to the use I made of these materials, original and secondary, not only because it is customary but also because it appears to be necessary, at least in certain eyes. One of the best of the latter-day authorities, in the course of his carefully documented exegesis, cautions against accepting the testimony of Lew Wallace as to what took place at a council of war preceding the march on Donelson. "Recollections of events long past are always to be suspected," he explains, "and especially when set down by a writer of fiction." Wallace then was doubly suspect. He had waited, and he had written *The Fair God* and *Ben-Hur*. He was a novelist.

Well, I am a novelist, and what is more I agree with D. H. Lawrence's estimate of the novel as "the one bright book of life." I might also agree with the professor quoted above, but only by considering each witness on his merit, his devotion as a writer to what should be his main concern. The point I would make is that the novelist and the historian are seeking the same thing: the truth — not a different truth: the same truth — only they reach it, or try to reach it, by different routes. Whether the event took place in a world now gone to dust, preserved by documents and evaluated by scholarship, or in the imagination, preserved by memory and distilled by the creative process, they both want to tell us *how it was*: to re-create it, by their separate methods, and make it live again in the world around them.

This has been my aim, as well, only I have combined the two. Accepting the historian's standards without his paraphernalia, I have employed the novelist's methods without his license. Instead of inventing characters and incidents, I searched them out — and having found them, I took them as they were. Nothing is included here, either within or outside quotation marks, without the authority of documentary evidence which I consider sound. Although I have left out footnotes, believing that they would detract from the work's narrative quality by intermittently shattering the illusion that the observer is not so much reading a book as sharing an experience, I have thought it proper to employ the three dots of elision to signify the omission of interior matter from quotations. In all respects, the work is as accurate as care and hard work could make it. Partly I have done this for my own satisfaction; for in writing a history, I would no more be false to a fact dug out of a valid document than I would be false to a "fact" dug out of my head in writing a novel. Also, I have tried for accuracy because I have never known a modern historical instance where the truth was not superior to distortion, by any standard and in every way. Wherever the choice lay between soundness and "color," soundness had it every time. Many problems were encountered in the course of all this study, but lack of color in the original materials was never one of them. In fact, there was the rub. Such heartbreak as was here involved came not from trying to decide what to include, but rather from trying to decide what to omit, and in the end the omissions far outnumbered the inclusions.

One word more perhaps will not be out of place. I am a Mississippian. Though the veterans I knew are all dead now, down to the final septuagenarian home-guard drummer boy of my childhood, the remembrance of them is still with me. However, being nearly as far removed from them in time as most of them were removed from combat when they died, I hope I have recovered the respect they had for their opponents until Reconstruction lessened and finally killed it. Biased is the last thing I would be; I yield to no one in my admiration for heroism and ability, no matter which side of the line a man was born or fought on when the war broke out. If pride in the resistance my forebears made against the odds has leaned me to any degree in their direction, I hope it will be seen to amount to no more, in the end, than the average American's normal sympathy for the underdog in a fight.

★

Picture Credits

★

Index

Numerals in italics indicate an illustration of the subject mentioned.

A

Alabama: 253-256; construction of, *252-253*

Alexandria, Virginia: 22, 23, 24, 26, 28, 29, 36, 63, 198

Anderson, Patton: 175, 176, 177

Anderson, R. H.: 41, 45, 46, 90, 99, 104, 113, 114, 115, 119, 121

Antietam, Battle of: *map* 109, 110-133, 157, 225; casualties, 131; Confederate dead at, *80-81;* and Emancipation Proclamation, 7, 137

Antietam campaign: *map* 91; and Special Orders 191, 90-92, 100

Antietam Creek: 108, *map* 109, 113, 114; bridges at, 111, 124, *127*

Aquia Creek: 19, 20, 22, 23, 54

Arkansas: 7, 156, 258

Army of Kentucky: reports of dissension in, 229-231

Army of Northern Virginia: effective strength and condition for Maryland invasion, 86; field telescope, *128;* morale in, 54-55, 238-239; and northern civilians, 85-86

Army of Tennessee: designation of, 232; dissension in, 260

Army of the Cumberland: 219-220

Army of the Ohio: 170, 219

Army of the Potomac: Burnside's reorganization, 216-217; Lincoln visiting with McClellan and general officers, *188-189,* 194-196; McClellan's farewell to, *204-205,* 206-207; morale in, 93, 108; pontoon bridging train, *216-217;* reenforces Army of Virginia, 16, 19, 22-23; regard for McClellan in, 61-62, 99-100, 195; strength of, 238

B

Banks, Nathaniel: 11, 22, 33, 56, 60, 93, 96, 112, *208,* 209, 210, 211, 212, 214

Barbourville, Kentucky: 67, 68, 184

Bardstown, Kentucky: 79, 150, 151, 155, 167, 168

Bates, Edward: 62, 267

Baton Rouge, Louisiana: 7, 156, 208, 232

Battery Robinette: 163-165, 166

Beauregard, P. G. T.: 161, 162, 173, 234-235, 257

Big Barren River: Federal troops at, *64-65*

Big Hill: 68, 69, 182-183

Blackburn's Ford: 35

Blockade: 258, 279

Bloody Lane: 121-*122,* 123

Bloss, J. M.: 94-95

Bolivar, Tennessee: 160, 161, 165

Bolivar Heights: 90, 103

Boonsboro, Maryland: 90, 95, 98, 99, 100

Bragg, Braxton: 155, 156, 231, 232, 245, 249, 256, 257, 260, 278, 279; and Davis, 186, 229-230, 232; Kentucky offensive, 7, 22, 67, 68, 70, 71, 72-74, 75, 76-79, 84, 149, 150-151, 155, 166-167; and Munfordville, 76-78, 83; and Perryville, 167-172, 175, 179, 180; withdrawal from Kentucky, 181-182, 183, 184, 185

Breckinridge, John C.: 156, 231-232

Bristoe Station, Virginia: 25, 26-27, 28, 30, 31, 35, 41, 60

Broad Run: 25, 27, 28, 30, 31, 35, 60

Buckeystown, Maryland: 98, 99

Buckingham, C. P.: 201-203, 204

Buckner, Simon Bolivar: 77-78, 175, 176

Buell, Don Carlos: 7, 66, 68, 73, 149, 150, 154, 166-167, 207; and defense of Tennessee and Kentucky, 74-75, 78, 79, 151-152, 155, 181, 183, 184; and Perryville, 168-171, 172, 173, 174, 175, 176, 177, 179-180; relieved of command, 187, 191, 194, 220

Bull Run: 29, 35, 49, 55

Bull Run, Second Battle of: *See* Second Bull Run, Battle of

Bull Run Mountains: 21, 30, 34

Burnside, Ambrose E.: 11, 16, 22, 31, 41, 52, 58, 96, 99, *202,* 210, 219, 278, 279; and Antietam, 112, 124, 125, 126, 129, 130, 131; appointed Army of the Potomac's commander, 202-204, 206; opening of Fredericksburg campaign, 215-126, 217-218, 239-241, 242

Burnside Bridge: 112, 124, 126, *127*

Butler, Benjamin: 207-208

C

Cameron, Simon: 267

Camp Dick Robinson: 181

Catlett's Station, Virginia: 17, *18-19,* 20

Catoctin Mountains: 89, 93, 95, 98

Cave City, Kentucky: 76, 78

Cedar Mountain, Battle of: 11, 22

Centreville, Virginia: 31, 33, 34, 35, 38, 55, 57

Chalmers, James R.: 75-76, 77, 78

Chambersburg, Pennsylvania: 196; Stuart's raiders in, *197*

Chantilly, Battle of: 58-59

Chaplin River: 170, 175, 176

Charleston, South Carolina: 234-235, 257

Chase, Salmon P.: 62, 63, 138, 141, 145, 200

Chattanooga, Tennessee: 7, 22, 73, 210, 219, 220, 230, 247, 250, 260

Cheatham, Benjamin: 175, 176

Chewalla, Mississippi: 161, 165

Cincinnati, Ohio: 71, 74, 79

Cleburne, Patrick R.: 70, 177-178

Columbia River: Confederate attacks on steamboats on, *233;* Confederate cavalry attack at,

226-227

Confederacy: army recruiting posters, 74; commerce raiders, 253-256; conscription in, 237-238; hopes for foreign recognition, 7, 84, 89, 144, 225, 250-253, 258, 278, 279; inflation in, 250, 279; public confidence in, 6, 250-251, 257-258; reaction to Emancipation Proclamation, 141-142; war weariness in, 279

Congress: Lincoln's message to, 271, 272-277; radical Republicans in, 215

Cooper, Samuel: 186, 244

Corinth, Battle of: *map* 161, 162-163, *164-165*, 225, 232; Confederate dead at, *146-147*

Corinth, Mississippi: 156, 159, 160, 163

Crampton's Gap: 98, 99, 103, 104, 106

Crittenden, T. L.: 155, 169, 170, 174, 177, 180, 220

Culpeper, Virginia: 15, 87, 200, 239

Cumberland Gap: 67, 71, 181, 184, 230

Curtis, Samuel: 160, 162, 243

D

Davis, Charles H.: 192, 194

Davis, Jefferson: 6, 7, 12, 40, 41, 49, 141-142, 145, 156, 213, 245-246, 250, 251, *259*, 269, 271-272, 278, 279; and Beauregard, 234; and Bragg, 229-230, 232, 260; commitment of, 257-261; criticism of, 260; general officers, reassignments, and support for, 229-237; and Johnston, 247, 249; and Lee, 84, 88, 89, 133

Davis, Jefferson C.: 152, *153*, 154, 155

Davis, Varina: 260-261

Decherd, Tennessee: 73, 74

Dumont, Ebenezer: 155, 168, 175

Dunker Church: 110, 112, 113, 115, 116, 119, 120, 123; Confederate dead at, *80-81;* truce parley at, *131*

E

Early, Jubal: 117, 120, 130

East Wood: 116, 118, 120

Emancipation Proclamation: 7, 137-145, 149, 200, 251, 271, 274, 276-277; commemorative copy of, *143*

Evans, Shanks: 41, 87

Ewell, Richard: 21, 25, 28, 30, 35, 36, 38, 39-40, 58; and Antietam, 113, 116

F

Fairfax Courthouse, Virginia: 58, 59

Falmouth, Virginia: 19, 217, 218, 240

Farragut, David: 191-192, 212

Flags (CSA): 1st Texas Infantry, *118*; (USA): 2d Wisconsin Infantry, *39*

Florida: 253-254

Forrest, Nathan B.: 7, 166, 220, 232

Fort Monroe: 22, 54, 211

France: consideration of recognition of Confederacy, 7, 251-253, 278, 279; and Emancipation Proclamation, 144

Frankfort, Kentucky: 71, 151, 155, 166, 167, 168, 170, 175

Franklin, William: 23, 57, 96, 98, 99, 106, 110, 217; and Antietam, 112, 123-124, 129, 130

Frederick, Maryland: 84, 93-94, 96, 98, 104, 131; Confederate troops in, *87;* McClellan in, *97-98*

Fredericksburg, Virginia: 11, 14, 19, 216, 218, *240-241*

G

Gainesville, Virginia: 25, 36

Galveston, Texas: 192, 243, 258

Garland, Samuel: *102*

Gibbon, John: 38, 39, 53, 62

Gilbert, Charles: 155, 169, 170, 173-174, 176, 177, 178, 179, 220

Gladstone, William E.: 251, 253

Grant, Ulysses S.: 74, 75, 155, 156, 157, 158, 159, 160, 162, 163, 165, 210, 211-212, 214, 219, 267, 277, 279

Great Britain: consideration of recognition of Confederacy, 7, 251-253, 278, 279; reaction to Emancipation Proclamation, 143-144, 225, 251; recognition of the Confederacy considered by, 89

Greeley, Horace: 56, *139,* 268

Gregg, Maxcy: 44, *45*

Groveton, Virginia: 35, 36, 40, 42, 43, 44, 54

H

Hagerstown, Maryland: 100, 110

Halleck, Henry: 6, 12, 22, 34, 47, 155, 161-162, 173, 191, 207, 208-209, 213, 216; and Antietam campaign, 96, 108, 130; and Buell, 75, 154, 184, 186-187; and Burnside, 217-218; and Grant, 211-212, 214; and McClellan, 23, 62, 63, 95, 97, 98, 196, 197, 199, 203; and Pope, 16, 19, 47, 55, 57, 58, 59; and Rosecrans, 219-221

Hampton, Wade: 14, 41, 86, 196

Hardee, William J.: 76, 78, *171,* 181, 182, 230, 231, 232; and Perryville, 171-172, 175

Harpers Ferry: 92, 98, 99, *104-105,* 110, 113, 115, 119, 128, 133, 195, 200; investment and capture of Federal garrison at, 89-90, 101, 103-106, 108

Harper's Weekly: 13, 267

Harrodsburg, Kentucky: 171, 175, 180, 181, 229

Hatchie River: 159, 160, 165, 214

Hay, John: 63, 96, 145, 223

Hayes, Rutherford B.: 102

Heintzelman, Samuel: 19, 22-23, 30, 34, 44, 48, 96

Henry Hill: 53, 56

Hill, A. P.: 12, 21, 25, 28, 29, 30, 35, 40, 44, 45, 50, 59, 107, 113; and Antietam, 115, 126, 128-129, 130, 132-133; quarrel with Jackson, 87-88, 107

Hill, D. H.: 12, 41, 86, 98, 99, 100, 101, 102, 103, 104, 105; and Antietam, 113, 114, 117, 119, 121, 122, 123, 125, 130; and Special Orders 191, 92, 94

Hindman, Thomas: 242-243, 244, *259*

Holly Springs, Mississippi: 156, 159, 165, 214

Holmes, Theophilus: 92, 242, 244, 246

Hood, John Bell: 11, 41, 43-44, 45, 46, 48, 52, 55, 87, 101, *114*, 239; and Antietam, 113, 114, 115, 116-117, 118, 130, 131

Hooker, Joseph: 30, 35, 96, *111*, 204, 207, 217; and Antietam, 111, 112, 115-116, 117, 118, 119, 120, 131

Hurlbut, Stephen A.: 160, 162, 212

I

Illustrated London News: pages from, *240-241*

Iuka, Battle of: 158-159

Iuka, Mississippi: 156

J

Jacinto, Mississippi: 157, 159, 160, 162

Jackson, Mississippi: 209, 235

Jackson, Thomas J. "Stonewall": 6, 7, 11, *21*, 63, 90, 92, 94, 239-240, 241, 248, 278; and Antietam, 113, 114, 115, 116, 119, 120, 125, 130, 131, 132, 133; and Antietam campaign, 90, 92; and Battle of Second Bull Run, 36-37, 39, 40, 41, 42, 43, 44, 45, 46, 47, 48, 49, 50, 51, 52, 53, 55; capture of Federal garrison at Harpers Ferry, 90, 103-104, 105, 106-107; capture of Federal supply base at Manassas, 27-29, 54; and Chantilly, 58-59; and Hill, 87; injury to, 86; and Second Bull Run campaign, 12, 13, 14, 20-21, 22, 24-26, 27-30, 31, 34, 35-36; unprepossessing appearance of, 27, 106-107

Johnston, Albert Sidney: 151, 261

Johnston, Joseph: 6, 19, 245, *248*, 259; appointed to command in the West, 247-250

Jones, D. R.: 41, 43

Jones, J. R.: 113, 116

K

Kearny, Phil: 30, 44, 53, *58*, 59

Kemper, James: 41, 43

Kentucky: civilian reaction to Confederate army, 67-68, 71, 150, 185; Confederate recruiting posters circulated in, *74*

Knoxville, Tennessee: 22, 184, 185, 229, 230, 231, 232

L

Lawton, Alexander R.: 40, 46, 113, 116

Lee, Fitzhugh: 14, 15, 18

Lee, Robert E.: 6, 7, 58, 59, 181, 185, 196, 198, 200, 218, 236, 240, 241, 242, 248-249, 256, 257, 259, 278, 279; advocacy of peace proposal, 88-89; and Antietam campaign, 83-84, 86, 87, 89-90, 91, 92-93, 99, 100-101, 102, 103, 106, 107, 149; and Battle of Antietam, 109, 110, 111, 112, 113, 114, 115, 119, 122, 125, 126, 127-128, 129, 130, 131, 132, 133; and Battle of Second Bull Run, 40, 41, 42, 43, 45, 46, 49, 50, 51-52, 54, 55, 56; and Davis, 229; death of daughter, 239, 241; injury to, 86; and McClellan, 207; Maryland proclamation,

88; recruitment needs of, 237-238; and Second Bull Run campaign, 11-14, 15-16, 17, 18-21, 22, 23, 24, 25, 26, 30, 34, 36; and Special Orders 191, 90-91

Lee, Robert E., Jr.: 55, 125

Lexington, Kentucky: 69, 71, 150, 151

Lincoln, Abraham: 6, 7, 22, 83, 108, 149, 154, 169, 184, 192, 207, 208, 209, 213; and Banks, 208-210, 211; and Burnside, 215, 216, 218, 278; and Cabinet, *134-135;* common touch of, 268-269; and congressional elections (1862), 201, 221, 225; criticism of, 221-222, 267, 270; and dismissal of Buell, 186-187; and Emancipation Proclamation, 137-145, 149, 225, 271, 274, 276-277, 278; faith of, 138-139, 144-145; frustrations with generals, 221, 225; and Grant, 210, 212, 214; growing strength of literary style, 270-277; and McClellan, 62-63, 95-96, 97, 98, *188-189*, 194-196, 198-200, 201, 203; and photography, 269; political cartoons, *268;* and public confidence, 267-270; review of executions, 222; and Rosecrans, 219; and Tad, 223-224; war aims, 208-210, 271-277

Lincoln, Tad: *223-224*

Lincoln, William: 223-224

Liverpool, England: Confederate shipbuilding in, *252-253*

London, Kentucky: 68, 181, 184

London *Spectator:* 141, 143

London *Times:* 143, 251

Longstreet, James: 87, 218, 239, 240, 241, 278; and Antietam, 113, 114, 122-123, 126, 129, 130, 132; and Antietam campaign, 90-92, 98, 99, 100, 101, 102, 103, 104; and Battle of Second Bull Run, 40, 41, 44, 45, 46, 47, 49, 50, 51, 52, 55; injury to, 86; and Second Bull Run campaign, 11, 12, 13, 14, 16, 20, 21, 30, 34, 36; at Thoroughfare Gap, 42, 43

Louisville, Kentucky: 71, 74, 75, 79, 149, 151, 152, 154, 155, 167, 169; supply line for, 66

Lovell, Mansfield: 160, 162, 163, 235

M

McClellan, George M.: 6, 7, 11, 19, 28, 41, 54, 75, 197, 238, 239, 278; and Antietam campaign, 91, 92, 93, 95-100, 101, 102, 103, 104, 106, 133, 149; and Battle of Antietam, 108-111, 112, 113, 114, 119, 123, 124, 129, 130, 131, 132; farewell to Army of the Potomac, *204-205*, 206-207; final dismissal of, 201-203; and Lincoln, *188-189*, 194-196, 198-200; and Pope, 23-24, 30, 36, 60-61; public criticism of, 198; replaces Pope in field command, 61, 62-63, 83, 90; and Special Orders 191, 94-95, 98, 100; withdrawal from Peninsula, 12, 22, 23

McClernand, John: 213-214

McCook, Alexander: 155, 169, 170, 174, 176, 177, 178, 220

McDowell, Irwin: 31, 32, 34, 38, 43, 44, 48, 50, 52, 53, 56, 60, 61, 93, 96, 191

McGuire, Hunter: 47, 120

Mackville, Kentucky: 169, 170

McLaws, Lafayette: 41, 86, 90, 92, 99, 101, 103, 104-106, 113, 114, 115, 119, 130

Magruder, John: 6, 41, 104, 242-243, 259

Manassas, Second Battle of: *See* Second Bull Run, Battle of

Manassas, Virginia: 21, 26, 30, 31, 38, 41, 42, 44

Manassas Junction, Virginia: 23; burned-out railroad cars at, *32-33;* Union supply base at, 14, 16, 27-29, 54

Mansfield, J. K. F.: 112, *117,* 118, 119, 120, 131

Martinsburg, (West) Virginia: 89, 90, 106, 133, 196

Maryland: Confederate hopes for support in, 84; Confederate invasion of, *map* 91

Maryland Heights: 90, 99, 103, 104, 119, 123, 131

Memphis, Tennessee: 159, 214, 258, 266

Memphis & Charleston Railroad: 156, 157, 160, 162, 164

Minnesota: Sioux uprising in, 63, 222

Monocacy River: 197, 198

Morgan, George: 71, 166

Morgan, John: 7, 166, 220, 232

Morton, Oliver P.: 152, 187

Muldraugh's Hill: 79, 150

Munfordville, Kentucky: action at, 75, *76-77,* 78

Murfreesboro, Tennessee: 74, 230, 232

N

Napoleon III: 89, 251-252, 253

Nashville, Tennessee: 73, 74, 75, 184, 220, 230, 231, 232, 258; railroad depot in, *182-183;* supply line for, 66

Negley, James S.: 184

Nelson, William: 68, *69,* 70, 71, 78, 79, 155, 182; death of, 152, *153-*154

New Orleans, Louisiana: 192, 208, 209, 243, 258

Newspaper cartoons: Federal generals and Jackson, *34;* Lincoln and Tammany Hall, *268;* Semmes, *256*

New York *Evening Post:* 267

New York *Illustrated News:* page from, *153*

New York Times: 201, 269

New York *Tribune:* 139, 194, 225

New York *World:* 142

Norfolk, Virginia: 54, 258

North: criticism of Emancipation Proclamation, 142; crusading war spirit in, 265-266; elections (1862), 200-201, 221

O

Ocmulgee: 255, 256

Ord, Edward O.: 156, 157, 158, 159

Oxford, Mississippi: 214

P

Paducah, Kentucky: 156, 159

Palmerston, Lord: 89, 251

Pemberton, Joseph: 234, 235, 236, 244, 245, 249

Pendleton, W. N.: 114, 132

Perryville, Battle of: 170-173, *map* 174, 175-180, 225

Perryville, Kentucky: 170, 177

Pocahontas, Mississippi: 160, 161, 162

Pocotaligo, South Carolina: 257

Point of Rocks, Maryland: 90, 92

Polk, Leonidas: 76, 78, 151, 167, 168, *178,* 180-181, 182, 183, 230-231, 232; and Perryville, 171, 172, 175, 176, 178, 179

Pope, John: 6, 7, 11, *13,* 18, 24, 28, 38, 62-63, 90, 119, 207, 215, 222; and Battle of Second Bull Run, 40, 41, 43, 44, 45, 47, 48, 49, 50, 52, 54, 55-56; dismissal of, 191; headquarters attacked by Stuart, 17; loss of confidence by, 57-58, 59; and Second Bull Run campaign, 12-14, 15, 16, 19, 20, 21, 23, 24, 25, 26, 30-35, 36; soldiers' dissatisfaction with, 56-57, 59-61, 93

Porter, David Dixon: 192, *193,* 194, 213

Porter, Fitz-John: 12, 19, 22-23, 34, *48,* 96, 207; and Antietam, 112, 129, 130, 132, 133; and Antietam campaign, 99; and Second Bull Run, 44, 46-49, 52

Port Hudson, Louisiana: 236

Potomac River: 88, 103, 108, 119, 127, 196, 197, 198, 200; Confederate army crossing, 84, *85,* 132

Price, Sterling: 155, 156, 157, 158, 159, 160, 162, 163, 164, 165, 181, 232, 236

Q

Quintard, C. T.: 180

R

Randolph, George: 245-246

Rapidan River: 12, 13, 14, 16, 23

Rappahannock River: 12, 13, 15, 16, 17, 20, 21, 22, 23, 25, 31, 40, 49, 54, 84, 217, 218, 239; fraternizing among pickets, *224;* fugitive slaves and Federal troops fording, *8-9*

Rappahannock Station, Virginia: 14, 17, 19, 20

Reno, Jesse L.: 16, 19, 31, 34, 44, 53, 58, 96, *102,* 112, 131

Richmond, Kentucky: 68, 69; Battle of: 68-70, 168

Richmond, Virginia: 6, 14, 15, 16, 18, 19, 28, 41, 54, 84, 86, 210, 216, 246, 247

Richmond *Dispatch:* advertisements for substitutes, *238*

Richmond *Examiner:* 141

Ripley, Mississippi: 160, 162, 165

Rosecrans, William S.: 156, 157, 158, 159, 160, 173, 210, 212, 219, 220, 232, 279; and Corinth, 161, 162-163, 164-165, 166

Russell, Lord John: 89, 144, 251, 253

S

Sabine City, Texas: 192

Sabine Pass: 192

St. Louis, Missouri: 159, 162

Salem, Virginia: 24, 25, 41, 202
Salem (Ill.) *Advocate:* 201
Salt River: 170, 171, 180
Schofield, John: 243, 244
Schurz, Carl: 221-222
Second Bull Run, Battle of, 36, *map* 37, 38-54; British reaction to, 89; casualties, 54; Federal retreat from, 53, *57,* 60
Second Bull Run campaign: 11-25, *map* 26, 27-63
Seddon, James A.: 246-247
Semmes, Raphael: 254-255, *256,* 257
Seward, William H.: 62, 137, 141, 142
Sharpsburg, Maryland: 101, 103, 104, 107, 108, *map* 109, 112, 113, 122, 125, 126, 128
Shelby, J. O.: 243, *244*
Shelbyville, Kentucky: 167, 232
Shenandoah Valley: 19, 23, 30, 54, 83, 89, 90, 239, 248
Shepherdstown, West Virginia: 103
Shepherdstown ford: 112, 114, 132, 149
Sheridan, Philip H.: 173, 176, 177
Sherman, William T.: 266-267, 279
Sigel, Franz: 34, 44, 53, 96, 217, 218
Sill, Joshua: 168, 170, 175, 181
Sioux uprising: 63, 222
Smith, Edwin Kirby: 7, 76, 167, 171, 180, 181, 182-183, 184-185, 186, 230, 231, 249, 256, 257, 278; Kentucky offensive, 22, 67-75, 79, 150-151, 155
Southern Illustrated News: page from, *213*
South Mountain: 98, 101; Battle of: 99, 101-102, 113, 131, 138
Special Orders 191: 90-91, *94,* 95, 100
Springfield, Kentucky: 169, 170
Stanton, Edwin: 62, 63, 138, 200, 202, 213, 267
Starke, William E.: 39, 46, 116
Stevens, I. I.: 58, 59
Stevenson, Alabama: 74, 230
Stevenson, Carter: 183, 231, 232
Stone Bridge: 35, 36, 53
Stuart, Jeb: 14, *15,* 16, 22; and Antietam campaign, 100, 106, 115, 117; Catlett's Station raid, 16-18; Chambersburg raid, 196-198, 238; and Second Bull Run campaign, 25, 28, 40, 45, 46, 49
Sudley Springs: 49, 58
Sumner, Edwin: 23, 57, 61, 216-217; and Antietam, 112, 113, 119, 120-121, 123, 124, 130, 131; and Antietam campaign, 96, 99, 133
Sumter: 254, 255
Susquehanna River: 92, 103
Sykes, George: 52, 53, 61, 129-130

T

Taliaferro, W. B.: 21, 25, 28, 35, 36, 37-38, 39, 40
Tammany Hall: 268
Taylor, Richard: 242-243, 259
Tennessee: Confederate raiding activity in, *226-227, 233*
Tennessee River: 220, 249

Terrill, William: 176, *177*
Thomas, George: 74, 75, 78, 79, 154, 155, 169, 170, 179-180, 220
Thoroughfare Gap: 21, 25, 34, 36, 44, 46; fighting at, *42, 43*
Toombs, Robert: 15, 87, 125-126, 127, 129
Transmississippi: Confederate operations in, 242-244
Trimble, Isaac: 28, 46
Turner's Gap: 98, 99, 100, 101-103, 106

V

Van Dorn, Earl: 155-156, *157,* 160, 232, 235, 236, 243; and Corinth, 148, 161, 162, 163, 164, 165-166, 181
Versailles, Kentucky: 171, 180
Vicksburg, Mississippi: 155, 192, 209, 210, 212-214, 232-234, 236, 244, 245, 246, 258, 260, 279
Virginia Central Railroad: 11, 84

W

Walden's Ridge: 73
Walker, John G.: 86, 90, 92, 93, 103, 105, 113-114, 119, 120, 130, 132
Wallace, Lew: 71
Ward, Artemus: 137
Warrenton, Virginia: 17, 26, 60, 200, 204, 216
Warrenton Junction, Virginia: 30, 206
Warrenton Turnpike: 25, 34, 35, 36, 41, 46, 47
Washington, D.C.: 6, 20, 21, 54, 56, 57, 58, 216, 248; construction work on Capitol, *275;* defenses of, 62, 63, 83, 93, 95, 96; White House and Treasury building, *262-263*
Waterloo Bridge: 17, 18, 22
Waud, Alfred: 18
Welles, Gideon: 62, 192-194
West Virginia: Federal presence in, 54
West Wood: 116
Wheeler, Joseph: 175, 177, 183, 232
White Plains, Virginia: 25, 41, 42
White's Ferry: 84
Whittier, John G.: 267
Wilcox, Cadmus: 41, 43
Wilder, J. T.: 76-78, 83
Williams, Alpheus: 96, 112, 118-119, 120
Williamsport, Maryland: 14
Winchester, Virginia: 89, 133, 200
Winder, Charles: 21, 39, 40

Y

Yancy, William: 237, 249-250
Yates, Richard: 187
Yell Rifles: 70
Yorktown, Virginia: 23

Z

Zouaves: 52
Zouave uniform: *53*

SHELBY FOOTE, THE CIVIL WAR,
A NARRATIVE
VOLUME 4   SECOND MANASSAS
TO POCOTALIGO

Library of Congress Cataloging-in-Publication Data
Foote, Shelby.
    [Civil War, a narrative]
    Shelby Foote, the Civil War, a narrative / by Shelby
Foote and the editors of Time-Life Books. — 40th
Anniversary ed.
        p. cm.
    Originally published: The Civil War, a narrative.
New York: Random House, 1958-1974, in 3 v.
    Includes bibliographical references and indexes.
    Contents: v. 4 Second Manassas to Pocotaligo
    1.United States—History—Civil War, 1861-1865.
I. Time-Life Books. II. Title.
E468.F7   1999   99-13486
973.7—dc21   CIP
ISBN 0-7835-0103-X

For information on and a full description of any
of the Time-Life Books series listed at right, please
call 1-800-621-7026 or write:
Reader Information
Time-Life Customer Service
P.O. Box C-32068
Richmond, Virginia 23261-2068

 Time-Life Books is a
division of Time Life Inc.

TIME LIFE INC.
PRESIDENT and CEO: George Artandi

TIME-LIFE BOOKS
PUBLISHER/MANAGING EDITOR: Neil Kagan
VICE PRESIDENT, MARKETING: Joseph A. Kuna
VICE PRESIDENT, NEW PRODUCT
DEVELOPMENT: Amy Golden
DIRECTOR OF MARKETING: Pamela R. Farrell

PROJECT EDITOR: Philip Brandt George
DIRECTOR, NEW PRODUCT
DEVELOPMENT: Elizabeth D. Ward
Deputy Editor: Kirk Denkler
Design Director: Ellen L. Pattisall
Marketing Manager: Peter Tardif
Copyeditor: Christine Stephenson
Editorial Assistant: Patricia D. Whiteford
Picture Associate: Susan L. Finken

Special Contributors: Matt Baumgardner, John
Drummond, Jennifer A. Gearhart, Kimberly Grand-
colas, Janet Dell Russell Johnson, Monika Lynde,
Barbara M. Sheppard (design and production); Christine Higgins (administration); Roy Nanovic (index).

Correspondent: Christina Lieberman (New York).

Director of Finance: Christopher Hearing
Directors of Book Production: Marjann Caldwell,
Patricia Pascale
Director of Publishing Technology: Betsi McGrath
Director of Photography and Research:
John Conrad Weiser
Director of Editorial Administration: Barbara Levitt
Manager, Technical Services: Anne Topp
Senior Production Manager: Ken Sabol
Quality Assurance Manager: James King
Chief Librarian: Louise D. Forstall

OTHER TIME-LIFE HISTORY PUBLICATIONS

Our American Century
World War II
What Life Was Like
The American Story
Voices of the Civil War
The American Indians
Lost Civilizations
Time Frame
The Civil War
Cultural Atlas
Echoes of Glory